SOUTH VIETNAM:

U. S. - Communist
Confrontation
in Southeast Asia

Volume 1

1961-65

INTERIM
HISTORY

SOUTH VIETNAM:

U. S. - Communist Confrontation in Southeast Asia

Volume 1
1961-65

Edited by Lester A. Sobel

Contributing Editors: Hal Kosut,
Howard M. Epstein

FACTS ON FILE, INC.   NEW YORK

SOUTH VIETNAM:
U.S.-Communist Confrontation
in Southeast Asia
Volume 1
1961-65

Copyright, 1966, by Facts on File, Inc.

Library of Congress Catalog Card Number: 66-23943

ISBN 0-87196-160-1

9   8   7   6   5   4

CONTENTS

INTRODUCTION

THE WIDESPREAD CONFUSION about the events in Vietnam can hardly be blamed on scarcity of information. The public has been flooded for years in a steady stream of news on the subject. Nor can there be any complaint about lack of variety in the reports, which are sometimes accurate but often inaccurate, frequently biased but occasionally objective, at times shallow but on occasion perceptive—and usually incomplete. Newspapers, television, magazines, radio, books—every medium is employed to inform us. Yet the more we read and hear about this troubled land, the less we appear to understand.

A major reason for the confusion seems to be that this great profusion of data, sweeping over us so relentlessly, is more than anybody should be expected to digest. Why, then, does FACTS ON FILE produce another book on Vietnam? The answer, obviously, is that we believe this book can help clarify the issues—and we believe there is a need for a factual, unbiased reference book that an intelligent reader can turn to when he wants to look up a specific item among the thousands of facts about the Vietnam situation.

This book is largely a journalistic narration of the events that make up the Vietnam story. Like most of the other volumes in the INTERIM HISTORY series, this book contains a large amount of material that appeared in one form or another in previous FACTS ON FILE publications. The book also includes material adapted or digested from the *Department of State Bulletin* and from other reports or publications of the Department of State, from the Senate Committee on Foreign Relations and from press sources on both sides of the Bamboo Curtain.

BACKGROUND

SOUTH VIETNAM exists as a separate state because of international agreements signed in Geneva July 21, 1954. The principal purpose of these accords was to end a 7½-year war between France and various nationalist and Communist elements in formerly French Indochina. The agreements ended the last vestiges of French rule in Indochina.

The 3 separate agreements were worked out at a conference held in Geneva May 8-July 21, 1954. Delegates from Great Britain and the Soviet Union served as co-chairmen of the conference. The other participants were: representatives of France, the U.S. and Communist China; delegates from Cambodia, Laos and Vietnam (the 3 former Associated States of Indochina); and representatives of the Viet Minh movement, which had won control of the northern part of Vietnam.

The Geneva conference agreements provided that:
• Vietnam would be provisionally partitioned approximately along the 17th Parallel. The northern part of the country was turned over to the Communists—the Viet Minh's Democratic Republic of Vietnam (generally referred to later as North Vietnam), under the leadership of Ho Chi Minh. The southern part (South Vietnam) was put under the control of the State (later Republic) of Vietnam, headed by French-backed former Emperor Bao Dai. (Bao Dai, who absented himself frequently and for long periods in France, was ousted Oct. 23, 1955 by a referendum in which Premier Ngo Dinh Diem became chief of state.)

1

● North and South Vietnam were to be reunified on the basis of "free elections" to be held throughout the country within 2 years—by July 20, 1956. "Competent representative authorities" of North and South Vietnam were to begin consultations on the elections July 20, 1955.

● An International Control Commission (ICC) consisting of representatives of India (chairman), Canada and Poland would supervise the carrying out of the agreements in North and South Vietnam. (2 similar ICCs were created to supervise the agreements in Laos and Cambodia, the 2 other former Associated States of Indochina.)

● Neither side was permitted to increase its military manpower or armament during the pre-unification period.

● "The establishment of new military bases is prohibited" throughout Vietnam. This applied specifically to any "military base under the control of a foreign state." North and South Vietnam were not permitted to form military alliances or to permit the use of their territories for hostilities or "an aggressive policy."

The U.S., a non-belligerent, did not sign the agreements. But the chief of the U.S. delegation, State Undersecy. Walter Bedell Smith, issued a statement asserting that the U.S. (a) "will refrain from the threat or the use of force to disturb" the agreements, (b) "would view any renewal of the aggression in violation of the aforesaid agreements with grave concern and as seriously threatening international peace and security" and (c) "shall continue to seek to achieve unity through free elections, supervised by the UN to insure that they are conducted fairly."

The South Vietnamese delegate, Foreign Min. Tran Van Do, also refused to sign the agreements—in protest against the provisions for *de facto* partition of Vietnam. But he also pledged that his government would not use force to oppose the agreement's terms.

When the day for consultations on unification elections arrived, the North Vietnamese régime announced its willingness to open the discussions. The South Vietnamese government, however, refused to participate. The South Vietnamese argued that free elections were impossible in the Communist-ruled North and that falsified totals from the more populous North Vietnam would outweigh any honest South Vietnamese vote. The U.S. supported South Vietnam in this stand. The South Vietnamese government also pointed out that it had not signed the Geneva agreements and was not bound by them.

U.S. involvement in Vietnam's wars had begun at least as early as 1950. State Secy. Dean G. Acheson had announced in Paris May 8, 1950 that an agreement had been reached with France for U.S. arms assistance to the 3 French-sponsored Associated States of Indochina. Pres. Harry S. Truman had announced June 27, 1950, at the outbreak of the war in Korea, that he had ordered "the dispatch of a military mission" to Indochina "to provide close working relations" with the French and native forces there. A U.S. Military Assistance Advisory Group (MAAG) of 35 men reached Indochina in August to teach the troops receiving U.S. weapons how to use them. Arrangements for additional U.S. military aid to Vietnam, Laos and Cambodia were concluded under a military aid agreement signed Dec. 23, 1950 by the U.S., France and the 3 Indochinese states. The U.S. cited this agreement Jan. 1, 1955 in pledging new military assistance to South Vietnam. After French officers relinquished command of South Vietnam's armed forces, an enlarged U.S. MAAG on Feb. 12, 1955 took over the job of training the South Vietnamese army.

Increasing guerrilla activity in South Vietnam by Communist-led irregulars was reported as early as mid-1957. U.S. military personnel suffered their first injuries of the Vietnamese war when terrorists dynamited MAAG and U.S. Information Service installations in Saigon Oct. 27, 1957. In the next attack on Americans, 2 MAAG members were killed and a 3d injured July 8, 1959 in a terrorist strike at an MAAG compound in Bienhoa, 20 miles northeast of Saigon.

The Communist-led struggle against the South Vietnamese régime was an outgrowth of an anti-French independence movement. This rebellion had started in the mid-19th century not long after France had taken control of Indochina.

The revolt alternately sputtered and flamed for nearly a century before the French finally withdrew from the country.

Victory came to the insurgents under the leadership of Ho Chi Minh (He Who Enlightens), a son of one of the early rebels. Ho was born Nguyen Tat Thanh May 19, 1890 in the central Vietnamese village of Hatinh. During a French crackdown on rebels in 1911, Ho fled to France as a galley hand on a French ship. Paradoxically, Ho found more freedom in France to agitate against the French than had been permitted in Indochina. In Paris he used propaganda and political weapons to labor for Vietnamese independence. Ho also changed his name to Nguyen Ai Quoc (Nguyen the Patriot) and became a founding member of the French Communist Party. He studied Communist techniques in Moscow in 1923-25 and in 1928, later was a Communist agent in China and founded the Indochinese Communist Party in 1930. He formed the Viet Minh (full name: Vietnam Doc Lap Dong Minh Hoa—League for the Independence of Vietnam) in the South China village of Chingsi May 19, 1941.

The Viet Minh guerrillas at first fought the Japanese, and Ho (who adopted the name Ho Chi Minh in 1943) was able to establish his forces in northern Indochina after the war. Because of their services against the Japanese, Ho's forces were aided initially by the U.S. Office of Strategic Services.

The French Mar. 7, 1946 recognized the autonomy of Northern Vietnam with Ho as president, but the Viet Minh kept up guerrilla pressure on the French in a campaign to win all of Vietnam. After the French defeat and the 1954 Geneva agreements, Ho's Viet Minh inspired the guerrilla and terrorist movement in South Vietnam in a continuation of the Communist program to control all of Vietnam. In Dec. 1960 this movement formed the National Liberation Front, which took charge of rebel political action. The name Viet Cong, which came into use in about 1956 to identify the guerrillas in South Vietnam, is a contraction of Vietnam Congsan (Vietnamese Communists).

GEOGRAPHIC ASPECTS OF THE STRUGGLE

(Abridgment of an article written by Dr. G. Etzel Pearcy, Geographer of the U.S. Department of State, for the Sept. 20, 1965 edition of the Department of State Bulletin)

A<small>LL</small> PHYSICAL RELATIONS between the United States and South Vietnam involve distances of global proportions. In a westerly direction 176° of longitude separate Washington from Saigon; in an easterly direction, 184°. Thus the capitals of the two countries are within about 250 miles of being halfway around the world from each other.

A direct, or great circle, route from Seattle to Saigon measures 7,400 miles. Were the flight to go via Honolulu, 1,625 miles would be added to the distance. By ship, the distance from San Diego to Saigon via the shortest sea route, skirting the coast of Japan, would run around 8,400 miles. Modern jet aircraft seem to shrink these overwhelming distances, but even the latest and fastest of naval vessels would require from a week to 10 days for the trip. In any event, the transpacific supply lines to South Vietnam are staggering in dimensions. Sustained operations through staging points for any significant volume of men and materiel present logistic problems too complex to evaluate simply by route distances or ton-miles.

The approach to South Vietnam is via its east coast. On the Asian continent much of the quadrant containing this area is generally hostile or nonaligned with the West, forcing U.S.

5

staging operations to take place primarily in the western part of the Pacific defense zone. 2 outlying areas presently controlled by the U.S. have reasonably strategic locations along supply routes: Guam, an unincorporated territory, and Okinawa in the U.S.-administered part of the Ryukyus. Even here mileages remain high: Guam to Saigon, 2,600 miles; Okinawa to Saigon, 1,825 miles.

South Vietnam, with its marginal position on the continent, can be readily approached. But its relatively small size and attenuated shape pose serious problems for its defense. Although a little larger than Florida in area, the country in the north narrows to no more than 33 miles in one place. Even Saigon, an "east coast" city, lies only 35 miles from the Cambodian boundary to the west. The widest part of the country, in the central portion, measures less than 130 miles. In contrast, South Vietnam's eastern coast curves in a long arc for almost 800 miles, nearly equal to California's arcuate west coast.

Geopoliticians cite compact shape as a decided asset for defense purposes and refer to France, with its hexagonal form, as approaching the ideal. South Vietnam represents the opposite extreme: a narrow ledge of land clinging to the great interior mountain system of Asia and presenting a classic example of exposed territory. So lengthy are the country's boundaries in relation to its size that those who would infiltrate have a rich choice of spots from which to select for entry.

Diversity of Topography

About 60% of South Vietnam consists of relatively high mountains and plateau lands. Maximum elevation is 8,500 feet, about 1,500 feet lower than in North Vietnam. Lowlands with little or no relief make up most of the remaining 40% of the country and are located chiefly in the Mekong Delta area.

Thus it can be seen that well over half of the countryside presents obstacles to penetration and movement but offers protection to offensive forces engaged in guerrilla-type warfare. And even in the lowlands, swamps and heavy vegetative

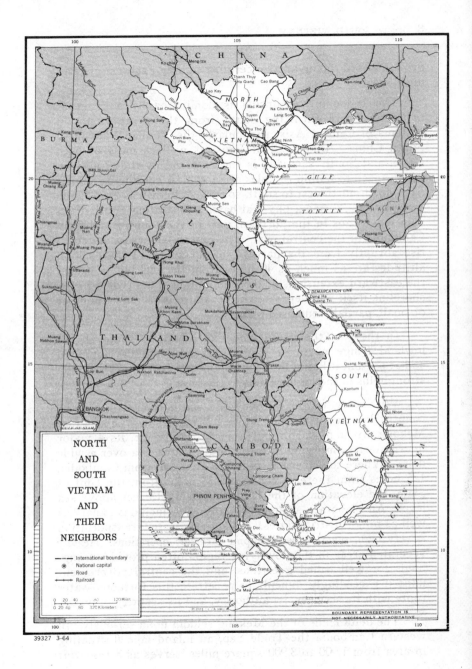

NORTH
AND
SOUTH
VIETNAM
AND
THEIR
NEIGHBORS

———— International boundary
⊛ National capital
———— Road
—+— Railroad

0 20 40   80   120 Miles
0 20 40   80   120 Kilometers

BOUNDARY REPRESENTATION IS
NOT NECESSARILY AUTHORITATIVE

39327 3-64

growth afford the invaders a certain immunity against government security forces.

The Indochina Peninsula is dominated by a series of mountain spurs thrusting south from the great mountain systems of Central Asia, particularly the Yunnan Plateau of South China. Almost all of Laos, as well as most of both North and South Vietnam, is encompassed by these outliers, which reach to within 50 miles of Saigon. A cordillera running from north-northwest to south-southeast, known as the Chaine Annamitique, forms a physical barrier separating South Vietnam from Laos in the northern part of the country and from Cambodia in the central part. The eastern slopes of the chain rise abruptly from the narrow coastal zone. In places high altitudes are as much as 40 miles from the sea, but in others the eastward extensions of these mountain spurs crowd to the shoreline itself and separate the coastal region into a number of small, partially enclosed plains.

In the past the impingement of mountain spurs on the lowland fringe north of Saigon has inhibited development, and at present it limits the scope of operations against guerrilla strongholds in the higher lands to the west.

With very few exceptions the southernmost ⅓ of the country lies at an altitude of less than 500 feet. The great Mekong River flows through this flat landscape, its 4 major distributaries emptying into the South China Sea over a wide delta. Where the river enters South Vietnam from Cambodia, 125 miles from the east coast and 55 miles from the Gulf of Siam, the elevation of the land is scarcely 15 feet above sea level. An elaborate system of waterways includes canals as well as minor distributaries. Reliance on water transportation is very high, severely handicapping strategic operations. Heavily vegetated areas in this low-lying region often provide strongholds for well-armed guerrillas, and the central government finds it exceedingly difficult to penetrate this tortuous water route with its services, its authority, and its security program.

The delta lands of the Mekong seldom flood seriously. In western Cambodia the Tonle Sap, an inland lake fluctuating in area from 1,000 to 3,900 square miles, serves as a reservoir to stabilize the flow of the lower Mekong. When the water rises, the surplus backs up into this lake and prevents heavy flooding. In turn, during low water the process is reversed and from the Tonle Sap the extra accumulation of water drains back into the river.

Notwithstanding this fortunate regulation by nature, there are seasons of relatively high water which further isolate the delta. But the South is spared the ravaging floods quite common to the Tonkin Delta in North Vietnam, except upon rare occasions when the Mekong picks up an unusually heavy load on its 2,600-mile course from Tibet.

Climate & Vegetation

The thermometer in South Vietnam never skyrockets; the highest temperature ever recorded at Saigon has only been 104° F. Nevertheless, a temperature which never goes much below 80° F. definitely has a debilitating effect on human energy, particularly when it is accompanied by high humidity. Sustained periods in the steaming lowlands of the Mekong Delta place a severe strain on anyone accustomed to the climate of higher latitudes. At higher elevations temperatures are more agreeable, but here other handicaps, such as pounding rainfall and dense vegetation, may well offset the advantage of a cool breeze.

The controlling factor in Vietnam's climate is its position deep in the tropics. Another basic climatic control is Vietnam's location on the southeastern margin of the great Eurasian land mass. Pressure differences between continent and ocean result in major air-mass movements which pour seaward during the winter and landward during the summer. This dynamically effective wind system, which reverses itself twice yearly, gives rise to a monsoon influence—a "when the rains come" type of climate.

For Southeast Asia in general the rainy season thus occurs in summer, but along the coast in the northern part of South Vietnam (Hué-Danang area) the wettest period lasts from September to January. This exception is caused by the northeast monsoon winds, which are normally dry but are onshore in this particular location and so contain moisture. In short, the monsoon does not appreciably alter temperature values but brings a notoriously wet season each summer and fall.

Heavy rainfall handicaps security measures in several ways. Mobility is reduced, equipment becomes difficult to maneuver, and better protection is offered the aggressor. Air action may be limited by the poor visibility resulting from high humidity and low cloud cover during the rainy season.

The quantity of rain falling in South Vietnam is impressive. At Saigon the annual precipitation amounts to 78 inches, of which 67 inches fall during the 6-month period from May to October. June and September average over 13 inches each, registering frequent downpours of torrential proportions. On the exposed east coast north of Saigon, steep slopes lift the moist, humid air as it blows landward and upward, unloading even greater amounts of water. Hué, onetime capital of the old Annamese Empire, annually receives 115 inches.

In their extreme form the unequal atmospheric pressures give rise to typhoons which pound the east coast of the Indochina Peninsula. These devastating storms occur from July into November; in October and especially in November they are concentrated on the Vietnamese coast south of the 17th Parallel.

Over ⅚ of South Vietnam has a cover of natural vegetation—rain forests, monsoon forests, and some savanna lands. When the original forest is cut away or burned, a secondary forest cover takes over in many places, poorer in timber but with heavier undergrowth. These tangles of vegetation are a marked disadvantage for forces seeking out an enemy which moves quickly on foot, with a good knowledge of the terrain. For example, roadways cleared through heavy vegetative growth must be maintained or they soon revert to the jungle. In contrast, dense foliage offers excellent concealment from both air and land observation. From such terrain guerrillas may operate with relative safety and on a time schedule of their own making.

Transportation

Transportation facilities in South Vietnam are too limited to provide unity and cohesion within the country. Physical factors handicap the development of communications to many remote and marginal areas; in numerous instances towns and villages have had little or no contact with the Central government.

The obstacles of inaccessibility also handicap those fighting against the guerrilla aggressors from the North. Inadequate lines of communication allow guerrillas to infiltrate large areas and remain under cover while at the same time they prevent effective offensive action to rout them. American military operations, ordinarily geared to efficient transportation systems, contrast markedly with those of the Viet Cong along the infiltration routes, where guerrillas slip in with their less-than-complex supplies and equipment.

Economic development on the Indochina Peninsula has been largely limited to the Mekong Delta region in the south, the Tonkin Basin in the north, and the lowlands fringing the coast between them. When Vietnam was partitioned in 1954, the southern part inherited only one of the larger lowland areas and about ⅗ of the string of coastal lowlands. Modern transportation facilities within the country do not generally extend beyond these areas.

Within South Vietnam there are only about 870 miles of operable railway lines, comprising for the most part the coastal line from Saigon to Dongha, 40 miles north of Hué and within 12 miles of the demarcation line from North Vietnam. From this longitudinal railroad, a few short spurs branch off, the most important of which reaches Dalat, high on the plateau of the same name. The slim traffic artery completely bypasses the extensive "back country" of South Vietnam with its thousands of hamlets and villages.

Highways in South Vietnam form a rather sketchy network but have much greater coverage than the railway lines. When Indochina was a part of France's colonial empire, the French established a road pattern in some ways resembling that of metropolitan France. The more important routes carry numbers, identifying them with major axes of travel between key points. For example, National Route 14 leads from Danang (Tourane) on the coast, 50 miles south of Hué, to the northern part of the Mekong lowlands and gives access to Saigon. The over-all route system, however, has been truncated, for it was developed to cover French Indochina. Now an appreciable proportion of the net lies in Cambodia, Laos, and North Vietnam.

Route 9 extends nearly straight westward from Dongha near the coast, through Laobao on the Laos boundary, to Savannakhet on the Mekong border between Laos and Thailand. This particular route, paralleling the demarcation line on the south for about 10 or 15 miles, is at least partially responsible for deflecting the infiltration route of the Viet Cong to the west into Laotian territory. Although the demarcation line itself crosses relatively empty countryside and would entice infiltrators, Route 9 provides some access for security measures.

The northern approach to South Vietnam for the Viet Cong is not limited to any given itinerary but corresponds to a band of rough landscape where improvised paths and trails can carry the traffic. This zone does not correlate in any way with the established road pattern for that part of the Indochina Peninsula. It serves as the principal access route from north to south; into it and from it finger a labyrinth of trails for assembly and deployment of the Viet Cong forces.

Water transportation plays a heavy role in the heart of the Mekong Delta. Some 3,000 miles of waterways crisscross these lowlands, giving access to areas where roads are difficult to construct and maintain. Unfortunately the lack of approach by land hampers security precautions, and the Viet Cong have installed themselves in certain of these low-lying and often saturated areas. Elsewhere in South Vietnam navigable waters are limited or altogether lacking.

In North Vietnam watercourses provide excellent transportation facilities in the delta of the Red River of Tonkin. Hanoi and the port city of Haiphong are both in the midst of true delta country, whereas Saigon lies somewhat off center of the Mekong Delta.

Air transportation in South Vietnam has superficially alleviated some of the problems involving appreciable distance and inadequate means of movement on the surface. Saigon is well known as one of the leading international air terminals in Southeast Asia, but in addition there are local flights from here to the larger cities in South Vietnam. The fact that the Viet Cong have been unable to overrun urban areas permits commercial air transportation to continue even during heated warfare.

The People of Vietnam

The Vietnamese people range from highly cultured and sophisticated individuals who dwell in the larger cities to tribal folk who eke a living out of the countryside by the most primitive of methods. Well-to-do Vietnamese in Saigon live in European-style homes, dress and entertain as do Westerners, and send their children abroad to school. Peasants may live in villages amounting to nothing more than collections of straw huts.

Throughout most urban centers French culture is at once apparent. The French language continues to be used by many of the better educated Vietnamese. Most administrative and educational practices of the former French colonial regime also continue in use. French methods persist in most of the routine necessary to the country's political and economic existence.

Any ethnological map of South Vietnam must be considered as a segment of a larger one encompassing the entire Indochina Peninsula and its environs. Ceaseless migrations during past millennia have brought numerous racial types and social patterns to the area. Predominant influences stem not only from what is now the Indo-Pakistan subcontinent and China proper, but from deep within the interior of the Asian Continent. Most of the present-day inhabitants of South Vietnam, however, may be directly related to the people of the old Annamite Kingdom in the eastern part of the Indochina Peninsula. Known racially as well as nationally as Vietnamese, they comprise about 85% of South Vietnam's some 16 million population.

As a powerful majority the Vietnamese south of the 17th Parallel dominate the country and represent a new national group. Height of the men averages around 5 feet 1 or 2 inches, and their weight around 120 pounds. The most common physical type is characterized by straight black hair, broad face, high cheekbones, dark eyes with an epicanthic fold of the eyelid, and light- or medium-brown skin.

Minority Groups

Several minority groups, while not great in total numbers, complicate the racial picture. The Chinese, forming the largest minority, have not fared especially well politically. Their skill and energy brought them economic success as entrepreneurs, but with the rise of nationalism a prejudiced policy of discrimination gave many the feeling of persecution. Under the French they were allowed to retain Chinese citizenship and could appeal to their motherland in the case of denied rights (before the Communist conquest of mainland China). But the Vietnamese government required that all Chinese become citizens of the new state in response to the special need for loyalty in the face of aggression from the North by a power friendly to their former homeland.

The second most significant minority are the *montagnards*. (The word in French means "dwellers in the mountains.") Estimates of their number range from 500,000 to 700,000. These highlanders live in relative isolation from the rest of the country, speak their own languages, and maintain distinctive cultural traditions. The remote and sparsely settled habitat of the *montagnards* is a region that is definitely vulnerable to guerrilla infiltration. Some steps have been taken by the Central government to lessen this danger. The Viet Cong have gone so far as to assure these primitive peoples in Communist propaganda that they may have their own autonomy "when the Communists conquer South Vietnam."

Another minority, the Khmers, are actually Cambodians living in South Vietnam. Numbering from 350,000 to 400,000, they are largely concentrated southwest of Saigon. Like the *montagnards,* they have not assimilated well with the Vietnamese. On the other hand, they have generally not proved to be a primary security problem.

The Chams, numbering only about 35,000, represent the least significant of the minorities. A fragmented remainder of a once great people, they are poor economically. Scattered through less desirable sections of the south-central part of the country, they live in humble little villages quite apart from the general flow of Vietnamese life.

Europeans, especially French, do not enjoy the privileges they once did under colonial rule. Nevertheless there are still some close associations between European and Vietnamese which prove mutually beneficial.

The last extended period of peace and stability for the inhabitants of what is now South Vietnam dates back to the pre-World War II years, and even that was marred by a serious economic depression. Any person under 40, then, could not be expected to have experienced any type of life other than a troubled one. Political instability has been the general rule. What progress has been made has been achieved in the face of serious handicaps.

Economic Pressures

In the 1954 split of territory between North and South Vietnam, the latter came out a poor 2d in natural resources. In mineral resources the division was especially uneven; North Vietnam has copious quantities of coal, zinc, phosphates, tin, and graphite, while South Vietnam's share, pending further investigation at least, is quite meager. Further, the French promoted greater industrial development in the North than in the South.

Partially offsetting these advantages of the North, however, is the fact that there is a considerably greater population pressure on the fertile lowlands around Hanoi and Haiphong than on those tributary to Saigon. As a result, in normal years South Vietnam exports rice, while North Vietnam traditionally has to import rice.

The economic pattern of South Vietnam is hardly a complex one. Agriculture provides the basic sustenance, ranging from rubber and rice as the prime products entering trade down to a number of provision crops for local consumption, including corn, cassava, and beans. Other products, commercial in nature, are tea, coffee, tobacco, sugar cane, and coconuts. By Western standards industrial processes are largely the community type, wherein simple manufactured goods are produced for domestic consumption.

The U.S., by its aid program, has done much in recent years to stimulate economic activity in South Vietnam, somewhat countering the war-induced decline in production and welfare. Projects include the improving of agricultural techniques, pest and insect control, an agricultural credit system, better transportation and communication facilities, and land reclamation.

Problems in Perspective

From a geographic point of view there can be no doubt that the U.S. faces disadvantages in Vietnam that far outweigh the advantages. While factors of relief, climate, and vegetation which handicap the defenders are not necessarily in themselves assets to the guerrillas, the guerrillas, of course, take advantage of the landscape as it is. They turn heavy foliage into camouflage, use light arms on terrain too rough for most conventional weapons, and seek strategic advantages during the monsoon season, when aircraft cannot be fully effective.

Tactics of the Viet Cong are likewise tailored to the cultural environment, including the abstract struggle for the minds and sympathies of the inhabitants. A recent estimate identifies well over a million villagers as dominated by Communists, with other millions subjected to some degree of Viet Cong control or pressure. Methods of obtaining cooperation from these rural inhabitants vary—from terrorism to the promise of concession. By holding small, scattered areas, the Viet Cong can erode government control more than they could if they gained larger but fewer blocks of territory. Hit-and-run tactics can be extended in more widespread fashion for greater psychological effect. Also, control of areas as close as possible to Saigon tends to give the impression that a rice-roots rebellion is closing in on the capital.

1961

The Viet Cong intensified their attacks on South Vietnamese targets early in 1961. Significant increases in guerrilla manpower and arms were reported. The U.S. Administration took steps to help South Vietnam's Ngo Dinh Diem régime by providing arms and training troops and by extending additional economic aid. Vice Pres. Lyndon B. Johnson visited South Vietnam to emphasize the U.S. determination to bolster the country against Communist aggression. There were reports of increasing involvement of U.S. combat instructors in the Vietnamese fighting.

U.S. Aids Diem Régime

Pro-Communist Guerrillas Step Up Attacks

Early in 1961 the Viet Cong movement intensified its guerrilla campaign to overthrow the U.S.-backed government of South Vietnamese Pres. Ngo Dinh Diem and to replace it with a Communist régime.

Few major battles were reported in this period, but it was said in March that the guerrillas were killing an average of 500 pro-government villagers and home guardsmen monthly in isolated skirmishes. The Communist guerrilla force was said at this time to total 9,000 men, most of them grouped in small combat units that avoided open battle with the much larger South Vietnamese army and easily eluded encirclement in remote rural areas.

The first large-scale guerrilla attacks were launched in March and April, during the South Vietnamese national elections. 400 guerrillas attacked the Kienhoa Province village of Truc Giang Apr. 1 but were beaten off by government troops. Nearly 100 guerrillas were killed Apr. 3 in an attack on Bencat, north of Saigon. The government charged Apr. 10 that the attacks had been launched to intimidate voters and prevent a fair election tally.

Despite the renewed guerrilla campaign, Pres. Diem and Vice Pres. Nguyen Ngoc Tho were reelected to 5th terms

Apr. 9. They received 85% of the ballots cast although their vote in politically sophisticated Saigon was less than 50% of the potential vote. They defeated opposition tickets led by Nguyen Dinh Quat and Ho Nhat Tan. Among Diem's election promises were pledges to build a bigger army, clamp down on official corruption, improve government efficiency, start a social insurance program and expand industry and agriculture. He said opposition parties would be permitted to operate only as consistent with "national discipline."

Diem was inaugurated for his new term Apr. 29. His new presidential cabinet, named May 29, included 3 "superministers": State Secretary for Coordination of Economic Development—Vice Pres. Nguyen Ngoc Tho; State Secretary for Coordination of Security Matters—Nguyen Dinh Thuan; State Secretary for Coordination of Social and Cultural Matters—Truong Cong Cuu. Diem reorganized the government May 27 in keeping with his election pledges of governmental reform.

U.S. Administration Pledges 'Every Possible Help'

State Secy. Dean Rusk reported at a press conference in Washington May 4 that Viet Cong forces in South Vietnam had grown to 12,000 men and had killed or kidnaped more than 3,000 persons in 1960. Rusk declared that the U.S. would give South Vietnam "every possible help, across the entire spectrum in which help is needed." He refused, however, to say whether the U.S. would intervene militarily.

Chrmn J. W. Fulbright (D., Ark.) of the Senate Foreign Relations Committee met with Pres. John F. Kennedy later May 4 and told newsmen that he (Fulbright) would support the sending of U.S. combat troops to South Vietnam and Thailand if the Administration deemed necessary. Fulbright conceded that he had opposed U.S. military intervention in Laos, but he said the Laotians had shown indifference to their fate whereas the South Vietnamese and Thai had proved willing to defend themselves against communism.

Pres. Kennedy announced at his press conference in Washington May 5 that Vice Pres. Lyndon B. Johnson would go to Asia on a "fact-finding mission" to help the Administration decide the nature and extent of U.S. aid needed by South Vietnam. The President said: "The problem of troops . . . and the matter of what we are going to do to assist Vietnam obtain its independence is . . . still under consideration."

Vice Pres. Johnson, accompanied by his wife and a party of 30 Congress members and officials, left Washington by air May 9 and arrived in Saigon May 11. Addressing the South Vietnamese National Assembly May 12, Johnson declared that the U.S. was ready "immediately" to help expand South Vietnam's armed forces and to "meet the needs of your people on education, rural development, new industry and long-range economic development." Johnson met with Pres. Diem May 12. He said at a reception later that day that the U.S. was ready to stand "shoulder to shoulder" with South Vietnam in its war against communism.

An agreement for increased U.S. military and economic assistance for South Vietnam was made public in a joint communiqué issued in Saigon May 13 by Johnson and Diem. The aid increases, expected to total $40 million, were to be used primarily (a) to strengthen the South Vietnamese civil guard (40,000 men; 32,000 more in training) and army (150,000 men; 20,000 more requested), and (b) to support social welfare and public works programs.

Johnson left Saigon May 13 to continue his Asian tour with visits to the Philippines, Thailand, India and Pakistan. (Johnson flew to Manila May 13 and told a joint session of the Philippine Congress: "America will honor her commitments to the cause of freedom throughout the community of free nations"; "we will . . . proceed either alone or with our free friends to preserve our position in Asia." Johnson flew to Bangkok, Thailand May 16, met privately several times with Field Marshal Sarit Thanarat May 16-18 and said at a Bangkok news conference May 17 that he had made it "abundantly clear" to Sarit that the U.S. would aid Thailand against any Communist pressure. The Vice President landed in Karachi May 20 on the final stop of his tour and conferred with Pakistani Pres. Mohammed Ayub Khan. In a speech at a Karachi civic reception, Johnson reiterated the U.S.'

pledges of support for Asian efforts to combat "subversion, infiltration and terror.")

Johnson returned to Washington May 24, reported to Pres. Kennedy at the White House and then met reporters. He told the newsmen that the Administration would request an additional $100 million for Asian economic and military aid, the bulk to be allocated to South Vietnam, Thailand and Pakistan. (This was done in a special message sent to Congress by Pres. Kennedy May 25.) Johnson said his trip had convinced him that the U.S. must support efforts on a "broad regional basis" to "banish the curse of poverty, illness and illiteracy" in Asia. He declared that no country he visited had requested U.S. troops and that the U.S. did not plan to send armed forces to Asia.

The specific terms of the accord signed by Johnson and Diem were negotiated in South Vietnam in June and July by a 6-member economic survey committee headed by Dr. Eugene Staley of the Stanford (Calif.) Research Institute. The committee's work was the subject of a report submitted to Pres. Kennedy July 29. The report urged U.S. aid for a 15% increase in South Vietnam's armed forces, the resettlement of indefensible villages in 100 self-contained "agrovilles" and a long-range development program intended to improve the general economy and internal communications. Estimated cost of the program submitted to Mr. Kennedy: $50-$100 million.

Viet Cong Called Poorly Armed

Viet Cong fighters were lightly armed, largely with second-hand or home-made weapons, according to an article in the London *Times* Sept. 27. The article, written by the *Times'* Saigon correspondent, said that the home-made weapons, "turned out from different gauges of iron pipe," included rifles, mortars, and grenades that fired scrap iron. The guerrillas also had French rifles, light machineguns and grenades acquired during the long Indochinese war, U.S.-made rifles, pistols, machine guns and mortars captured more recently from the South Vietnamese army and "a few Skoda weapons of dubious antecedents."

Intelligence officers were cited as saying that "the best and most complex arms go to the 27 regular battalions of the Viet Cong," the "hard core" units occupying "fairly well-defined bases . . . usually in impenetrable jungles or marshland." According to the *Times* article: "On the approach of government columns, the Viet Cong battalions melt into the bush or retreat across the frontier into the comparative safety of Cambodia or Laos. Supporting these regular units, and in much closer contact with the villages, is another terrorist formation made up of what are called 'local troops on the district level.' These men are true guerrillas, constantly on the move from one village to another. . . . They are grouped into about 43 regional companies and 21 sections with special tasks, including propaganda and tax-collecting. The total strength of the Viet Cong troops and guerrillas is estimated at between 12,000 and 14,000 combatants."

In an effort to improve its operations against the Viet Cong, the South Vietnamese government appealed to Britain for technical help in fighting terrorism. In response to this request, 3 British officials who had been involved in the anti-terrorist campaign in Malaya arrived in Saigon in September to act as advisers on police and intelligence work. The leader of the group, R. G. K. Thompson, had served as defense secretary in the Malayan Federation.

Fighting Intensified, Government Revamps Forces

A Viet Cong campaign launched in May had been continued throughout the summer and fall, and small guerrilla units were reported to have penetrated Saigon's outskirts. The South Vietnamese army announced May 24 that its forces had been reorganized into 3 tactical commands, corresponding to the country's southern, central and northern regions, to cope with the guerrilla offensive. Maj. Gen. Duong Van Minh was named army commander-in-chief.

Viet Cong attacks were renewed after May 14 in the region between Saigon and Dalat, and major guerrilla activity was reported to have begun May 23 in the northern mountain region near Hué.

The South Vietnamese government announced June 2 that more than 140 Viet Cong fighters had been killed in recent attacks, 67 of them in a raid on a village 55 miles south of Saigon. More than 200 guerrillas were reported killed in fighting the following week; 100 of these were said to have been killed when 500 Viet Cong fighters attacked Phouclong, 200 miles southwest of Saigon.

169 guerrillas were killed July 16 when a 500-man Viet Cong unit was ambushed and surrounded by a 700-man South Vietnamese force in the Plaine des Joncs (Plain of Reeds) marsh area 80 miles west of Saigon. The battle was described as the bloodiest in South Vietnam since the 1954 armistice ended the revolt against France.

The South Vietnamese government announced Aug. 2 that all able men aged 25 to 33 had been ordered into the armed forces to help combat increased guerrilla attacks.

The *N.Y. Times* reported Aug. 21 that full-time Viet Cong forces had grown to 13,000-15,000 men and that casualties on both sides had reached 1,000 monthly.

The South Vietnamese government announced Sept. 4 that 302 guerrillas had been killed and 357 captured during August. Army casualties were listed as 73 killed, 50 missing, 191 wounded.

1,500 guerrillas Sept. 19 attacked and reportedly overran Phouc Minh, the capital of Phuoc Thanh Province. Several provincial officials and most of the defending forces' officers were reported to have been killed in the attack on the city, 60 miles north of Saigon. 2 South Vietnamese army companies were reported Sept. 22 to have been annihilated in Viet Cong attacks on Daclac Province.

The government's Psychological Warfare Department reported Oct. 7 that casualties for the period Sept. 20-Oct. 4 totaled 371 Viet Cong and 171 army troops killed, 322 Viet Cong captured and 59 government troops missing.

Pres. Diem declared Oct. 2 that the Viet Cong guerrilla campaign had grown into a "real war." Addressing the National Assembly, Diem said that the enemy "attacks us with regular units fully and completely equipped." He warned that the enemy "seeks a strategic position in Southeast Asia in conformity with the orders of the Communist International." Diem said that South Vietnamese army units had halted the guerrilla advance in the southwest but that renewed Viet Cong attacks were under way in the central and northeastern highlands. The attacks were accompanied by massive infiltration and propaganda in rural villages.

A state of emergency was decreed throughout South Vietnam by Diem Oct. 18 as a result of the increased Viet Cong attacks and of severe floods in southern rice-producing areas. The emergency decree, ratified the same day by the National Assembly, empowered Diem to suspend constitutional processes and take any action necessary for national security.

The *N.Y. Times* reported from Saigon Nov. 1 that more than 500 Viet Cong members were believed to have been killed in recent fighting with South Vietnamese forces. The engagements were said to include: (1) an attack in which South Vietnamese troops recaptured Phuoc Thanh, 60 miles northeast of Saigon, and killed 100 guerrillas; (2) a clash in which 70 Viet Cong were killed near Giao Thanh, a coastal town south of Saigon. Saigon reports said Nov. 2 that 50 paratroops and 100 guerrillas had been killed and wounded in fighting in Phuoc Thanh Province, 35 miles from Saigon.

South Vietnamese authorities had announced Oct. 3 that Communist guerrillas Oct. 1 had kidnaped Col. Hoang Thuy Nam, a state undersecretary and liaison officer to the International Control Commission (ICC) for Vietnam. Hoang's mutilated body was discovered in the Saigon River near Saigon Oct. 16.

South Vietnam formally charged North Vietnam Oct. 24 with aggression intended to overthrow the Diem régime. The complaint, lodged with the ICC, accused North Vietnam of an "intensive program of subversion, terror and direct aggression aimed at conquering the South and adding it to the Communist bloc."

The South Vietnamese charges were supported by the U.S. State Department in a 2-volume "white book" entitled *A Threat to Peace.* The U.S. "white book," published Dec. 10, contained copies of documents captured from North Vietnamese sources. The State Department document charged that the North Vietnamese government directed and controlled the Viet Cong movement. It warned that South Vietnam stood in "clear and present danger of Communist conquest." Such a conquest, the State Department predicted, would "doubtless seal the fate of Laos, where the Communists already control half the country," and would endanger Cambodia's neutrality and the position of Thailand.

U.S. Agrees to Train Combat Troops

Nguyen Dinh Thuan, State Secretary for the Coordination of Security Matters in Pres. Diem's cabinet, had met with Pres. Kennedy June 14 to transmit a message from Diem requesting that U.S. military instructors be used to train Vietnamese soldiers "directly," instead of training Vietnamese who in turn would serve as combat instructors. Thuan and U.S. officials reached agreement June 16 on a program for the direct training and combat supervision of Vietnamese by U.S. instructors.

The deterioration of the South Vietnamese military situation in the fall brought reports that the Kennedy Administration was considering U.S. intervention to prevent the Diem régime's overthrow. A State Department statement issued Oct. 2 said the U.S. was "pressing ahead with urgent measures to increase the ability of the South Vietnamese soldier to defend his country." It was reported that the Administration had decided to send U.S. combat and training formations to Communist-threatened areas of South East Asia if necessary. But State Department press officer Lincoln White told newsmen Oct. 11 that "there has been no such decision. Furthermore, . . . Vietnam assures us . . . that with U.S. material assistance and training services, it can handle the present Communist aggressive attacks."

The U.S.' reported decision to intervene militarily was said to have been transmitted to other SEATO (South-East

Asia Treaty Organization) nations at the 15th semi-annual meeting of the alliance's military advisers, held in Bangkok Oct. 3-6. A final communiqué issued by the advisers Oct. 6 said only that they had "decided upon practical measures to increase . . . the effectiveness of SEATO defenses to defeat any aggression."

Pres. Kennedy announced at his news conference in Washington Oct. 11 that he had directed retired Gen. Maxwell D. Taylor to "go to Saigon to discuss . . . ways in which we can perhaps better assist . . . Vietnam in meeting . . . [the] threat to its independence." Responding to reporters' queries as to whether he was considering sending U.S. troops to South Vietnam, Thailand or Laos, Mr. Kennedy said that "we're going to wait till Gen. Taylor comes back" with information and "then we can come to conclusions." (In a personal message to Pres. Diem on South Vietnam's 6th independence day Oct. 26, Pres. Kennedy again pledged that "the United States is determined to help Vietnam preserve its independence, protect its people against Communist assassins and build a better life." Mr. Kennedy told Diem that he would be able to "consider with you additional measures that we might take to assist . . . Vietnam" after he received Taylor's report.)

Taylor flew to Saigon Oct. 18. He met with Pres. Diem immediately after his arrival and consulted Oct. 19 with South Vietnamese army leaders and Lt Gen. Lionel C. McGarr, head of the U.S. Military Advisory Group. Taylor flew Oct. 21 to Dongha, 450 miles north of Saigon on the border between North and South Vietnam, to inspect South Vietnamese units in the field; he conferred again with Diem in Dalat Oct. 21 and toured the Mekong River delta area by plane Oct. 22. Taylor conferred with U.S. officers in Saigon Oct. 23 and met again with Diem Oct. 24. He left for Thailand Oct. 25. Taylor urged in a farewell statement that South Vietnam begin a "national mobilization" in the "political, economic, military and psychological fields." He expressed "great confidence in the military capability of South Vietnam to cope with anything within its borders." (Taylor flew to Bangkok Oct. 25 for a 5-day visit and talks with Thai Premier Sarit Thanarat.)

Taylor returned to Washington Nov. 3 after a stopover in Manila. He told newsmen that his report to the President would stress Diem's ability "to prevail against the Communist threat" to his country. Taylor reported to Pres. Kennedy immediately after his return.

Taylor's trip to South Vietnam was assailed by the USSR and North Vietnam's Communist régime as a prelude to U.S. military intervention in Southeast Asia. Political commentaries on Moscow radio had charged Oct. 12 that the Taylor mission was proof of the U.S.' "openly aggressive" plans to send troops into Vietnam. North Vietnam protested to the International Control Commission for Vietnam Oct. 14 that the purpose of Taylor's visit was to "intensify United States intervention in South Vietnam and prepare the way for introducing United States troops" there. It said the Taylor mission itself violated the Geneva armistice accords.

U.S. Military Personnel & Helicopters Arrive

The U.S. aircraft ferry-carrier *Core* arrived in Saigon Dec. 11 with 33 U.S. Army helicopters and 400 air and ground crewmen assigned to operate them for the South Vietnamese army. The helicopter consignment followed an announcement by State Secy. Rusk Dec. 8 that the U.S. was consulting with its allies on the provision of joint economic and technical defense support for Vietnam. Rusk said South Vietnam was in "clear and present danger" of Red conquest.

The U.S. Military Assistance Advisory Group in Vietnam had been limited by the Geneva accords of 1954 to a strength of 685 officers and men. Most were instructors in the use of arms and equipment supplied under U.S. aid programs. Other U.S. troops were in South Vietnam as guerrilla warfare instructors and specialists. It was reported Nov. 12 that 4 U.S. F-101 reconnaissance jets were engaged in photo-spotting of guerrilla units in remote areas vulnerable only to air attack.

The *N.Y. Times* reported Dec. 20 that uniformed U.S. troops and specialists were "operating in battle areas with South Vietnamese forces" and although not in combat, were authorized to fire back if fired on. The troops, said to number about 2,000, were described as operating aircraft and transport and communications facilities. The *Times* reported that the U.S. had delivered $500 million worth of military equipment to South Vietnam in the past 7 years, $65 million worth in 1961.

Saigon dispatches had reported Nov. 9 that Air Force Globemasters had begun transporting large amounts of equipment to South Vietnam from Clark Field in the Philippines. The equipment was said to be intended for a small force of B-26 bombers, fighters and helicopters scheduled to be given to South Vietnam together with services of 200 air and ground crew instructors.

It was reported in Washington Dec. 16 that Diem had agreed to U.S. demands for a joint program to assess South Vietnam's need for rapid and radical reforms to assure economic and military efficiency. The reports, circulated by Kennedy Administration officials, came after intensive negotiations between Diem and U.S. Amb.-to-South Vietnam Frederick E. Nolting, Jr. It had been reported from Saigon Nov. 26 that Diem had refused to accept U.S. demands that his régime be liberalized, but an agreement reportedly was reached after the U.S. threatened to recall Nolting and curtail its aid. In return for Diem's assent to the reforms, the U.S. was said to have promised a heavy increase in its economic and military aid programs. Pres. Kennedy informed Diem in a letter made public Dec. 15 that "we shall promptly increase our assistance to your defense effort."

1962

U.S. involvement in the Vietnamese war grew during 1962, and U.S.-operated helicopters were in use by February to ferry South Vietnamese troops into combat. The Soviet government, reacting to the new development, accused the U.S. of fighting an "undeclared war" in Vietnam. In a dramatic display of domestic opposition to Pres. Diem's régime, 2 dissident South Vietnamese Air Force pilots bombed Diem's palace in February but did not hurt the president. In a long-range program to clear key areas of guerrillas, South Vietnam began consolidating scattered rural populations in fortified "strategic villages." The International Control Commission for Vietnam accused North Vietnam of "subversion and aggression" in South Vietnam but simultaneously charged South Vietnam and the U.S. with violating the 1954 Geneva accords.

U.S. Intervention Grows

The Viet Cong assault, which struck at the Ngo Dinh Diem government in nearly all parts of South Vietnam, was viewed by the U.S. as a major attempt to extend Communist influence throughout Southeast Asia. It was feared that if the Viet Cong campaign succeeded in undermining the Diem régime, not only South Vietnam but neighboring Cambodia and Laos, the latter also torn by Communist-provoked civil war, would come under Communist control. The U.S. response to this threat was to increase the flow of military aid to the Diem government. With the arms and equipment came thousands of U.S. technicians and military officers to train and guide South Vietnamese forces in its use. By the end of 1961, U.S. personnel had been operating with Vietnamese units in combat areas, although they technically were not in combat and were not authorized to fire except in self-defense. The U.S. intervention in the South Vietnamese war grew substantially during 1962.

Social Aid Planned by U.S. & South Vietnam

The U.S. and South Vietnamese governments announced Jan. 4 that they would cooperate in starting "a broad economic and social program aimed at providing every Vietnamese with the means for improving his standard of living." The program was planned as part of U.S. efforts to strengthen South Vietnam against the Viet Cong. The U.S. had exerted

30

pressure on the Diem government to institute reforms that would enable it to combat the Communist rebels effectively in the social and economic as well as the military field. Diem had resisted most of the suggested political reforms.

The program was to be financed by South Vietnam by heavy duties on luxury imports and by a new tax system. The U.S. would provide advice, support essential imports and finance specific projects. State Department officials said U.S. expenditures for South Vietnam would rise "appreciably" above the $136 million worth of economic aid provided in 1961. The announcement stressed that the U.S. "simultaneously" would act to strengthen South Vietnam militarily.

Goals of the development program: (1) the training of village officials; (2) rural clinic and inocculation programs; (3) expansion of education; (4) improvement of communications; (5) road construction; (6) aid to farmers; (7) pest control; (8) resettlement of villagers endangered by guerrillas; (9) Mekong delta flood reconstruction; (10) public works to end unemployment; (11) industrial development.

(Viet Cong guerrillas continued their terror campaign in January, particularly in the Mekong River delta area. The *N.Y. Times* reported Jan. 9 that 300 guerrillas had attacked and captured Khanh Binh Tay, near the Gulf of Siam. The Mekong campaign apparently was aimed at disrupting South Vietnam's rice production.)

USSR Accuses U.S. of Violating Geneva Accords

In an exchange of notes between the USSR and Britain, the Soviet government Jan. 10 denounced the U.S. for "gross interference" in South Vietnam's internal affairs and for "open violations of the international agreements on Indochina." The U.S. bore primary responsibility for the "present worsening of the situation in South Vietnam," the note charged. It also accused South Vietnamese Pres. Ngo Dinh Diem of abolishing all democratic liberties and creating "a military dictatorship based on ruthless terror." The British reply, in a Feb. 16 *aide-mémoire*, rejected the Soviet charges against the U.S. and asserted that "the rebellion in South

Vietnam has been fomented, organized, in part supplied, and wholly directed from the North."

In a statement issued in Moscow Mar. 17, the Soviet Foreign Ministry charged the U.S. with fighting an "undeclared war" against the "national liberation movement" led by the Viet Cong. The Soviet statement, circulated as a diplomatic note to all participants in the 1954 Geneva conference on Indochina, demanded (1) "the discontinuation of [U.S.] delivery of armaments and war materials to South Vietnam"; (2) "the immediate evacuation of United States military personnel from South Vietnam"; (3) "the liquidation of the American military command on the territory of that country." The Soviet statement said: "The U.S., by continuing to increasingly intervene in the domestic affairs of South Vietnam, flagrantly violates the Geneva agreements of 1954 on Vietnam and creates a serious threat to the peace in that region. In defiance of the Geneva agreements, which ban the introduction into Vietnam of any military units and additional military personnel, . . . some 5,000 American servicemen are now in South Vietnam . . . and are directly participating in military operations against the local population."

The British government Apr. 16 rejected the USSR's request for joint measures against the U.S.' involvement in South Vietnam. (The British note was in response to the USSR's Mar. 17 message, which had appealed to Britain, as co-chairing power of the 1954 Geneva conference on Indochina, for joint measures against the U.S. involvement in Vietnam.) The British note asserted that the major cause of the South Vietnamese guerrilla war and of the threat to the peace of Asia was the Viet Cong subversive campaign fostered by Communist North Vietnam. It suggested that instead of seeking measures against the U.S. involvement, the USSR respond to Britain's prior request for a joint appeal to North Vietnam to end its intervention in South Vietnam.

The USSR answered Britain July 3 with a note that again condemned the U.S.' intervention in the civil war but defended North Vietnam's "interest" in the fighting. It said that "naturally the Vietnamese in the north feel warm sympathy and fraternal solidarity toward the population of South

Vietnam and express support for their just fight for . . . independence."

U.S. Helicopters in Combat

South Vietnamese troops recaptured the guerrilla-held village of Hung My Feb. 4 in a surprise airborne attack mounted with U.S. helicopters and crews. A helicopter was shot down in the operation, but its crew was saved, and the craft later was repaired and flown out. 15 helicopters were used in the attack; they first shuttled troops to an assembly point near the village, then flew them directly into the village, behind the guerrillas' positions. Officials conceded, however, that the attack had failed in that 130 Viet Cong guerrillas had escaped and only 3 were captured. Hung My was situated at South Vietnam's extreme southern tip.

A 2d U.S. helicopter was shot down and crashed without loss of life Feb. 6 in a similar raid.

U.S. Forms Vietnam Command

The Defense Department announced Feb. 8 that a new U.S. military command was being formed in South Vietnam to coordinate all U.S. military support for the Diem government. The new unit, the U.S. Military Assistance Command (MAC), Vietnam, was to be commanded by Gen. Paul D. Harkins, former U.S. Army deputy commander-in-chief in the Pacific. (Harkins, promoted from lieutenant general to full general for his new assignment, arrived in Saigon Feb. 13.) MAC, Vietnam was to supervise the U.S. Military Assistance Advisory Group, commanded by Lt. Gen. Lionel C. McGarr, and was to direct all U.S. troops and other personnel on advisory, training and support missions with South Vietnamese forces. A Pentagon spokesman said Feb. 9 that the new command was a demonstration of the U.S. belief that "this is a war we can't afford to lose" and that "we're drawing a line" against Communist subversion in South Vietnam.

(According to the N.Y. Times Feb. 8, the U.S. currently had nearly 5,000 military personnel in South Vietnam. Most were engaged in training and technical work, but many were on ground and air support missions. The UPI reported from Washington Mar. 8 that a Defense Department summary of U.S. military aid to South Vietnam had listed the total as nearly $750 million. Arthur Z. Gardiner, director of the U.S. operations mission in South Vietnam, told newsmen in Saigon Mar. 7 that economic aid currently was being provided at the rate of $200 million annually.)

Political Controversy in the U.S.

The mounting U.S. involvement in South Vietnam's civil war was the subject of several statements by American political leaders in February. Pres. Kennedy, replying to reporters' questions on the subject, said at his press conference Feb. 7: The South Vietnamese war "is a subterranean war, a guerrilla war of increasing ferocity. . . . [The U.S.] has been assisting Vietnam economically to maintain its independence . . . and also [has] sent training groups out there, which have been expanded in recent weeks, as the attacks . . . have increased. We are out there on training and on transportation, and we are assisting in every way we properly can. . . ."

The Republican National Committee's publication *Battle Line* charged in its Feb. 13 issue that Mr. Kennedy had been "less than candid" about U.S. involvement in the Vietnam fighting. The bulletin called on Mr. Kennedy to "make a full report" on the extent of this involvement. It said: The U.S. should be informed if it was "moving toward another Korea", "the people should not have to wait until American casualty lists are posted"; "we would ask Pres. Kennedy if it isn't time to drop the pretense that the United States is merely acting as military adviser to South Vietnam."

Asst. State Secy. W. Averell Harriman told the Senate Foreign Relations Committee Feb. 13 that the Kennedy Administration had "no present plans for commitment of American combat forces" in the Vietnamese fighting.

Pres. Kennedy said at his Feb. 14 news conference that all major U.S. moves to support the South Vietnamese government had the approval of "a very strong bipartisan concensus" of Republicans and Democrats. He said he had been

as "frank" as possible, consistent with security, on the nature
of the U.S.' involvement in Vietnam. He reiterated that "the
training missions that we have there have been instructed
that if they are fired upon, they are of course to fire back, but
we have not sent combat troops in [the] generally understood
sense of the word."

Commenting on charges that Mr. Kennedy had concealed
the extent of the U.S. involvement in the South Vietnamese
civil war, ex-Vice Pres. Richard M. Nixon said Feb. 15: "I
don't agree at all with any partisan or other criticism of the
U.S. build-up in Vietnam. My only question is whether it
may be too little and too late. . . . I support Pres. Kennedy
to the hilt, and I only hope he will step up the build-up and
under no circumstances curtail it because of possible criticism."

Communists Threaten U.S. with Retaliation

The increasingly overt U.S. involvement in Vietnam brought
warnings of retaliatory measures from Communist China and
the Soviet Union.

A Communist Chinese Foreign Ministry statement broadcast Feb. 24 by Peiping radio said the U.S. intervention was
"a direct threat" to Communist North Vietnam and hence
"seriously affects the security of China and the peace of
Asia." The statement charged that the new U.S. command
in South Vietnam was "by no means merely one for military
assistance, but an operational command of the United States
imperialists for direct participation." "The United States is
already in an 'undeclared war' in South Vietnam," the Chinese
statement said.

Soviet Deputy Foreign Min. Valerian A. Zorin said at a
UN press conference Feb. 26 that the U.S. risked becoming
"bogged down in a very disadvantageous and politically unjustified war" in South Vietnam. He warned that the U.S.'
continued involvement could "entail very unpleasant consequences."

State Secy. Dean Rusk said at a Washington news conference Mar. 1 that the South Vietnamese war could be ended
easily if the Communist nations halted their intervention and

encouragement of the Viet Cong. Although he declared that the U.S. was always ready to discuss peace, he expressed doubt that it would be useful to convene international talks on Vietnam, as proposed by the Soviet bloc. Rusk said: "There can be peace overnight in Vietnam if those responsible for the aggression wish peace. It is as simple as that."

Dissidents Bomb Diem's Palace

The South Vietnamese presidential palace in Saigon was bombed and partially burned Feb. 27 (Feb. 26 U.S. time) by 2 dissident South Vietnamese Air Force pilots flying U.S.-supplied AD-6 fighter-bombers.

Pres. Diem was in the palace when the planes attacked but was not injured. Mr. and Mrs. Ngo Dinh Nhu, the president's influential brother and sister-in-law, also in the palace, were unhurt except for minor injuries to Mrs. Nhu when she fell during the raid. The only person known to have been killed during the raid was Sidney Ambrose, 49, an American technician, who fell from a roof while watching the attack.

The attacking planes were piloted by First Lt. Pham Phu Quoc and Lt. Nguyen Van Cu. They had taken off from the Bienhoa airfield to attack targets in guerrilla-held areas. Instead, they veered toward Saigon and strafed and bombed the palace. Despite official South Vietnamese denials, reporters insisted the planes had dropped napalm bombs. Following the raid, which was unopposed, the 2 pilots flew toward Cambodia. Pham was captured near Saigon after his plane was hit by ground fire and crashed. Nguyen reportedly crash-landed in Cambodia and was arrested.

Apparently only the 2 pilots were involved in the attack. Tanks and government troops surrounded the palace after the raid, but no disturbances occurred.

The *N.Y. Times* reported Mar. 13 that Phan Huy Quat, president of South Vietnam's opposition Committee on National Union, had appealed to U.S. Amb. Frederick Nolting Jr. to intercede for liberalization of the Diem government. Quat reportedly contended that many honest Vietnamese nationalists and the bulk of South Vietnam's population had been alienated from the régime by its suppression of political and civil rights. He appealed to Nolting to urge that non-Communist opposition leaders be freed from jail and loyal nationalist groups be permitted to present their grievances. Nolting had told South Vietnamese in a Saigon speech Feb. 15 that "my government fully supports your elected constitutional government" despite the criticism of the Diem régime by what he called misguided "skeptics." Nolting conceded that there had been delay in carrying out promised reforms and local aid programs, but he declared that the only hope for success against the Viet Cong lay with "the dedicated and courageous leadership of your president."

(Stanley Millet, a U.S. professor who had spent a year in South Vietnam, reported in *Harper's* in September: "In that entire year I never heard a single Vietnamese voice raised in defense of the Diem régime. High and low, government officials, professors, army officers and students condemned it and yearned for a change—a *coup d'état* which would rid them of Diem before the Communists crushed him.")

AMERICANS JOIN FIGHTING

U.S. Pilots Fly Combat Missions

U.S. State Department officials confirmed Mar. 9 that American pilots were flying combat-training missions with South Vietnamese airmen over guerrilla-held areas of South Vietnam. They would neither confirm nor deny that these missions involved bombing and strafing attacks on Viet Cong strongholds. Saigon dispatches of the UPI and Reuters had reported earlier Mar. 9 that the U.S. pilots were involved directly in attacks and that in most cases the Vietnamese airmen flew as co-pilots. The UPI said that such use of U.S. pilots had been going on for 2 months and that it had been justified as an emergency measure pending the training of combatable South Vietnamese airmen. *The Wall St. Journal* reported from Saigon Mar. 6 that the U. S. Army helicopters used to ferry South Vietnamese troops on raids against the guerrillas usually had American crewmen manning machineguns to return ground fire.

U.S. Air Force helicopters, manned by U.S. crews, prepare to airlift South Vietnamese soldiers into combat against Viet Cong in early Feb. 1962. This mission was against guerrilla-held village of Hung My. (Wide World photo)

U.S. personnel were reported by Western newsmen to be taking a direct part in most major South Vietnamese combat actions. Among examples of U.S. intervention:

● U.S. helicopters flew troops to besieged villages in Tay Ninh and Phuoc Thanh Provinces Mar. 4, and Viet Cong units were forced to retreat after losing 110 killed in the 2 battles.

• The civil guard post of Bo Tuc, near the Cambodian frontier, was rescued Mar. 4 when South Vietnamese planes strafed 500 guerrilla attackers and U.S. planes dropped 500 paratroops with their American advisers. The guerrillas were said to have escaped, leaving 56 dead.

• South Vietnamese troops were flown by helicopters into an attack Mar. 6 on Viet Cong-held Cai Ngai village, at the southern tip of the country. At least 25 guerrillas were killed in the action and accompanying strafing, but the bulk of the Communist force escaped. 5 helicopters were hit by ground fire; one was brought down but later was repaired and flown out.

• Helicopters airlifted a battalion of South Vietnamese troops into action Mar. 13 against a force of 500 guerrillas operating along the Upper Mekong River in Kien Hoa Province. It was reported Mar. 14, however, that the main body of guerrillas had escaped.

Pres. Kennedy said at his news conference in Washington Mar. 14 that while "a good many Americans" were serving in Vietnam, none could properly be termed "combat troops." He added that "if there were a basic change in that situation in Vietnam which calls for a Constitutional decision [on whether to send troops], I . . . would go to the Congress."

Defense Secy. Robert S. McNamara confirmed at a Washington news conference Mar. 15 that American servicemen in South Vietnam had exchanged fire with Communist guerrillas. McNamara was the first high-ranking Kennedy Administration official to confirm the reports that U.S. troops had been involved directly in the fighting. He said: "I think our mission in South Vietnam is very clear. We are there at the request of the South Vietnamese government to provide training. . . . There has been sporadic fire aimed at United States personnel, and in some minor instances they've had to return that fire." U.S. advisers had taken part in "combat-type training missions" with Vietnamese troops, but "Americans are under instructions not to fire unless fired upon." (McNamara left Washington for Honolulu Mar. 20, accompanied by Adm. Harry D. Felt, U.S. Pacific commander, for his 3d Hawaiian meeting of 1962 on the South Vietnamese situation. Returning from these talks, McNamara told newsmen in San Francisco Mar. 22 that U.S. assistance had enabled the South Vietnamese to take the offensive.)

15 H-34 combat helicopters of the U.S.' 362d Marine Medium Helicopter Squadron landed in South Vietnam Apr. 15 from the aircraft carrier *Princeton.* The Marine helicopters, to be based near Soctrang, capital of Ba Xuyen Province, 100 miles southwest of Saigon, were to reinforce the 3 U.S. Army helicopter companies already in South Vietnam. They were the first Marine air units sent to Vietnam.

State Undersecy. George W. Ball warned Apr. 30 that the South Vietnamese war would be a "slow, arduous" struggle of the sort not liked by Americans. Addressing the Detroit Economic Club, Ball asserted, however, that the war could be won if the U.S. maintained its support for the South Vietnamese government and made possible the defeat of the guerrillas by arms and attrition.

Operation Sunrise Shifts Villages

South Vietnam's first long-range counteroffensive against the Viet Cong, dubbed Operation Sunrise, was launched Mar. 22 in Binh Duong Province, 35 miles north of Saigon. The operation, described in Saigon dispatches Mar. 26, was aimed at (1) clearing key areas of guerrillas; (2) regrouping local populations in fortified "strategic hamlets"; (3) giving these villages government services and facilities for self-defense.

According to the Mar. 29 *N.Y. Times,* many villagers were resisting the move to fortified hamlets. Homer Bigart reported from Bencat that in several such operations South Vietnamese troops had surrounded villages in an effort to prevent the men from fleeing and then had burned the villages to the ground after transferring the remaining occupants—women, children, aged persons and families volunteering for resettlement. Bigart reported that a U.S. adviser had found 630 Vietnamese women and children, ill-housed and ill-fed in a fortified village described as a "stockade." U.S. advisory personnel in South Vietnam were said to have backed Operation Sunrise because of the success of the similar anti-guerrilla program in Malaya.

A sharp increase in South Vietnamese combat operations took place in April. Among major operations reported during the month:

• The South Vietnamese government reported Apr. 7 that its forces, forewarned by spies, had repelled an attack by 1,200 guerrillas in a 4-hour battle in the Tra Bong District, 330 miles northeast of Saigon. It was the biggest guerrilla offensive in months. 45 Viet Cong were reported killed. South Vietnamese casualties were 16 dead and 33 wounded.

• A U.S. military source in Saigon Apr. 11 reported the death of 12 Viet Cong guerrillas, presumably killed by T-28 fighter-bombers piloted by Americans.

• 29 U.S. helicopters—the largest such force yet used in South Vietnam—airlifted about 600 South Vietnamese troops to the Mekong River delta in Kein Phong Province (80 miles southeast of Saigon) Apr. 22 to raise to 1,200 the number of government troops used in a "mopping up" operation there.

• 87 guerrillas were reported killed and 3 captured in a Mekong River delta battle at Cantho Apr. 24.

• The U.S. reported Apr. 24 that 69 guerrillas had been killed in a running battle with government troops 34 miles southwest of Saigon.

• 20 guerrillas were reported killed Apr. 25 when a Viet Cong attack on Binh Chanh, 12 miles south of Saigon, was repulsed.

More than 200 Viet Cong guerrillas were killed in 7 battles during the latter part of April, the South Vietnamese government reported Apr. 28.

McNamara Denies Plan to Use U.S. Combat Men

Defense Secy. McNamara, accompanied by Gen. Lyman L. Lemnitzer, chairman of the Joint Chiefs of Staff, arrived in Saigon May 9 to confer with U.S. and South Vietnamese officials, reportedly in an effort to eliminate friction between them and to encourage Pres. Diem's régime to a more effective prosecution of the war.

'Strategic hamlet' in South Vietnamese jungle. Government gathered scattered families into these fortified villages.

(Wide World photo)

McNamara told newsmen that "there is no plan for introducing [American] combat forces in South Vietnam." He toured South Vietnamese battle areas by plane and helicopter May 9-10 and met with Diem late May 10 for a strategy discussion attended by Adm. Felt and Gen. Harkins. He left for Washington May 11 after saying at a Saigon news conference that he was "tremendously encouraged" by developments in South Vietnam and that he saw no reason for a large scale increase in U S military aid to the Ngo government.

U.S. Seeks Allies' Aid

State Secy. Rusk, attending an ANZUS Council meeting in Canberra, Australia May 9, appealed to the U.S.' Pacific allies for "a helping hand" in Vietnam. A communiqué issued later May 9 by Rusk, Australian External Affairs Min. Sir Garfield Barwick and New Zealand Prime Min. Keith J. Holyoake said the ANZUS powers (Australia, New Zealand, the U.S.) were prepared to back the South Vietnamese. Barwick said Australia would send aid and a few technical experts but no combat troops. (30 Australian specialists in guerrilla warfare arrived in Saigon in August to help train South Vietnamese troops.)

A report made public May 27 by the U.S. House Foreign Affairs Committee asserted that SEATO "offers no security" to the nations of Southeast Asia and might even have had a harmful effect by hampering the creation of effective defense arrangements. The report, written by a bipartisan group of committee members, traced the pact's ineffectiveness to its requirement of unanimity and "the lack of support of Britain and France." The study concluded that "either the [SEATO] rule of unanimity should be abolished or the treaty itself should be terminated."

NORTH VIETNAMESE INVOLVEMENT

ICC Accuses Hanoi of Intervention

A report of the International Control Commission (ICC) for Vietnam, disclosed in part in Hanoi and Saigon May 25, charged that Communist North Vietnam was fostering the guerrilla war by "subversion and aggression" in South Vietnam.

The report was first disclosed when Hanoi radio broadcast sections of it. The Hanoi broadcast reported that North Vietnamese Defense Min. No Nguyen Giap had rejected the report and had charged Gopalaswami Parthasarathy, Indian chairman of the ICC, with subservience to U.S. "warmongers" in South Vietnam. Saigon sources asserted May 25 that the report had been adopted by the Indian and Canadian members of the ICC but had been opposed by the Polish member.

The report, based on investigations of truce violation charges, was submitted to the British and Soviet governments. It condemned North Vietnam for violations of the 1954 Indochina armistice agreement but also held that the U.S. had violated the pact with its military buildup in South Vietnam. The report cited evidence that Hanoi had sent troops and supplies into South Vietnam. It also accused South Vietnam of violating the 1954 Geneva accords by accepting the U.S. aid and establishing "a factual military alliance" with the U.S.

The British government disclosed June 25 that it had proposed to the USSR that mobile inspection teams be established on the border between North and South Vietnam. The disclosure was made with the publication of a British note delivered to the USSR June 14 and of the ICC report. The British note called on the USSR for joint action to halt the flow of weapons and men across the border.

South Vietnam informed the ICC June 30 that Communist Chinese artillery, bazookas and munitions were in use by the Viet Cong guerrillas and had been captured by government forces. It charged that the Chinese weapons could have come only through North Vietnam and that this proved North Vietnam had violated the Geneva pacts.

Diem Government Cancels Elections

The government-controlled Saigon press reported June 8 that the Diem régime had taken steps to postpone National Assembly elections that were constitutionally required in August. The Assembly named a special committee to study proposals for a constitutional amendment to extend deputies' terms from 3 to 4 years.

Presidential decrees published May 17 had forbidden the holding of any meeting without prior governmental permission. Persons planning meetings for any purpose were required to apply for permission 7 days in advance.

The U.S. embassy in Saigon announced June 2 that it had asked all Americans in South Vietnam to obey a new "protection of morality law" under which the Diem régime had banned all dancing, boxing, animal fights and beauty contests. Mrs. Ngo Dinh Nhu, the president's sister-in-law and originator of the "morality law," declared June 12 that dancing was akin to "promiscuity." Mrs. Nhu, a member of the National Assembly, an influential figure in South Vietnam's Roman Catholic minority and frequently Pres. Diem's official hostess, said that Americans should share South Vietnam's wartime "austerity" or go home.

Fighting Grows in Intensity

Viet Cong forces were reported to have launched mass attacks in May on areas under government control, and massive South Vietnamese counter-attacks followed. Thousands of South Vietnamese troops and Viet Cong fighters were locked in battle in these attacks, reported throughout the country:

• U.S. Army and Marine helicopters flew South Vietnamese troops into the Plaine des Joncs (Plain of Reeds) area in the Mekong River delta May 2 and 6 in surprise raids on Viet Cong forces. 10 guerrillas were reported killed May 2 and 57 killed May 6.

• A 1,000-man Viet Cong force reportedly killed 13 civilians May 4 in an attack on a land development center 90 miles west of Saigon.

• More than 1,000 South Vietnamese troops—flown into the area by U.S. helicopters—engaged in 5 separate clashes with the Viet Cong May 12 in one of the year's biggest battles in the Mekong delta about 75 miles southwest of Saigon. 2 helicopters were shot down but recovered. U.S. Col. Frank Butner Clay, senior adviser to the South Vietnamese 7th Division, derided early reports that 300 guerrillas had been killed; he said he doubted that more than 20 had been slain.

• The South Vietnamese 7th Division reportedly killed 95 guerrillas and captured 35 (including 10 wounded) May 23-24 in an attack on a Viet Cong force trapped on the southern edge of the Plaine des Joncs. It was the worst Communist defeat in the area since 169 guerrillas were slain in Kien Tuong Province in July 1961.

The South Vietnamese government reported May 26 that 227 guerrillas had been killed and 82 captured during that week's fighting.

• The Viet Cong reportedly killed 24 members of a 1,200-man private army (the Sea Swallows) commanded by the Rev. Nguyen Lac Hoa, a Catholic priest, in an attack May 29 on the village of Phy My, about 170 miles southwest of Saigon on the Camau Peninsula. A May 30 report listed more than

100 guerrillas killed in a counter-attack that day, but 26 Sea
Swallows members were killed, 18 wounded and 2 reported
missing.

Several U.S. servicemen serving in technical or advisory
capacities with South Vietnamese forces were killed in fighting with guerrillas in June and July: Sgt. Robert Gardner of
Nashua, N.H. was killed June 13 in fighting in the Quang
Nam Province area. Capt. Walter R. McCarthy Jr. of Brooklyn,
N.Y. and an unidentified U.S. lieutenant were killed June
16 in a Communist ambush of an armored convoy 35 miles
north of Saigon; 15 South Vietnamese soldiers and a number
of civilians were killed in the attack, in which the convoy,
bound from Bencat to Saigon, was destroyed by about 200
guerrillas. Capt. Don J. York of Asheville, N.C. was killed
July 14 in a guerrilla ambush of a South Vietnamese army
convoy 40 miles north of Saigon; 22 South Vietnamese troops
were killed in the action. 4 Americans were reported killed
or missing July 15 in the crash of a U.S. Army helicopter
shot down by guerrillas 20 miles north of Kontum, near South
Vietnam's western border with Laos; Lt. Col. Anthony J.
Tencza of Fairfax, Va. and CWO Joseph Goldberg of Sanford,
N.C. were killed in the crash; Sp/5C James E. Lane of Spring
Lake, N.C. and Sp/5C Harold L. Guthrie of Burlington,
N.C. were missing. An unidentified U.S. pilot was killed July
16 in the crash of a South Vietnamese Air Force C-47 near
Kontum, in the central highlands; 22 Vietnamese also died
in the crash.

The fighting grew in intensity during June, July and August,
and thousands of South Vietnamese troops were air-lifted
into action against the Viet Cong guerrillas aboard U.S. military helicopters. Hundreds of engagements were fought, and
the South Vietnamese government reported June 30 that in
only 30 days—to June 28—860 Viet Cong members had been
killed, 180 wounded and 1,200 captured. Government losses
in the same period reportedly were 300 killed, 500 wounded
and 200 missing.

Viet Cong radio broadcasts monitored in Saigon and reported Aug. 4 by the *N.Y. Times* expressed concern at the
large numbers of guerrillas admitted to have been killed or

lost in South Vietnamese army attacks in the Plaine des Joncs in July. Conceding that 100 Viet Cong had been killed and that 50 were missing, the broadcasts charged that guerrilla commanders had courted defeat by disobeying orders to disperse in small bands when attacked by superior force. The broadcasts admitted that the Plaine des Joncs stronghold had been betrayed to government troops by the local peasantry.

Some 4,000 South Vietnamese ground, air and naval troops, supported by U.S. planes, undertook a 16-day campaign against the Viet Cong in the Camau Peninsula Aug. 15-30. The South Vietnamese army reported Aug. 31 that 499 guerrillas had been killed in the drive.

Despite the apparently-growing Viet Cong vulnerability to attack, Kennedy Administration officials quoted by the *N.Y. Times* Aug. 22 estimated that the guerrilla forces had increased from 12,000-15,000 men at the end of 1961 to a current total of 20,000. These officials expressed the view that the 2 sides in the South Vietnamese civil war had fought to a virtual stalemate.

South Vietnam reported Sept. 6 that its troops had killed 54 Viet Cong in a battle near the Cambodian border and 63 in fighting near Saigon Sept. 4; the government claimed that these 2 battles brought the number of guerrillas killed in the past week to 308. The government said Sept. 10 that its forces, supported by U.S. helicopters, had killed 40 guerrillas, wounded 7 and captured 4 in fighting that day in Kien Phong Province, 80 miles west of Saigon. South Vietnamese troops killed more than 100 guerrillas and captured 8 in a battle Sept. 9 in the Plaine des Joncs, according to a U.S. report Sept. 13. (South Vietnam said 116 Communists were killed.)

Some 2,500 South Vietnamese soldiers, supported by U.S. helicopters, fighter-bombers and amphibious forces killed at least 153 Viet Cong (according to a U.S. report) Sept. 18 in fighting around the Plaine des Joncs village of Anhu. 38 guerrillas were captured. The estimate of the number killed was raised Sept. 19 to 168, one of the largest Viet Cong death tolls to be reported for any single day.

Viet Cong Leader Proposes Neutral, Coalition Régime

Nguyen Van Hieu, secretary general of the Viet Cong movement's South Vietnam National Liberation Front, told newsmen in Moscow July 8 that the Viet Cong's ultimate aim was a coalition government and a neutral state, both on the model of Laos. He welcomed as a "positive initiative" a proposal by Cambodian Prince Norodom Sihanouk to transform South Vietnam, Laos and Cambodia into an Asian neutral zone. Hieu denied that the National Liberation Front was Communist or that it had any contact with Communist North Vietnam. He said it comprised 20 political parties and religious groups opposed to the Diem régime.

Hieu listed the following South Vietnamese as president and vice presidents of the front's policy-making central committee: Nhuyen Huu Tho, president of the front, a non-party lawyer imprisoned under the Bao Dai régime; Dr. Phung Van Cung, non-party physician; Co Chi Cong, a "veteran" Communist revolutionary; Huynh Tan Phat, an architect and general secretary of the Vietnamese Democratic Party; Son Vong, a Buddhist Khmer monk of Cambodian nationality; Ybih Aleo, a Protestant and leader of South Vietnam's Ede ethnic minority.

(The formation of a new political movement in Viet Cong-held areas of South Vietnam had been announced Jan. 18 by Communist North Vietnam's Hanoi radio. The announcement said that the new organization, the Vietnam People's Revolutionary Party, had been founded in South Vietnam in 1961 at a meeting held by leaders of the Viet Cong movement and other groups opposed to Diem's "dictatorial" régime. The party was described as Marxist-Leninist and the principal instrument of the "national liberation movement" in South Vietnam. A statement issued Jan. 18 by North Vietnamese Foreign Min. Ung Van Khiem said that the new party would assume the status of a government and would seek the support of Soviet bloc nations.)

Long War Seen, Diem's Effectiveness Questioned

Speaking with newsmen on his arrival in Honolulu July 23 for a new round of talks on the South Vietnam situation

Defense Secy. McNamara asserted that the war against the Viet Cong would be long and costly but could be won if the U.S. maintained its support of the Diem government. "It will take years rather than months," McNamara said, "but the Communists eventually will be defeated." (McNamara had said at a Washington news conference July 6 that "we can't expect termination of a war . . . [in] months. It will be years before it is concluded. . . .") On leaving Honolulu July 24, McNamara declared that the South Vietnamese were "beginning to hit the Viet Cong insurgents where it hurts most—in winning the people to the side of the government."

McNamara's confidence in an eventual South Vietnamese victory and his view of the Diem régime's progress were not shared by 2 *N.Y. Times* correspondents, both of whom had served in South Vietnam. Writing in the *Times* July 25, Homer Bigart asserted that the U.S., "by massive and unqualified support of the [Diem] régime, . . . has helped arrest the spread of Communist insurgency. . . . But victory is remote. The issue remains in doubt because the Vietnamese president seems incapable of winning the loyalty of his people." Jacques Nevard reported July 29 that "the furthest any American in a position to know . . . is willing to go is to say that Pres. Ngo Dinh Diem's régime has a 50-50 chance of defeating the Communist guerrillas. Many others . . . believe the odds are slimmer than that."

Gen. Maxwell D. Taylor, newly-designated chairman of the U.S. Joint Chiefs of Staff, visited South Vietnam Sept. 10-13 for talks with Diem and the commanders of the U.S. military assistance operations and to tour Vietnamese battle areas. Taylor, at a Saigon news conference Sept. 13, lauded the "resistance of the Vietnamese people to the subversive insurgency threat" and praised their "great national movement, assisted to some extent . . . by Americans." Replying to reporters' questions of his view of the Diem régime's apparent lack of popularity, Taylor declared that once the "strategic hamlets" program was effective and the South Vietnamese could be assured protection against the Viet Cong, then "I believe the emphasis will shift from military more to economic and social activities."

(Pham Huy Co, a physician and opponent of the Diem régime, had announced in Tokyo Aug. 17 the formation of a 30-member National Council of the Vietnamese Revolution. The council, made up of non-Communist opposition groups, held that South Vietnam could defeat the Viet Cong rebels only if a new government were formed to eliminate the alleged corruption and dictatorial abuses of the Diem régime.)

"Guarded optimism" about the eventual outcome of the Vietnamese war was expressed by Roger Hilsman Jr., director of State Department intelligence and research, in an address in Chicago Sept. 18. Hilsman, a guerrilla warfare officer during World War II, asserted that the U.S.' "vigorous" support had given the South Vietnamese "new confidence." He said: (a) More than 2,000 "strategic hamlets," 1,000 of them radio equipped, had been created. (b) None of the hamlets had "gone over" to the Viet Cong or had sold their arms to the guerrillas; all had "fought well," and only 5% had lost their radios to the Viet Cong. (c) In one week in August, "over 600 Viet Cong were killed as against less than 100 killed among the pro-government forces," and ⅔ of the Communists' casualties were inflicted by village defense units. (d) The Viet Cong's defection rates had gone up while the guerrilla recruitment program had faltered.

Diem declared Oct. 9, in an address at the opening session of the National Assembly in Saigon, that there had been an "incontestable turn" for the better in the war on the Viet Cong. He said that South Vietnam's armed forces, currently estimated at nearly 200,000 full-time troops, had "reversed" the advantages won by the Viet Cong in 1961. He said: "Everywhere we are taking the initiative . . . passing to the offensive, sowing insecurity in the Communists' reputedly impregnable strongholds, smashing their units one after another." (The National Assembly voted Oct. 26 to extend for another year Diem's power to rule by decree.)

(In Saigon Dec. 2 Sen. Mike Mansfield, D., Mont., became the first major U.S. official to refuse to make an optimistic public comment on the progress of the civil war. In South Vietnam as Pres. Kennedy's personal representative, the Senate majority leader rejected an "encouraging" departure statement prepared by the embassy and limited his comment to praise of Diem's personal integrity.)

U.S. Helicopter Crews 'Fire First'

American helicopter crewmen were reported Oct. 15 to have begun to fire first on any Viet Cong formations encountered during their missions with South Vietnamese troops. The "fire-first" actions were attributed to crews of heavily-armed Bell HU-IA helicopters in use for the first time as escorts for troop-carrying helicopters. The reports were repeated from Saigon despite a Defense Department statement in Washington that there had been no alteration of orders limiting U.S. personnel to shooting back if fired upon.

The AP reported Oct. 15 that 3 HU-IAs—each of which carried 2 heavy machineguns and 16 rockets—had carried out an offensive strike against a Viet Cong stronghold in a mountainous area 55 miles northwest of Saigon. Although crewmen of the H-21 troop-carrying helicopters used in Vietnam already had exchanged fire with the guerrillas, they had observed the "return fire" orders and had been limited by their light armaments and their machines' vulnerability.

15 of the turbine-powered HU-IAs reportedly were in Vietnam; they were flown by U.S. Army crews but carried no national insignia.

7 Americans were killed Oct. 6 when their Marine H-34 helicopter crashed in a mountainous area near Quangngai, 330 miles north of Saigon. An unidentified U.S. soldier was killed Oct. 6 during a helicopter-borne raid in Dinh Tuong Province, south of Saigon. 3 Americans were killed Oct. 15 when their L-28 observation plane was shot down by Communist ground fire near Banmethuot in the central highlands.

It was reported from Saigon Oct. 19 that Operation Morning Star, a major South Vietnamese effort to clear Tayninh Province, north of Saigon near the Cambodian border, had ended in relative failure. More than 5,000 South Vietnamese troops were said to have been ferried into action for 8 days by U.S. helicopters but were said to have killed only 40 Viet

Cong and to have captured only 2 others. 25 more guerrillas were said to have been killed by fire from HU-IA attack helicopters, one of which was lost during the operation. U.S. officials termed the operation a waste of manpower and disclaimed responsibility for it.

Government troops launched a 4-day attack Nov. 1 near Vinh Long in the Mekong delta. 12 U.S. troop-carrying H-21 helicopters, 5 rocket-armed HU-IA escort helicopters and 600 South Vietnamese infantrymen were involved. South Vietnamese government sources estimated enemy losses as possibly as high as 250.

U.S. military sources reported 64 Viet Cong killed Nov. 7 and 8 in the Plaine des Joncs, where 2 battalions of government troops were flown into battle by U.S. helicopters.

Operation An Lac (Peace & Goodwill), a major drive to gain control of the Darlac Province highland area in central South Vietnam, was launched in November by U.S. advisers and government forces with these reported aims: (a) to isolate the Viet Cong in the south; (b) to harass guerrillas in the region until they were on the defensive; (c) to win over the primitive mountain tribesmen (*montagnards*). The operation was scheduled to last 4 months and had been allocated more than a regiment of government troops. (Failure of the program was indicated by the government's admission Dec. 20 that the Viet Cong had opened a new offensive in the region.)

The most ambitious government effort to penetrate the guerrilla-held "D Zone," main Communist rest and supply area, was launched Nov. 20, when 800 troops were airlifted into the region by 56 helicopters. Although 5,000 Viet Cong were believed to be in the area, 9 days of the top secret operation resulted only in 2 guerrilla deaths (government figure 10). At least 4 South Vietnamese paratroopers were killed and 20 injured during jumps. The campaign was planned to last 3 weeks, but participating units were reassigned by Dec. 4. The operation involved up to 2,000 men.

Outnumbered government troops Nov. 25 killed 124 attacking Viet Cong at the outposts of Phuoc Chia and Phuoc

Lam near the North Vietnamese border. U.S. military sources called the action perhaps the most decisive single victory of the war for the South Vietnamese.

Year-End Assessment

The first year of large-scale U.S. military aid to South Vietnam ended without decisive gains for either the government or the Communist Viet Cong.

Maj. Gen. Charles J. Timmes, who succeeded Lt. Gen. Lionel C. McGarr as head of the U. S. Military Assistance Advisory Group, called 1962 "a year of training" for anti-Communist forces. By Dec. 31 Timmes' men had trained 65,000 Self Defense Corps members to defend their villages. The Diem government had about 200,000 regular troops opposing an estimated 25,000 trained Communist guerrillas. (Active Viet Cong sympathizers were said to number 150,000.) 11,000 U.S. military advisers and technicians were said to be working with South Vietnamese forces by the year's end. Planned U.S. aid to South Vietnam during fiscal 1963 included $200 million in economic assistance and more than $75 million in military aid.

At least 51 U.S. servicemen were reported to have been killed in South Vietnam between Dec. 1961 and the end of 1962. U.S. Defense Department spokesmen had reported Oct. 8 that to that date 43 Americans had been killed in Vietnam —13 directly as a result of enemy action and 30 in plane crashes and other accidents not directly attributable to combat. 8 more Americans were reported killed between Oct. 15 and Dec. 23, all of them in action against Viet Cong guerrillas.

1963

South Vietnamese Buddhists began a waive of riotous demonstrations during 1963. The Buddhists, whose protests were countered by armed police and troops, accused Pres. Diem, his government and his Roman Catholic family of anti-Buddhist discrimination. Several Buddhist monks and nuns burned themselves to death publicly to dramatize their protests. Students and intellectuals joined the demonstration movement, and the protesters won widespread sympathy abroad. U.S. spokesmen warned the Diem régime that it would be wise to end repressions and try to win the support of all South Vietnamese. But the U.S. Administration emphasized that it would not end its support of South Vietnam's war against Communist aggression. The anti-government unrest culminated in a military *coup d'état* in which the Diem régime was overthrown and Diem slain.

U.S. INVOLVEMENT

Senators Question U.S. Support

A U.S. Senate report Feb. 24 questioned the current high level of U.S. military and economic aid to the South Vietnamese government in its fight against the Viet Cong. The report, suggesting that South Vietnam expend "further effort" in its struggle for "survival," declared that "there is no interest of the United States in Vietnam which would justify, in present circumstances, the conversion of the war . . . primarily into an American war to be fought primarily with American lives."

The report, submitted to the Senate Foreign Relations Committee by a 4-man panel headed by Senate majority leader Mike Mansfield (D., Mont.), was the result of an investigation of the U.S. aid program in Southeast Asia requested by Pres. John F. Kennedy in 1962. The other subcommittee members were Sens. J. Caleb Boggs (R., Del.) and Claiborne Pell (D., R.I.) and ex-Sen. Benjamin A. Smith (D., Mass.).

The report also dealt with the U.S. aid program in Laos, Cambodia, Thailand, Burma and the Philippines. In submitting the subcommittee's findings to Sen. James W. Fulbright (D., Ark.), committee chairman, Mansfield said emphasis had been placed on South Vietnam because the U.S.'

greatest effort in Southeast Asia was centered in that country: an annual aid expenditure of $400 million and the stationing of 12,000 Americans there "on dangerous assignment."

Points made in the report:

• The U.S. should thoroughly reassess its "over-all security requirement on the Southeast Asia mainland" with a view to carrying out an orderly reduction in the U.S. aid programs. But "extreme caution" should be used in reducing such aid, "for if the attempt is made to alter the programs via a Congressional meat-axe cut . . . it runs the risk of not merely removing the fat but of leaving a gap which will lay open the region to massive chaos and, hence, jeopardize the present pacific structure of our national security."

• "Although not intended for combat," U.S. soldiers "have been in combat. More than 50 men have lost their lives— about ½ in battle—in Vietnam" since "the program of intensified assistance" began in 1961.

• The subcommittee, while deploring the size of U.S. aid needed to help the Vietnamese defeat the Viet Cong, conceded that it would be risky to reduce such aid.

• "In the very best of circumstances outside aid in very substantial size will be necessary for many years," even after Saigon forces defeat the Viet Cong.

• The "intensification [of U.S. aid] has carried us to the start of the road which leads to the point at which the conflict could become of greater concern and . . . responsibility to the U.S. than it is to the government and people of South Vietnam."

Mansfield, recalling his visit to South Vietnam in 1955, said: "What is most disturbing is that Vietnam now appears to be as it was then, only at the beginning of coping with its grave inner problems. All of the current difficulties existed in 1955, along with the hope and energy to meet them. But it is 7 years later and $2 billion of U.S. aid later. Yet, substantially the same difficulties remain, if, indeed they have not been compounded."

South Vietnamese newspapers and radio stations, ignoring all critical points of Mansfield's findings, merely announced that the Senator had reported to Pres. Kennedy on his trip to Southeast Asia.

Under a U.S.-South Vietnamese accord made public May 9, the Saigon régime agreed to pay for the operation of the U.S.-financed Operation Sunrise "strategic-hamlet" program. The South Vietnamese government promised to defray the entire $17 million cost of shipping U.S. economic and military equipment, supplies and food to villages fortified against Viet Cong attacks. This included the cost of transportation, road repair and other related activities. South Vietnam planned to pay for the program by deficit financing through borrowing from its Central Bank. Heretofore, South Vietnam had refused to transfer budgeted funds for the strategic-hamlet program. Its refusal had prompted the U.S. in the fall of 1962 to speed up deliveries by authorizing a $10 million cash transfer through the purchase of South Vietnamese piasters. Pres. Kennedy later directed U.S. agencies to avoid such cash transfers wherever possible because they aggravated the U.S.' balance-of-payments deficit. The U.S.-South Vietnamese agreement also provided for retaining the current number of U.S. advisers at provincial and local levels. South Vietnam previously had sought to reduce the number and influence of such advisers. (2,000 American advisers were reported to be on duty with provincial administrators.)

U.S. Amb.-to-South Vietnam Frederick Nolting Jr. had appealed to a group of South Vietnamese officials in Saigon Feb. 11 to display "less touchiness and more of a willingness to face the bad along with the good in the months and years of efforts ahead." Nolting's statement was believed to have been the U.S. government's reply to Vietnamese criticism of U.S. newsmen's reports on the fighting. The Vietnamese had been particularly irate over U.S. newspaper accounts of the Jan. 2 battle of Ap Bac in which government troops had failed to prevent a trapped Viet Cong battalion's escape. The Vietnamese had criticized U.S. military advisers for giving a private analysis of the battle to U.S. reporters. Nolting, calling for "frankness between" U.S. and Vietnamese officials, sug-

gested that both sides "refrain from idle remarks and unneces-
sary comments and from spreading allegations and rumors
which . . . play directly into Communist hands." Nolting's
speech was the highlight of a ceremony marking the transfer
to South Vietnam of more than $1 million worth of U.S.
equipment.

U.S. to Continue Helicopter Combat Aid

The State Department had confirmed Jan. 5 that the
U.S. would continue to support South Vietnamese troops.
with helicopters. It reported: "In 1962, U.S. Army aviation
units flew over 50,000 sorties in support of operations in
Vietnam, approximately ½ of which were combat support
sorties. During the period Jan. 1-Nov. 30, 1962, 115 U.S.
Army aircraft were hit by ground-fire, only 9 of which were
shot down."

The U.S. was reported Apr. 11 to have reinforced its
military units in South Vietnam in the past month with about
100 troops of the Hawaiian-based 25th Infantry Division. The
men, serving as machine gunners aboard Army H-21 helicopters that ferried South Vietnamese troops into fighting
areas, freed mechanics for maintenance service. The mechanics
previously had been required to serve also as gunners.

Communists Charge U.S. Uses Gas

The Soviet military newspaper *Krasnaya Zvezda* (*Red
Star*) charged Mar. 9 that U.S. "interventionists" in South
Vietnam had used "asphyxiation gases" and "noxious chemicals" in fighting the Viet Cong. The newspaper said that
"hundreds of people perished, great quantities of cattle were
poisoned."

Peiping radio charged Mar. 9 that the U.S. had sprayed
chemicals "to poison innocent South Vietnamese people and
devastate crops." The broadcast said 5,000 persons had been
poisoned and that public meetings had been held in Hanoi,
North Vietnam "to censure the atrocities." Peiping radio said
the Chinese Red Cross had protested the use of "chemical

poisons by U.S. imperialism to murder civilians and destroy crops in South Vietnam."

The Communist charges apparently referred to a tactic of spraying a weed killer from U.S. planes to destroy heavy foliage used as hiding places by the Viet Cong.

The U.S. State Department said Mar. 9: "We have never used poison gas in South Vietnam, and there is no truth in Communist reports that we are using it now"; the chemicals employed by U.S. pilots were "non-toxic to humans and animals when used in the prescribed manner, that is, sprayed on trees and underbrush in the open air."

ANTI-GOVERNMENT ACTIVITY

Buddhist Unrest Shakes Diem Régime

Thousands of South Vietnam's Buddhists, led by their priests and nuns, took to the streets during 1963 in angry demonstrations against the government of Pres. Ngo Dinh Diem and his Roman Catholic family. The demonstrations were met by force. Police and troops fired on marchers, killing several persons and creating the first martyrs of a protest movement that was to become increasingly political in its aims. To these deaths were added those of a number of Buddhist priests and nuns who soaked their robes in gasoline and publicly burned themselves to death in protest against the repression of the Diem régime.

The first of the clashes was reported May 8 when South Vietnamese soldiers and police dispersed a protest demonstration by 9,000 Buddhists in Hué, 400 miles north of Saigon. 9 persons were killed. Buddhist witnesses said the casualties were caused by police hand grenades and gunfire from armored cars. The government said the casualties resulted from grenades thrown from the crowd. The demonstrators were protesting a government order that forbade the display of Buddhist religious flags and the staging of parades to commemorate Buddha's birthday (May 8).

Buddhist leaders met with Pres. Diem in Saigon May 15 and demanded that the government (a) withdraw its ban

Buddhist monk Quang Duc starts series of self-immolations by burning himself to death in Saigon June 11 in protest against Diem régime's alleged persecution of Buddhists.

(Wide World photo)

against religious flags; (b) grant Buddhism the same legal standing as Roman Catholicism (Buddhists comprised an overwhelming majority of the population); (c) "stop terrorizing the [Buddhist] faithful"; (d) grant Buddhists the freedom to preach their religion; (e) indemnify the victims of the May 8 clash and punish officials responsible for the incident.

In response to the Buddhist demands, the government June 1 replaced 3 officials of the Hué area. One of them was Maj. Dang Si, who reportedly had ordered troops to fire on the Buddhist demonstrators May 8.

The Buddhist leaders rejected the government's action as insufficient and announced that the public demonstrations would be resumed and continued until all their demands were met.

400 Buddhist priests and nuns staged a 40-hour protest demonstration in front of the National Assembly in Saigon May 30. About 500 Buddhist students June 3 demonstrated before the Hué office of the chief government delegate for the northern coastal region. 67 rock-throwing students were injured and 35 arrested in a clash with about 300 soldiers. Buddhist demonstrations also were held in Quangtri and Uhatrang, in the northern part of the country.

Diem appealed for an end to the Buddhist unrest in a speech broadcast to the nation June 7. He conceded that some government officials were to blame for the manner in which the Buddhist dispute was being handled. He said "that some of our compatriots, including the cadres of various branches of the public as well as private services, have not yet reached a substantial degree of understanding . . . regarding their duty towards the people."

(Gen. Paul D. Harkins, commander of the U.S. military mission in Vietnam, was reported June 10 to have warned U.S. military personnel to shun duty with any Vietnamese military units involved in the suppression of Buddhists.)

First Priest Commits Suicide by Fire

A Buddhist monk, Quang Duc, 73, committed suicide in a Saigon street June 11 in protest against the government's policies. While 700 other Buddhist monks formed a circle around him, gasoline was poured over the priest and ignited. The demonstration was in violation of a government ban against such public protests. In a further act of defiance, the Buddhists displayed their religious flag while marching back to their pagoda and then flew it from the roof of the structure.

In a broadcast immediately after the suicide, Pres. Diem deplored the fact that it had occurred at a time when the government was negotiating with Buddhist leaders in an effort to settle the dispute. Denying that there was "any scheme to unjustly crush Buddhism," Diem declared "that behind the Buddhists . . . there is still the constitution, that is, myself."

Thousands of Buddhists rioted in Saigon June 16 as they attempted to break through police lines to attend Quang Duc's funeral services at a pagoda. The Buddhists charged that during the ensuing clashes one of their followers was killed by a police bullet and 5 others were injured. The police denied that any fatalities had occurred and said 30 policemen had been injured by flying bricks. About 250 persons were arrested.

Accord Fails, Demonstrations & Suicides Resume

A 5-point agreement aimed at ending the Buddhist-government dispute was signed in Saigon June 16. Formal negotiations had started June 14. According to the text of the agreement, made public June 17: (1) the government would compensate the families of the 9 Buddhists killed by soldiers in Hué May 8 (a government commission was to determine the extent of government responsibility for the incident); (2) Buddhist priests were to be allowed to teach their religion freely; (3) arrests and mistreatment of Buddhists were to stop; those in custody were to be released; (4) Buddhists would be permitted to fly their flags on condition that the national flag was displayed at the same time; (5) the National Assembly would reconsider a law regarded by the Buddhists as favoring Christianity over Buddhism.

Buddhist leaders charged July 15 that government officials had ignored the Saigon agreement and that Buddhists were still being subjected to "acts of a terrorist nature." They announced that the mass demonstrations against the Diem régime would be resumed. Government appeals July 18-19 for a renewal of negotiations were rejected by the Buddhists. Again charging that government officials were sabotaging Diem's conciliation efforts, the Buddhists July 19 listed these conditions for resuming negotiations: public identification of secret police who had been attacking Buddhist demonstrators; the release of Buddhist prisoners; removal of barbed wire from Saigon's main pagodas.

About 60,000 Buddhists defied government prohibitions and staged rallies July 30 in Saigon, Dalat, Nha Trang, Quon Nhon and Hué in memory of Quang Duc, the monk who had burned himself to death June 11.

A 2d Buddhist monk burned himself to death Aug. 4 in Phanthiet, 100 miles east of Saigon, in protest against the government's religious policies. Government troops, who had arrived too late to stop the suicide, carried away the monk's body. The monk had come from a pagoda where other Buddhist leaders had been holding 48-hour protest fasts since July 30.

A 3d Buddhist monk, Thich Thanh Thuc, 17, committed suicide by burning himself to death with gasoline at a pagoda near Hué Aug. 13.

In a Saigon address Aug. 3, Mrs. Ngo Dinh Nhu, wife of Pres. Diem's brother, assailed the Buddhists as "so-called holy men" who had used Communist tactics in their anti-government protests. Mrs. Nhu, a Roman Catholic, called Quang Duc's suicide "murder." "What else can be said when they [Buddhist leaders] murder their own kin and their own peers in a most barbaric manner under the pretext of defending a faith that has never been under attack," she said.

Ngo Dinh Nhu, Diem's chief adviser and head of the secret police, warned in a Saigon interview Aug. 3 that if the Buddhist crisis was not soon resolved "it will lead toward a *coup d'état*" that would be anti-American and anti-Buddhist.

Thich Thinh Khiet, South Vietnam's supreme Buddhist monk, sent a message to Buddhist leaders Aug. 14 appealing for a halt in the suicide-protests. The suicides, nevertheless, continued: A Buddhist nun, Dieu Quang, in her 20s, committed suicide by setting herself afire Aug. 15 in the coastal town of Ninh Hoa, and a Buddhist monk, 71, burned himself to death at a Hué pagoda Aug. 16.

Troops Attack Buddhist Centers

The Diem government struck back at the Buddhist protest movement in August. Charging that Buddhist leaders were acting as tools of the Communists, the régime used military force to seize and occupy the country's major pagodas and arrest large numbers of priests and student demonstrators. The government's action precipitated a crisis in its relations with the U.S., which considered the repressive tactics unacceptable and a hindrance to the war against the Communist-led Viet Cong guerrillas. U.S. Pres. Kennedy, himself a Roman Catholic, personally denounced the anti-Buddhist action and demanded that the Diem government take steps to reform itself to regain the loyalty of the South Vietnamese public.

South Vietnamese troops and police attacked and occupied Buddhist pagodas throughout the country Aug. 21. Hundreds of Buddhist priests were reported to have been beaten and arrested. All prominent Buddhist leaders were reported seized.

Diem imposed nationwide martial law later Aug. 21 amid reports that a military coup was about to be launched against his government. Diem imposed censorship and ordered a 9 p.m.-5 a.m. curfew. In the broadcast proclaiming martial law, Diem declared that the "government's extremely conciliatory goodwill in settling" the Buddhist dispute had been abused "by a number of political speculators who had taken advantage of religion." Diem said they had engaged in "repeated illegal actions in order to create a confused situation."

The anti-Buddhist raids were concentrated on pagodas in Saigon, Hué, Quangtri, Quangnam and Nhatrang. One of the worst clashes reported occurred in Hué, where the city's Tu Dam pagoda was said to have been destroyed by the attackers. 6,000 Hué residents later rioted and fought armed troops in the streets. In Saigon, soldiers and police stormed the Xa

Loi pagoda (Buddhist headquarters for their anti-government campaign) with small arms, grenades and tear-gas bombs and reportedly killed several persons. Witnesses said monks and nuns were beaten and 300-500 Buddhists were arrested in the Saigon attack. (The Xa Loi pagoda was reopened Aug. 31. The reopening followed Buddhist acceptance Aug. 30 of a government demand to reorganize the lay General Buddhist Association and to replace imprisoned association president Mai Tho Truyen.)

3 high-ranking Vietnamese diplomatic officials resigned Aug. 22 in protest against the government's anti-Buddhist policies. They were: Foreign Min. Vu Van Mau, a Buddhist; Amb.-to-the U.S. Tran Van Chuong, a Confucian; Chuong's wife, a Buddhist, Saigon's permanent observer at the UN. (The Chuongs were the parents of Mrs. Ngo Dinh Nhu, who had converted from Buddhism to Roman Catholicism on her marriage to Nhu in 1943.) Truong Cong Cuu, coordinating state secretary for Cultural and Social Affairs, was named acting foreign minister.

U.S. Opposes Anti-Buddhist Crack-Down

The U.S. State Department Aug. 21 denounced the armed action against the Buddhists as a reversal of the Diem government's promises to the U.S. to reconcile its differences with the religious sect. The department deplored what it said were repressive measures taken against Buddhist leaders. Pres. Kennedy, when advised of the new situation, immediately called an emergency meeting of top Administration officials. (State Secy. Dean Rusk had said at a Washington news conference Aug. 16 that the U.S. was "deeply distressed" by the Buddhist crisis. Rusk said: "We are especially distressed because we regret anything which seems to create disunity" at a time when the government was successfully waging war against the Viet Cong guerrillas.)

The U.S. and South Vietnam became involved in a dispute Aug. 26 over whether the army or the Diem government had been responsible for the Aug. 21 attacks against the Buddhists. A State Department statement on South Vietnam, issued Aug. 26, said: "Current information makes it clear that these attacks . . . were carried out by the police, supported by small groups of Special Forces troops not under the command of the Vietnamese forces [Ngo Dinh Nhu controlled the Special Forces' palace units as well as the police]. . . . The top leadership of the Vietnamese army was not aware of the plans to attack the pagodas, much less the brutal manner in which it was carried out."

A Vietnamese government communiqué Aug. 28 denied the State Department assertion. The communiqué said: "All responsible army chiefs unanimously . . . proposed and obtained from [Diem] . . . permission to establish martial law, as well as the referred-to measures [against the Buddhists], and it is the army which has directly taken all measures to accomplish this mission."

(According to reports filed from Saigon by U.S. newsmen, Nhu had been the prime instigator of the move against the Buddhists. Nhu reportedly had been angered by the government's conciliatory policy toward the Buddhist protest movement and by its failure to crush it. Mrs. Nhu was said to have shared his views and to have pressed for action by the government. Maj. Gen. Tran Van Don, newly appointed armed forces head, reportedly had not been informed of the decision to attack the Buddhists Aug. 21 until he was called to the presidential palace and informed of his promotion.)

It was reported that U.S. South Vietnamese relations were further aggravated by Amb. Lodge's rejection of a South Vietnamese government request that he turn over 2 Buddhist monks who had received asylum in the U.S.' aid mission headquarters during the Aug. 21 raids. Lodge was said to have been called to the South Vietnamese Foreign Affairs Ministry, where the request was made by Acting Foreign Min. Truong Cong Cuu. The 2 monks left the U.S. mission Sept. 1 and went to a Saigon pagoda, where a group of government-approved Buddhist leaders assured them of their safety.

3 other Buddhist monks, including Tri Quang, 2d in command of the General Buddhist Association, requested and were granted asylum in the U.S. embassy in Saigon Sept. 1.

The monks had been in hiding since the Aug. 21 raids. The U.S. Sept. 3 and 6 formally rejected a South Vietnamese government request to hand over the 3 monks.

Pres. Kennedy declared in a TV interview at Hyannis Port, Mass. Sept. 2 that South Vietnam's repressive actions against the Buddhists "were very unwise." Mr. Kennedy said the U.S. was "prepared to continue to assist" the Saigon government in fighting the Communist Viet Cong guerrillas. But, he added, "I don't think that the war can be won unless the people support the effort, and . . . in the last 2 months, the [South Vietnamese] government has gotten out of touch with the people." Only "changes in policy and perhaps with personnel" could enable Diem's régime to regain the people's support, the President said.

Mrs. Nhu assailed Pres. Kennedy Sept. 11 as an "appeaser." Arriving in Belgrade to attend a meeting of the Interparliamentary Union, Mrs. Nhu said: ". . . Pres. Kennedy is a politician, and when he hears a loud opinion speaking in a certain way, he always tries to appease it somehow . . . if that opinion is misinformed, the solution is not to bow to it, but the solution should be to inform."

(Cambodia severed diplomatic relations with South Vietnam Aug. 27 in protest against alleged border violations and the alleged Vietnamese persecution of Buddhists.)

Students & Professors Active in Protests

The focal point of anti-government unrest shifted Aug. 22-25 from the Buddhists to Saigon University professors and students, who expressed strong opposition to the Diem government's policies.

Police Aug. 22 arrested several university professors for refusal to sign a government loyalty oath. Many students boycotted classes in protest. Others tore down posters urging citizens to join the army. More than 500 students staged an anti-government rally at the school Aug. 23. The students ousted secret policemen who tried to break into the meeting. The students pledged to carry on the anti-government campaign in the place of arrested Buddhist leaders.

The government closed Saigon University and all public and private secondary schools in the city Aug. 24, as student unrest continued to spread.

Police and soldiers Aug. 25 thwarted a city-wide strike and rally called by Saigon students in protest against the arrests of Buddhists and students. One demonstrator was shot to death and at least 600 students were arrested. Large-scale arrests of students were carried out in other parts of Saigon. The UPI reported that 1,000 to 2,000 students had been placed in detention camps.

At least 800 Saigon high school students were arrested Sept. 7 in anti-government demonstrations. The youths, many of whom threw rocks at police, shouted slogans attacking the Diem régime, Nhu, and Mrs. Nhu. The students criticized U.S. support of the Diem family and hailed the South Vietnamese army because it "does not fight students." (Regular army troops were not used against the students; only Nhu's Special Forces units and combat policemen were used.) Gen. Ton That Dinh, military governor of Saigon, said in a communiqué Sept. 8 that teen-agers arrested Sept. 7 would be sent to a re-education camp for an indefinite term; arrested demonstrators older than 20 would be drafted into the army.

About 1,500 students at an all-boys high school in Saigon were arrested Sept. 9 after a 2-hour anti-government demonstration despite the governor's warning. More than 100 more teen-age students were arrested during a demonstration at a Saigon high school Sept. 12.

In spite of continued student unrest, the government Sept. 16 lifted the nationwide martial law, curfew and press censorship that had been imposed Aug. 21. Administrative power given to the army during the emergency period was returned to civilian officials.

The South Vietnamese government announced Oct. 19 that it had smashed an "organized rebellion by students and intellectuals" aimed at overthrowing the Diem régime. The announcement said "a number of persons have been arrested," including Nguyen Manh Cuong, reportedly head of the group, called the Revolutionary Council for Religious Freedom &

Human Rights. South Vietnamese police also were said to be continuing the arrests of other students in a move to smash their underground movement. Some students freed several weeks previously were rearrested.

3 U.S. newsmen were severely beaten by Vietnamese plainclothes policemen in Saigon Oct. 5 after they had watched a Buddhist monk burn himself to death with gasoline. The death was the 6th such suicide since June 11. The newsmen were attacked as 2 of them tried unsuccessfully to keep the police from seizing the camera of NBC-TV correspondent Grant Wolfkill, who had taken pictures of the suicide. The 2 other newsmen were John Sharkey, also of NBC, and *N.Y. Times* writer David Halberstam. State Secy. Dean Rusk announced in Washington Oct. 5 that Amb. Henry Cabot Lodge had protested the attack "on the newsmen to the Vietnamese government in the most serious terms."

McNamara & Taylor Probe Situation in Vietnam

Defense Secy. Robert S. McNamara and Gen. Maxwell D. Taylor, chairman of the Joint Chiefs of Staff, visited South Vietnam Sept. 24-Oct. 1 to determine whether the country's military situation had suffered as a result of the clash between the government and the Buddhists. The 2 U.S. officials returned to Washington Oct. 2 and reported their findings to the President and to the National Security Council.

A White House statement issued later Oct. 2 made it clear that the U.S. intended to continue its military support of South Vietnam and that it aimed at a victory over the Viet Cong by 1965. The statement acknowledged that the South Vietnamese political situation was grave, but it denied that the political unrest had affected the war effort.

Excerpts from the White House statement: "The security of South Vietnam is a major interest of the United States as of other free nations. We will adhere to our policy of working with . . . South Vietnam to deny this country to communism. . . . The military program in South Vietnam has made progress . . . though improvements are being energetically sought. Major United States assistance . . . is needed only until the insurgency has been suppressed or until the national security forces . .. of South Vietnam are capable of suppressing it. Secy. McNamara and Gen. Taylor reported their judgment that the major part of the United States military task can be completed by the end of 1965. ... They reported that by the end of this year the United States program for training Vietnamese should have progressed to the point where 1,000 United States military personnel ... can be withdrawn."

The statement disclosed that the U.S. policies outlined had been based on the reports of Amb. Henry Cabot Lodge as well as those of McNamara and Taylor. It had been reported from Saigon that Lodge and other U.S. embassy and civilian officials in South Vietnam believed the Diem government's anti-Buddhist policies had seriously undermined its capacity for effective war against the Communists. Lodge's views were said to be opposed to those of Gen. Paul D. Harkins, chief of the 14,000-man U.S. military mission in Vietnam, who was reported to have insisted to McNamara and Taylor that the anti-Communist campaign was progressing on schedule.

Despite Pres. Kennedy's earlier assertion that the U.S. planned to continue unabated its military and financial support of South Vietnam, it was apparent by October that economic pressure had been applied to the Diem régime to force it to institute reforms. The *N.Y. Times* reported Oct. 7 that the U.S. had suspended commercial export assistance to South Vietnam. Under the program, imports, mostly from the U.S., were purchased with dollars and bought by Vietnamese merchants with local currency. The U.S. was reported Oct. 21 to have taken these 2 additional economic reprisals against the Diem régime: (1) The U.S. had warned that it would deny funds to the Special Forces if its troops were used for political and security missions instead of fighting the Viet Cong; (2) the U.S. refused to renew the annual agreement providing the Saigon government with grants of surplus food, which was sold for local currency used to pay Vietnamese troops.

The CIA chief of operations in South Vietnam, John H. Richardson, flew back to Washington Oct. 5 after having been recalled for consultations by Pres. Kennedy amid reports that Amb. Lodge was seeking his replacement because of a dispute over the military and political situation in Vietnam. According to the *N.Y. Times,* Lodge had complained that his position as head of the U.S. mission in Vietnam conflicted with that of Richardson, who did not confine his operations to gathering and analyzing intelligence information but who worked closely on operational matters with Ngo Dinh Nhu; Lodge and many State Department officials often had favored a tougher attitude than the CIA toward the South Vietnamese government in its handling of the U.S.-supported war against the Viet Cong.

DIEM RÉGIME OVERTHROWN

Military Coup Deposes & Slays Diem

Discontented South Vietnamese army officers overthrew the government in a violent *coup d'état* Nov. 1-2. They ousted Ngo Dinh Diem as president, killed Diem and his brother, Ngo Dinh Nhu, and installed a civil-military government. Reforms were pledged to revitalize the nation in its war against the Viet Cong guerrillas. The new government was recognized almost immediately by the U.S.

The leaders of the coup were identified as: Maj. Gen. Ton That Dinh, military governor of Saigon; Maj. Gen. Duong Van Minh, military adviser to Diem; Maj. Gen. Tran Von Don, armed forces chief. A civilian-military government assumed office Nov. 4. It was headed by ex-Vice Pres. Nguyen Ngoc Tho, a Buddhist, as premier.

The coup was launched Nov. 1. Army insurgents blocked off roads to Saigon's airport and arrested Nhu's Special Forces units stationed there. Marine forces, camped outside the city, sped into Saigon and seized control of the Interior Ministry's communications center, naval headquarters, the police compound and the Defense Ministry. The rebels, assisted by artillery and planes, attacked the presidential palace where Diem and Nhu were holding out with 1,500 loyal troops. Palace soldiers fought back, as did Special Forces soldiers and some Vietnamese naval units, which fired at insurgent planes attacking military headquarters. But the pro-government naval units were quickly subdued.

South Vietnamese secret police chief Ngo Dinh Nhu, shown with his wife and children, was slain with his brother, Pres. Ngo Dinh Diem, in **coup d'état** Nov. 2. Mrs. Nhu had become a symbol to anti-Diem elements of the Diem régime's oppression and of its alleged pro-Catholic and anti-Buddhist bias.

(Wide World photo)

Diem and secret police chief Nhu died Nov. 2. Rebel leaders said both had committed suicide; later reports indicated that they had been assassinated.

A communiqué issued by the rebel leaders Nov. 1 said that under Diem's régime "the people's lawful rights were trampled upon" and that "the rottenness and corruption of

South Vietnamese Pres. Ngo Dinh Diem was slain Nov. 2 after his régime was overthrown by military coup. (Wide World photo)

the Ngo Dinh Diem clique destroyed the confidence of the people." The communiqué added: "While we were fighting on the battlefield [against the Viet Cong] . . . we felt we were being disgracefully utilized . . ."; "we have carried out a revolution to save the country and to rebuild a powerful army not controlled by incompetent cadres or unjust rule."

The leaders of the coup Nov. 2 established a provisional civilian-military junta, suspended the constitution and dissolved the National Assembly. Buddhist leaders imprisoned by the Diem régime were released. Thich Tri Quang, Buddhist high priest, returned to Saigon's Xa Loi pagoda from the U.S. embassy, where he had taken refuge at the start of the government-Buddhist crisis in August. The police reported Nov. 4 that about 150 political prisoners had been released. Many South Vietnamese political exiles returned to the country.

Casualty figures listed by the rebels in the Saigon fighting: 9 insurgents killed and 46 wounded; 4 palace guards killed and 44 wounded; 20 civilians killed and 146 wounded.

Brothers' Deaths Described

Conflicting accounts of the deaths of Diem and Nhu were given Nov. 2 by informants close to the new junta. At first military sources said they had been killed earlier that day as they attempted to escape through a palace tunnel shortly before rebel marines seized the building. A later report said that the 2 brothers had escaped from the palace and had sought refuge in a Roman Catholic church in the Saigon suburb of Cholon, where they were seized by rebel forces. The report said that while they were being brought to military

73

headquarters in Saigon in an armored personnel carrier, orders were given to kill them in the car, and both were dead when the vehicle arrived at its destination. This story later was substantiated by photographs purporting to show the bodies of Diem and Nhu lying on the floor of the armored vehicle in which they reportedly had been shot.

Diem and Nhu were buried in secrecy in Saigon Nov. 6.

Ngo Dinh Luyen, a brother of Diem, resigned Nov. 2 as ambassador to Britain and as minister to Belgium, the Netherlands and Austria. In a statement issued in London, Luyen charged that the coup leaders had "murdered my brother and camouflaged it as suicide." Another brother of Diem, Ngo Dinh Can, ruler of Hué, was turned over to junta authorities by U.S. officials Nov. 5 and brought to Saigon Nov. 6 to stand trial. Can had gone to the U.S. consulate in Hué Nov. 5 to seek refuge. U.S. authorities handed him over to the Vietnamese after receiving assurances that he "would receive due process of law."

(Col. Le Quang Tung, commander of Nhu's Special Forces, was reported to have been arrested Nov. 1 and later executed.)

The deaths of Diem and Nhu were reported to Mrs. Nhu while she was stopping in Beverly Hills, Calif. Nov. 2 during a tour of the U.S. Mrs. Nhu, believed to have wielded great influence in the Diem government, charged that the U.S. had instigated and supported the revolution against her brother-in-law's régime. She declared that "whatever happens to my family will be an indelible stigma against the United States." Mrs. Nhu had arrived in the U.S. Oct. 7 for a planned 20-day visit despite the evident displeasure of the Kennedy Administration, which had refused to officially acknowledge her presence or to extend diplomatic courtesies to her. Barred by the coup from returning to South Vietnam, she left the U.S. Nov. 13 and went first to Rome, where she was reunited with her younger children, who had been in Vietnam during the coup but had not been harmed. She later moved to Paris and was granted a residence permit by the French government.

(Mrs. Nhu and U.S. Amb.-to-South Vietnam Lodge had become embroiled in a controversy Sept. 26 over disparaging remarks that Mrs. Nhu was reported to have made about Americans serving in Vietnam. Mrs. Nhu had been quoted as saying a few days earlier: The U.S.' "younger officers . . . are acting like little soldiers of fortune. They do not know what is going on. With their irresponsible behavior, they have forced senior officers into following a confused policy." Lodge replied that her words were "shocking." "These men," he said, "should be thanked and not insulted" for risking their lives for Vietnam. Mrs. Nhu later claimed that her words had been misinterpreted.)

The Soviet government newspaper *Izvestia* Nov. 2 expressed satisfaction with the "ignoble" end of Diem but said that "judging from Saigon dispatches and from Washington's reaction, new American puppets have come to power." The USSR maintained no relations with South Vietnam.

(The properties of the Diem and his family were seized by the South Vietnamese government Dec. 25. The government also took over the holdings of 16 close associates of the Ngo family and of 5 organizations allegedly used by the Ngos to consolidate their power. The properties seized belonged to Diem and his 4 brothers: the late Ngo Dinh Nhu, Archbishop Ngo Dinh Thuc, currently in Rome; ex-Amb.-to-Britain Ngo Dinh Luyen; ex-Gov. Ngo Dinh Can, in a Saigon prison awaiting trial. Mrs. Nhu, in Paris, also had her property confiscated. The Ngo family reportedly had possessed large interests in the construction, shipping, real estate and fishing industries and in the cinnamon and rice trade.)

Junta Forms Civilian-Military Government

The victorious junta announced the formation of a new South Vietnamese government Nov. 4. The cabinet: Premier, Economic Affairs, Finance—Nguyen Ngoc Tho; Defense—Maj. Gen. Tran Van Don, acting joint chief of staff; Foreign —Pham Dang Lam; Information—Gen. Tran Tu Oai; Education—Pham Hoang Ho; Public Works & Communications—Tran Ngoc Hoanh; Labor—Nguyen Le Vai; Security—Maj. Gen. Ton That Dinh.

Pledging that the new government would not become a dictatorship, a military broadcast Nov. 4 asserted that "the best weapon to fight communism is democracy and liberty." The broadcast said the new government was on the side of the West and that its armed forces were dedicated "to fight communism."

Information Min. Tran Tu Oai declared in Saigon Nov. 6 that "the mission of the provisional government will not end until real democracy is established." Oai spoke at a news conference at which Maj. Gen. Duong Van Minh and Prime Min. Nguyen Ngoc Tho introduced members of the new government for the first time. (Oai said that the deaths of Diem and Nhu were "accidental suicides." Oai said the brothers were shot to death when Nhu tried to grab the pistol of the officer arresting them.)

The establishment of a "Council of Sages" was announced by the government Nov. 6. The council, to be composed of non-governmental civilians, was to advise the régime on ways to "carry out the revolutionary policy in conformity with the people's aspirations." The junta Nov. 7 removed the nation-wide curfew it had imposed following the coup. It also ordered the end of news censorship.

U.S. Backs New Régime

The U.S. recognized the provisional government Nov. 7, one day after the new régime had requested recognition. State Secy. Rusk predicted Nov. 8 that the anti-Diem coup would provide the Vietnamese with the "impetus" to combat the Viet Cong guerrillas. Rusk said the U.S. hoped the new régime "will be able to rally the country . . . so that [it] can be independent and free and secure." Resumption of the U.S.' commodity-import program for South Vietnam was announced by Washington officials Nov. 9.

Lyndon B. Johnson became President of the U.S. Nov. 22 on the assassination of John F. Kennedy. Mr. Johnson pledged Nov. 24 that his Administration would continue to pursue the U.S. policies on South Vietnam that had been established by Mr. Kennedy.

Defense Secy. McNamara conducted a 2-day fact-finding mission in South Vietnam Dec. 19-20 on Pres. Johnson's orders. The President had sent McNamara to Vietnam after U.S. officials there reportedly had expressed concern about chances of winning the war against the Communist guerrillas unless the new Saigon government pressed the fighting more effectively. McNamara reported back to Mr. Johnson Dec. 21. After receiving McNamara's briefing on recent Viet Cong successes, the Administration confirmed that it had abandoned its previously-announced goal of withdrawing most U.S. military personnel from South Vietnam by the end of 1965. (220 U.S. troops had left Vietnam by plane Dec. 3; they were part of a 1,000-man force that was to have been withdrawn by Dec. 25.) McNamara reportedly told Mr. Johnson and other U.S. officials that the Viet Cong, capitalizing on the overthrow of the Diem régime Nov. 1, had overrun "a substantial number" of strategic hamlets.

Soviet Premier Nikita S. Khrushchev predicted Dec. 27 that U.S. forces would be ousted from South Vietnam. Speaking at a Moscow reception in honor of a visiting Algerian delegation, Khrushchev said: "The French colonizers [of South Vietnam] have been replaced there by American imperialists. . . . There is not the slightest doubt that the people of South Vietnam will throw out the American invaders with even less ceremony . . . than the French colonizers."

Attacks on Catholics Reported

The Rev. Robert Willichs, 56, a Belgian priest, charged in Saigon Dec. 22 that Buddhists, instigated by Communists, had attacked Roman Catholics in mid-November in 9 provinces of central South Vietnam, an area of high Catholic-Buddhist tension. Willichs said that Buddhists had beaten Catholics, burned their homes and desecrated their churches. In one incident, Willichs reported, a Buddhist mob in Danang (400 miles north of Saigon) had killed 2 Catholics and injured 20. Willichs charged that government officials had participated in some of the attacks.

Premier Tho, a Buddhist, denied Dec. 23 that government officials had permitted or participated in the outrages. He said the government had reassured Roman Catholic leaders that his régime supported religious freedom and equality. Tho attributed the anti-Catholic violence to "Communists and crypto-Communists."

The UN General Assembly had accepted without vote Dec. 13 a decision to discontinue an investigation it had ordered of the alleged repression of Buddhists in South Vietnam. The decision had been made by a 7-nation fact-finding commission, headed by Abdul Rahman Pazhwak of Afghanistan, which had conducted an inquiry in South Vietnam from Oct. 25 until Nov. 1, when the Diem régime was overthrown. UN Assembly Pres. Carlos Sosa Rodriguez said Buddhist oppression by the government had ceased to be an issue after Diem's ouster.

CIVIL WAR

Operations Indecisive in 1963

South Vietnam's war against the Communist-led Viet Cong guerrillas continued throughout 1963. Vietnamese government troops, supported by U.S. helicopter forces and often led by U.S. advisers, inflicted heavy casualties on the guerrillas but failed to dislodge them from the wide areas of the country they controlled.

The Viet Cong struck back during the confused period following the overthrow of the Diem government. Taking advantage of the ensuing dislocation of government forces, they began an offensive that swept over the network of fortified hamlets created by the Diem régime, forcing the abandonment of many of them. Each side suffered nearly 3,000 casualties in the November fighting, according to generally accepted estimates; of those lost by the Viet Cong, nearly 80% were believed to have been killed in action.

There also was a growing number of casualties suffered by the 16,500-man U.S. military mission in Vietnam. By the end of the year, nearly 200 Americans had been killed since Dec. 1961, approximately 50% of them in combat.

South Vietnamese mother flees with her children from her burning home near Tay Ninh. Her village had been attacked and burned by South Vietnamese rangers because it had been used as a Viet Cong supply depot.   (Wide World photo)

Adm. Harry D. Felt, commander-in-chief of U.S. forces in the Pacific, had arrived in Saigon Jan. 9 on an Asian inspection tour. Felt said Jan. 11 that the Viet Cong faced "inevitable" defeat despite the difficulties existing between South

Vietnamese commanders and U.S. military advisers. Gen. Paul D. Harkins, commander of the U.S. Military & Advisory Group in South Vietnam, said Jan. 10: The South Vietnamese troops were "gallant and courageous" and had suffered 10,000 lives lost in combat in the past year.

Major Actions Summarized

The following major military engagements were reported in South Vietnam during 1963:

• Viet Cong gunfire Jan. 2 hit 14 of 15 U.S. Army helicopters ferrying troops of South Vietnam's 7th Infantry Division to attack a 400-man guerrilla force in the Mekong River delta village of Ap Bac, 30-50 miles southeast of Saigon. 5 of the helicopters were shot down; 3 U.S. military advisers were killed, and 10 were wounded. The Viet Cong scored a clear victory in the ensuing 2-day battle, in which 65 South Vietnamese soldiers were reported killed and at least 100 wounded. South Vietnam reported Jan. 2 that 101 guerrillas had been killed, but American advisers said that only 41 bodies had been counted.

• 39 government mountain troop trainees were killed and 26 wounded Jan. 3 in a Viet Cong attack on their camp at Pleimrong, deep in Communist territory. 50 Viet Cong were killed. 2 soldiers of a 12-man American unit that had been training the recruits were wounded. The attack occurred while ½ of the U.S. unit and ½ of a South Vietnamese strike force were away from the camp on patrol. 11 camp trainees who had concealed their Viet Cong membership and more than 200 pro-Communist villagers assisted the Viet Cong in the raid. The Americans, who had fed, clothed and provided medical care for the villagers, were unaware of their pro-Communist leanings. The Viet Cong had enlisted the sympathies of the villagers 2 months before the Americans had established the training camp in Nov. 1962. Just prior to the attack, the 11 Viet Cong trainees cut the camp's barbed wires, permitting the Viet Cong easy entry. More than 40 other trainees joined with the Viet Cong during the attack. South Vietnamese authorities were reported Jan. 22 to have arrested 42 pro-Communist villagers for their rôle in the attack.

• Viet Cong forces Jan. 6 reportedly overran a strategic government hamlet 235 miles northeast of Saigon. The government said Jan. 8 that its troops had killed or wounded more than 700 guerrillas in 2 operations that ended Jan. 7; both battles reportedly occurred north of Saigon, one near the Cambodian border, the other in a Communist enclave known as "D Zone"; government losses were listed as 21 killed and 130 wounded.

• A guerrilla force of 300 men Feb. 5 killed 34 government soldiers and wounded 27 others in an ambush near the Camau Peninsula village of Thoi Binh. In another Camau Peninsula clash Feb. 5 government marines and sailors stormed Viet Cong land positions on the Cua Long River from speedboats and landing craft. 29 Viet Cong were killed.

• A U.S. soldier was killed Feb. 24 as Viet Cong ground fire downed 2 of 3 U.S. Army H-21 helicopters that had been airlifting government soldiers about 100 miles north of Saigon. U.S. helicopters were ordered, effective Feb. 26, to shoot first at enemy soldiers while escorting government troops. Heretofore, the helicopters had been required to refrain from shooting until fired on.

• A 7,000-man South Vietnamese force Mar. 13 launched a major attack in the Plaine des Joncs (Plain of Reeds) near the Cambodian border in an effort to wipe out guerrillas operating within the Mekong delta area. 20 guerrillas were killed by government planes. As government troops began to return to their bases Mar. 16, military sources said the operation had failed because heavy government supply movements and aerial reconnaissance several days prior to the attack had alerted the Communist troops.

• A Viet Cong arms-manufacturing base, located in dense jungle 55 miles northwest of Saigon, was captured Mar. 24-25 by South Vietnamese paratroopers supported by fighter planes and amphibious weapon-carriers. 24 Viet Cong were killed and 11 South Vietnamese troops injured in the operation.

• Viet Cong units Mar. 30 ambushed a government civil guards company near the coastal community of Phan Thiet,

95 miles north of Saigon. 28 government soldiers were killed
and 18 wounded.

• Viet Cong forces Apr. 13 attacked a Vietnamese paratroop
company in the Tayninh Province jungles, about 40 miles
northwest of Saigon. In a 2-hour fight, 18 Vietnamese troops
were killed and 27 wounded; 15 Viet Cong were killed.

• Guerrilla forces Apr. 24 surrounded and wiped out a company of government civil guards near Quangngai, 325 miles
north of Saigon.

• 41 South Vietnamese soldiers and a U.S. Army master
sergeant were killed in a Viet Cong attack Apr. 27 on a battalion (300-400 men) of government regulars about 40 miles
northeast of Kontum.

• A U.S. lieutenant and 2 South Vietnamese soldiers were
shot to death by guerrillas May 6 on the road between Bencat
and Benduong, 30 miles north of Saigon.

• Viet Cong guerrillas May 16 ambushed a column of Vietnamese army trucks on a mountain road. 21 government soldiers were killed and 25 wounded.

• U.S. sources reported May 20 that Vietnamese troops had
killed 40 Viet Cong guerrillas that day. The Vietnamese government reported that its troops had killed 90 Viet Cong and
captured 25 in an attack on a rebel training center on the
Cambodian border.

• Guerrillas May 23 overran a Vietnamese outpost in Bay
Xuyen Province, 150 miles southwest of Saigon. 34 government soldiers were reported killed or captured.

• Guerrillas ambushed a Vietnamese engineer unit June 7
and killed 16 men. It was reported June 15 that Viet Cong
had twice ambushed Vietnamese troops in the Mekong delta
in the previous 3 days; 63 Vietnamese soldiers were reported
killed, 100 wounded and 29 missing. Government sources
said their troops had killed 114 Viet Cong during the operation.

• 3 U.S. Special Forces soldiers were killed July 18 when a
Viet Cong force ambushed a convoy 70 miles northwest of
Saigon near the Cambodian border.

• South Vietnam troops were reported July 26 to have ignored U.S. military advisers' protests in abandoning their fortified Rang Rang base in the Communist-dominated "D Zone" in the mountainous jungle north of Saigon. U.S. officials were particularly angered over the abandonment of 800 buried antipersonnel mines in the area.

• U.S. military sources in Saigon reported Aug. 6 that 90 Viet Cong had been killed in a 4-hour battle in the Camau Peninsula July 30. 3 government soldiers were killed.

• 2 U.S. pilots were killed and 3 other Americans injured when rebel gunfire shot down their helicopter Aug. 30 in the Tayninh area, 55 miles north of Saigon.

• At least 80 Communist guerrillas were killed in a Sept. 8-9 clash near Gocong, about 25 miles south of Saigon. 26 government troops were killed.

• Viet Cong units captured the Camau Peninsula towns of Cainouc and Damdoi but were ousted in a government counterattack Sept. 11. At least 90 persons, including civilians and soldiers, were said to have been killed in the ground fighting for Damdoi.

• A South Vietnamese regiment killed 122 guerrillas in a surprise attack Sept. 16 near Goden, 15 miles south of Saigon.

• 2 U.S. Marine helicopters crashed in the Danang area about 350 miles north of Saigon Oct. 8, and all 12 Americans aboard (9 Marines and 3 Navy men) were killed.

• About 40 Vietnamese government troops were believed to have been killed in a clash with a Viet Cong battalion Oct. 19-20 in the Chuong Thien Province village of Loc Ninh. An estimated 30 Communists were killed.

• A U.S. military spokesman reported in Saigon Oct. 29 that government troops had slain 44 guerrillas in a battle at 3 fortified hamlets in Quangngai Province Oct. 28-29.

• The government reported Nov. 25 that Viet Cong units had wiped out the 2 fortified strategic hamlets of Dake Rode and Polei Kobay, about 250 miles north of Saigon. After the attack, more than 1,000 tribesmen were missing from the 2 villages.

• Vietnamese officials said Nov. 25 that 150 guerrillas had been killed in 2 days of operations that had started Nov. 21 in the Mekong delta.

• Vietnamese forces suffered heavy casualties Dec. 1 in successfully defending a fortified post in Tayninh Province, about 60 miles northwest of Saigon. 42 civil guardsmen and 15-20 members of their families were killed in the Viet Cong attack. Guerrilla losses were estimated at 50.

• South Vietnamese troops Dec. 21 ambushed a Viet Cong guerrilla company near the U Minh jungle in Chuong Thien Province, about 110 miles southwest of Saigon. A U.S. military spokesman said 20 to 30 guerrillas were killed.

• South Vietnamese government forces Dec. 25 rejected a Viet Cong bid for a 24-hour Christmas cease-fire and continued operations. The Saigon régime said Dec. 26 that the Communists had attacked Vietnamese points in at least 4 provinces.

Viet Cong Urged to Defect

Pres. Ngo Dinh Diem, in a nationwide radio appeal Apr. 17, had promised Viet Cong guerrillas and their sympathizers clemency and material benefits if they abandoned the war against his government. In his radio address, Diem proclaimed a *"Chieu Hoi* [Open Arms]" program. He called on the Viet Cong to "return and uphold the just cause of the fatherland and to contribute their efforts along with those of all our people in order to build . . . a new society where every citizen will be able to develop totally and in full freedom."

Asserting that the offer was "inspired by the ideal of respect for the human being," Diem said the program "provides for appropriate measures in favor of all those . . . deceived, exploited or enrolled by force by the Communists—who have a new awareness and decide from today to rally to the side of the government." Diem announced that he had established a "special committee" to work among prospective Viet Cong defectors within the government's "strategic hamlet" program.

Diem said: Clemency applicants "having families and means of subsistance will be authorized to join their families or to reside" in the community "of their choice"; "those having no [such] means" "can be assured of assistance"; "those having skills and ability—after" they "have proved by concrete acts their total detachment from communism—will see their services accepted"; law violators "condemned or . . . subject to court trial will have the opportunity to . . . redeem themselves by . . . patriotic acts that will enable them to benefit from measures of indulgence or pardon."

Diem had issued a similar clemency appeal to the Viet Cong in February. The government reported that as a result of this plea, 2,787 persons had defected from the Communist ranks and had joined "the people"; 1,789 of them were peasants who lived in Viet Cong strongholds.

Strategic Hamlet Program Suspended

The South Vietnamese junta ordered a halt, at least temporarily, to the construction of new strategic hamlets, the fortified centers aimed at providing rural villagers with a defense against the Viet Cong guerrillas. The suspension of the program was disclosed Dec. 2.

A council directive to provincial officials said: (a) Peasants were not to be forced to move into the strategic hamlets; (b) officials were not to insist that peasants contribute to the financial upkeep of the hamlets; (c) "labor contributions" were to be requested only for programs that would directly benefit hamlet residents.

Maj. Gen. Duong Van Minh, junta chairman, said existing strategic hamlets would be "consolidated" by government security, economic and welfare services that the Diem régime had failed to provide.

The strategic hamlet program, originated by the Diem régime, had caused great resentment, particularly in the Mekong delta, where thousands of peasants were forced to leave their homes to build the fortified villages. Several thousand peasants were said to have left delta hamlets since the overthrow of the Diem régime.

Cao Daiists to Join Government Forces

The dissident Cao Dai religious sect announced Dec. 27 that it would join the South Vietnamese government in the war against the Viet Cong guerrillas. The pledge was made by Cao Dai leader Tran Van Vin at a temple ceremony in the Daiist center of Tayninh, 50 miles northwest of Saigon. The ceremony was attended by a Vietnamese military delegation headed by Maj. Gen. Duong Van Minh, chairman of the ruling military junta. Minh had been urged by U.S. officials to rally public support for the war against the Communists.

Maj. Gen. Le Than Tat, Cao Dai military leader, said Dec. 27 that he and about 200 Cao Dai officers were available to serve in the regular South Vietnamese army. Previously the Cao Dai had insisted on serving in separate units.

De Gaulle Proposes Neutral State

French Pres. Charles de Gaulle proposed Aug. 29 that Vietnam (North and South) be transformed with France's help from a divided, warring country into a unified, neutral state that could assume a new rôle in Asia. De Gaulle offered French aid and cooperation if Vietnam was prepared to accept such a policy and throw off the foreign "influence" currently wielded by the U.S. and Communist nations.

Referring to "the work which France accomplished in the past in Cochin-China, Annam and Tonkin [the 3 former provinces of French Indochina that made up North and South Vietnam], the ties which she retains in the whole country and the interest she has in its development," de Gaulle said that France appreciated "the rôle this people would be capable of playing in the present situation of Asia . . . once it is able to carry on its activity in independence from exterior influence, in internal peace and unity." He said France would be ready "to set up a cordial cooperation with this country" under such a policy.

The French proposal was rebuffed by Pres. Kennedy Sept. 2 as irrelevant to the current situation in Vietnam. In a TV interview, Mr. Kennedy emphasized his rejection of any policy that would lead to the withdrawal of U.S. troops from Vietnam before the Viet Cong menace there had been eliminated.

1964

The war against the Viet Cong grew in intensity throughout 1964. Major complications in fighting the war were caused by widespread internal unrest in South Vietnam and by the instability of the government, which underwent repeated shifts. In the U.S., criticism of Johnson Administration policy became more vehement as the Presidential campaign progressed and continued after the elections were over. The U.S. Administration repeatedly rejected proposals that North Vietnamese territory be attacked to block supply routes along which arms and men were sent from North Vietnam to the guerrillas in the South. In August, North Vietnamese PT boats attacked U.S. destroyers in the Gulf of Tonkin, and the U.S. retaliated with air raids on North Vietnamese coastal installations. The U.S. Congress then voted to give Pres. Johnson advance authority to take any action he found necessary in the Southeast Asian crisis.

DEEPENING CRISIS

Junta Centralizes Power but Falls in Coup

Maj. Gen. Duong Van Minh, chairman of the military junta (the Military Revolutionary Council) that had ruled South Vietnam since the overthrow of Pres. Ngo Dinh Diem Nov. 2, 1963, issued decrees Jan. 6 centralizing government and military power in the hands of himself and 2 other senior officers. Maj. Gen. Tran Van Don, defense minister and vice chairman of the junta, was appointed commander-in-chief of the armed forces; Maj. Gen. Le Van Kim, secretary general of the junta and foreign affairs commissioner, was named chief of staff of the armed forces' Joint General Staff.

The Revolutionary Council was overthrown Jan. 30 in a bloodless *coup d'état* carried out by dissident military officers. The rebel troops, numbering about 3,000, were led by Maj. Gen. Nguyen Khanh, commander of the army's First Corps. Gen. Minh, junta chairman, was placed under house arrest. Rebel soldiers took up key positions in Saigon, and Khanh occupied the junta's headquarters. Insurgent forces blocked the main highways into Saigon during the night. The rebels ousted Premier Nguyen Ngoc Tho and arrested him along with these 5 junta leaders: Maj. Gen. Tran Van Don; Maj. Gen. Le Van Kim; Maj. Gen. Mai Huu Xuan, national police chief; Maj. Gen. Ton That Dinh, interior minister; Brig. Gen. Nguyen Van Vy, deputy chief of staff.

Khanh said the coup was aimed at thwarting a French-led plot to neutralize South Vietnam. He charged that the arrested junta leaders had been in contact with French agents and that the plot had been timed to coincide with France's recognition of Communist China, announced Jan. 27. He declared that 3 months after the Diem régime had been deposed, the military junta had failed to solve the country's problems and was "anti-revolutionary." Khanh named himself to replace Minh as junta chairman. Minh was later released and agreed to serve the new régime as an adviser. (The 5 arrested junta leaders were released from detention May 30.)

Khanh appointed himself premier of a new cabinet Feb. 8. Minh was appointed head of state, a titular position without authority. The cabinet included Phan Huy Quat as foreign minister. Khanh was reelected chairman of the Military Revolutionary Council Mar. 22, and Minh was reappointed as the Council's supreme adviser. Khanh announced the formation of an executive steering committee and the extension of Council representation to the Self-Defense Corps and the Civil Guard in moves to strengthen the Council.

Communist Nations Arm Viet Cong

A U.S. military spokesman in Saigon reported Jan. 4 that arms shipments from Communist nations to the Viet Cong guerrillas in South Vietnam had increased considerably in the previous 6 months. As a result, the Viet Cong were "better equipped and better organized than 12 months ago." Other military sources said that ¾ of the arms shipments had been sent in Communist-bloc vessels from Chinese and North Vietnamese ports to Sihanoukville, Cambodia. The equipment reportedly was then routed to Pnompenh, Cambodia and transshipped to South Vietnam on the Mekong River.

The U.S. spokesman said that "the fact that Cambodia is a transit point does not prove collusion" of the Cambodian government with the Communists. (U.S. officials had complained that Cambodia's border guard was "wholly inadequate" to police the South Vietnamese frontier.) The spokesman said South Vietnamese troops in Dec. 1963 had captured

Chinese machineguns, rifles and ammunition in western Dingh Tuong Province, near the Cambodian border.

Buddhist Sects Unite Politically

South Vietnam's 11 main Buddhist sects Jan. 4 announced the formation of a politically-oriented Unified Vietnam Buddhist Church. The announcement was made at the conclusion of a 4-day convention in Saigon. The new movement's goal was confirmed in its charter, which established an Institute for Secular Affairs, described by Buddhist leaders as the church's political and social arm. The institute, headed by a strong 8-member leadership group, was to conduct its organizational work in each of South Vietnam's 42 provinces and their districts. The charter also established an 8-member Institute for Religious Affairs, whose head would be titular leader of all Vietnamese Buddhists.

(Premier Khanh May 15 signed a decree granting Buddhists the same rights as Catholics. The decree, abolishing legislative restrictions imposed by the former Diem régime, permitted the sect to accept money from private sources and to acquire land and buildings for religious purposes. More than 35,000 Roman Catholics demonstrated in Saigon June 7 and accused the government of discriminating against their faith.)

Village & Hamlet Reforms Urged

A South Vietnamese-U.S. report made public Jan. 14 warned that the war against the Viet Cong guerrillas in the critical Mekong River delta "cannot ever be won" unless South Vietnam's new government effected major reforms in the villages and strategic hamlets. The report was submitted by 4 Vietnamese officials and one U.S. aide; it was based on the findings of a 21-man survey team the 5 officials had supervised in Long An Province, south of Saigon, scene of recent Communist military successes. The survey team had questioned 1,500 peasant families in 15 villages.

Major points of the report: (a) steps should be taken to correct corruption, mismanagement and neglect by local officials in the strategic hamlets; (b) the government should halt the forcible removal of peasant families into the hamlets because such action aroused peasant resentment; (c) South Vietnamese regular forces had failed to reinforce part-time militia when they came under Communist attack in the villages and hamlets; (d) the government's education system was "too mechanical to cope with the Viet Cong propagandists," who made "the young" their "prime targets."

Nguyen Ngoc Tho, then premier, had pledged Jan. 9 that his government would carry out military and civil reforms as called for by the U.S. to help win the war. But he said the government could not yet fulfill the "pressing claims of the people who yearn for democratic liberty."

A comprehensive reform program to give South Vietnam "a solid foundation for the task of national salvation and development" was announced Mar. 7 by Gen. Nguyen Khanh, Tho's successor as premier. Khanh's 15-page policy paper called for decentralization of government agencies and for the assignment of younger leaders to positions of responsibility. Khanh placed great emphasis on the program of strategic hamlets. He said: "The previous . . . program followed the principle of building too many hamlets too quickly. We shall . . . insist on quality rather than quantity, giving equal stress to the security factor and to [raising] the living standard of the population." Other Khanh proposals: (a) improvement of social security measures; (b) a peasant land reform program; (c) expansion of irrigation projects to the central coastal plain.

Khanh's régime Mar. 30 began a "clear and hold" program of training army officers to run local governments properly as a means of retaining areas recaptured from the Viet Cong. The first 40 of the country's 237 military district chiefs (all army officers) started a 2-week program in Saigon that included courses in holding local elections, finance and accounting, economic and social development and local politics. Addressing the opening class, U.S. Amb. Henry Cabot Lodge said: The trainees "epitomize the idea of government of the people. After the enemy is driven out, it is up to you to govern the community with the help of local militia so that the Viet Cong won't come right back."

U.S. Hopes to Withdraw Troops, Ponders Policy

U.S. Defense Secy. Robert S. McNamara told the House Armed Services Committee Jan. 27 that the U.S. still hoped to withdraw most of its 15,000 troops from South Vietnam before the end of 1965. In testimony made public Feb. 18, McNamara said some U.S. commanders already had received orders to complete their training missions with the South Vietnamese forces and start shipping their personnel back to the U.S. Recalling that the major U.S. military assistance program to South Vietnam had started in 1961, McNamara said it was "reasonable to expect that after 4 years of such training, we should be able gradually to withdraw certain of our . . . personnel." McNamara said that although he did not believe that the U.S. "should assume the primary responsibility for the war in South Vietnam," some U.S. personnel would "have to stay there until the counterinsurgency operation has been successfully completed."

A U.S. fact-finding mission headed by McNamara visited South Vietnam Mar. 5-12 to survey the South Vietnamese government's reported political instability and the progress of the war against the Viet Cong guerrillas. Accompanying McNamara were Gen. Maxwell D. Taylor, chairman of the Joint Chiefs of Staff, and other top Administration officials. Both officials conferred with Premier Khanh and other Vietnamese leaders and with U.S. military and political advisers in the country. McNamara and Taylor returned to Washington Mar. 13 and delivered a preliminary report to Pres. Johnson. They then presented a full review of the situation Mar. 17 at a meeting of the National Security Council, presided over by the President. A White House statement after the meeting said the U.S. would increase military and economic aid to support Khanh's new plan for fighting the Viet Cong more effectively. Major provisions of Khanh's program included a national mobilization, increased pay and status for the paramilitary forces and "significant additional equipment" for the armed forces. In a speech in Washington Mar. 26, McNamara said the U.S. was determined "to answer the call of the South Vietnamese, . . . to help them save their country for themselves." He said "the situation in South Vietnam has unquestionably worsened, at least since last fall," and he assailed neutralization proposals for Vietnam. McNamara announced Mar. 29 that the U.S. would provide South Vietnam with $50 million annually (in addition to the current yearly assistance of $500 million) to finance the expansion of its armed forces by 50,000 men.

(An agreement providing South Vietnam with $31,200,000 worth of U.S. surplus commodities in 1964 had been signed in Saigon Jan. 14. The transaction, the largest single Food for Peace agreement with South Vietnam, provided for the shipment of surplus cotton, tobacco, wheat, flour and condensed and evaporated milk. U.S. Amb. Lodge said the commodities would be sold to commercial importers and 90% of the sales proceeds would be turned over to the government to help finance the war against the Viet Cong. Lodge said the remaining 10% was "available for loans to private industry." U.S. aid officials earlier Jan. 14 had turned over to South Vietnam $5 million worth of railroad equipment to replace rail facilities that had been destroyed by the Viet Cong.)

Sens. Ernest Gruening (D., Alaska) and Wayne L. Morse (D., Ore.) assailed the U.S.' Vietnam policy in Senate speeches Mar. 10 and demanded that the U.S. withdraw its forces. Sen. Thomas Dodd (D., Conn.) upheld Administration policy in a Mar. 11 reply to Morse and Gruening. He urged action to "turn the war against North Vietnam, the home base of the aggressor."

Sen. Hubert H. Humphrey (D., Minn.) said in a TV talk Mar. 29 that the U.S. had no choice but to continue to support the Saigon régime because the other alternatives—withdrawal or extending the war to North Vietnam—were unacceptable. Although opposing neutralization for Vietnam as "folly," Humphrey envisaged the possibility for negotiating an agreement for the "neutralizing of all the area included in Indochina," if and when the Vietnamese situation became stabilized.

Ex-Vice Pres. Richard M. Nixon, returning Apr. 15 from a 24-day trip through Asia, proposed extending the war in South Vietnam into North Vietnam and Laos. Arriving in

New York from Tokyo Apr. 15, Nixon told reporters that "we should strengthen our policy toward Communist activities in Asia rather than move along the lines suggested by Sen. [J. W.] Fulbright." In a speech before the N.Y. Chamber of Commerce Apr. 16, Nixon called for military action against Communist bases in North Vietnam and Laos and said the "enemy can no longer have privileged sanctuary." He said that any softening of U.S. policy toward Communist China would be the "straw that broke the camel's back in Southeast Asia." The U.S. "has gone too far in catering to neutrals," he declared. In Washington Apr. 18, Nixon said in a speech before the American Society of Newspaper Editors that South Vietnamese troops should go "in hot pursuit" of Communist guerrillas into Laos and North Vietnam. To win the war there, the initiative must be carried north, he asserted.

Acknowledging that "a total solution to the [Vietnamese] problem cannot be achieved solely by military means," U.S. Amb. Lodge said in the Apr. 17 issue of *Life* magazine: "At this rough and dangerous stage there is no substitute for force." He suggested that the terms of U.S. military advisers in South Vietnam be extended.

State Secy. Dean Rusk visited South Vietnam Apr. 17-20 to emphasize U.S. support of Premier Khanh and his régime's war against the Viet Cong. Rusk returned to Washington Apr. 20 and reported to Pres. Johnson. Rusk warned May 22 that "if the Communists persist in their course of aggression" in South Vietnam the war there could be expanded. In an address before the American Law Institute in Washington, Rusk said: The Viet Cong "aggression" against South Vietnam "was initiated and is directed by Hanoi. It is led by cadres in the North by Hanoi and . . . is equipped and supplied by Hanoi." North Vietnam "in turn has been guided, and in material ways, assisted by Peiping" with arms captured in South Vietnam. U.S. withdrawal from Southeast Asia "would mean not only grievous losses to the free world in Southeast and Southern Asia but a drastic loss of confidence in the will and capacity of the free world." U.S. withdrawal "would also bring us much closer to a major conflagration." "We are not going to abandon people who are trying to preserve their independence and freedom. This is the signal which must be read with the greatest care . . . , especially in Hanoi and Peiping. . . . There is a simple prescription for peace—leave your neighbors alone."

At a joint Washington news conference held Apr. 21, the Senate and House Republican leaders, Sen. Everett M. Dirksen (Ill.) and Rep. Charles A. Halleck (Ind.), charged that the Johnson Administration had concealed the extent of U.S. involvement in the Vietnamese war. Reading from the personal letters of an Air Force captain killed in Vietnam in March, the GOP leaders contended that the U.S. was fighting the war and not just training and supporting South Vietnamese in a war among Vietnamese. Halleck declared: "If we are going to war, let us prepare the American people for it." Dirksen added: "Let's have the whole brutal thing out on the table and let the American people see it for what it is." The letters read by Dirksen and Halleck were written by the late Capt. Edwin G. Shank of Winimac, Ind. to his wife. Excerpts read by the 2 Congress members: "I don't know what the U.S. is doing. They tell you people we're just in a training situation and they try to run us as a training base. But we're at war, we are doing the flying and fighting. Morale is very bad." "The Vietnamese 'students' we have on board are airmen basics. . . . The only reason they are on board is, in case we crash, there is one American 'adviser' and one Vietnamese 'student.' . . . They are . . . a menace to have on board."

McNamara and Taylor visited Saigon May 12-13 on another fact-finding mission. (McNamara came from Bonn where he had urged West German leaders May 9-11 to expand technical aid for South Vietnam.) In a statement prior to returning to the U.S. May 13, McNamara said "excellent progress" had been made in the war against the Viet Cong. McNamara and Taylor returned to Washington May 14 and reported to Pres. Johnson with a proposal for increased economic and military support of South Vietnam. McNamara said later at a White House news conference that victory over the Viet Cong "was not going to come soon," that it was going to be a "long hard war." He reported on his fact-finding mission at a meeting of the National Security Council May 15. Some Congressional leaders who attended the meeting said later that McNamara's report had been "very gloomy" and that the campaign against the Viet Cong apparently had deteriorated. (Nguyen Van Troi, 17, a Viet Cong terrorist, was executed by firing squad in Saigon Oct. 15 for having attempted to assassinate McNamara. Troi was arrested May 9 while placing an explosive charge under a Saigon bridge over which McNamara's car was to have passed on his arrival in South Vietnam May 12.)

Sen. Barry Goldwater (Ariz.), campaigning for the Republican Presidential nomination, suggested May 24 that "low-yield atomic weapons" be used to defoliate South Vietnamese border jungles affording protective cover for Communist supply lines from Communist China and North Vietnam. Speaking on the ABC radio-TV program "Issues and Answers," Goldwater also proposed non-atomic bombing of bridges, roads and railroads used as Communist supply routes.

High-ranking U.S. officials held a meeting in Honolulu June 1-2 to plan U.S. strategy to cope with the mounting crisis in Southeast Asia. The meeting had been called May 28 by Pres. Johnson, who reportedly had asked that the conferees recommend measures to counteract strong Communist pressures in Laos and South Vietnam. Most of the conferees returned to Washington June 3 and reported to Mr. Johnson. Among those attending were McNamara, Rusk, Taylor, CIA Director John A. McCone and State Undersecy. George W. Ball.

Gen. Paul D. Harkins, 60, left South Vietnam June 20 and was succeeded as head of the U.S. Military Assistance Command there by his deputy, Lt. Gen. William C. Westmoreland, 50 (whose appointment had been announced Apr. 25). In a final official statement, made June 18, Harkins expressed optimism about the progress of the war against the Viet Cong but acknowledged that the war effort had been set back by about 9 months as a result of the anti-Diem coup. Westmoreland, a specialist in guerrilla warfare, was reported June 23 to have been named as "executive agent" to supervise civilian as well as military assistance programs in Bin Duong,

Hau Nghia and Long An Provinces around Saigon. The appointment was the first step in a plan, eventually to be extended to all provinces, to give the U.S. military mission greater responsibilities than its civilian counterpart.

De Gaulle Proposes New Neutrality Plans

Pres. Charles de Gaulle of France proposed Jan. 31 that the Western powers negotiate with Communist China to neutralize Southeast Asia. De Gaulle said at a news conference in Paris that his recognition of Communist China was part of a wider French plan for settling the continuing crisis in Southeast Asia, particularly in Vietnam, Laos and Cambodia. He said: "There is in Asia no political reality . . . that does not concern or affect China. There is . . . neither a war nor a peace imaginable on this continent without China's being implicated in it. Thus it would be . . . impossible to envisage, without China, a possible neutrality agreement relating to the Southeast Asian states."

Pres. Johnson said Feb. 1 that he would be prepared to consider any plan that would insure the "neutralization of both North Vietnam and South Vietnam." "But I see no indication of that at the moment," he said. As long as Communist-inspired unrest in South Vietnam persisted, Mr. Johnson declared, "I think that the present course we are conducting is the only answer, . . . and I think that the operations should be stepped up there." The President specified that the U.S. had pledged full backing for the new régime installed by Gen. Khanh. (Mr. Johnson had said Jan. 1 in a message to Gen. Duong Van Minh, then chairman of the junta: The U.S. "shares the view of your government that single 'neutralization' of South Vietnam is unacceptable. As long as the Communist régime in North Vietnam persists in its aggressive policy, neutralization of South Vietnam would be another name for a Communist takeover.")

The Ministerial Council of the Southeast Asia Treaty Organization (SEATO) held its 10th annual meeting in Manila Apr. 13-15. The conference was marked by opposition within SEATO to France's proposals for neutralization of Southeast Asia. France abstained from voting on a section of a final communiqué, issued Apr. 15, that pledged SEATO support for South Vietnam against the Viet Cong. The section was approved by Australia, Britain, New Zealand, Pakistan, the Philippines and the U.S. It said: The SEATO council "agreed that defeat of the Communist campaign is essential not only to the security of Vietnam but to that of Southeast Asia. . . . The council agreed that members of SEATO should remain prepared . . . to take further concrete steps with their respective capabilities in fulfillment of their obligations under the treaty." The communiqué accused North Vietnam of directing, supplying and supporting the Viet Cong. Foreign Min. Maurice Couve de Murville, head of the French delegation, voted for the rest of the communiqué, which expressed SEATO determination to oppose overt Communist aggression in the area covered by SEATO.

At the opening meeting of the SEATO council's closed session Apr. 13, Couve de Murville praised U.S. support of Saigon's war effort but said he did not think South Vietnam could defeat the guerrillas. He based his doubts on what he called lack of public support for Premier Khanh's régime and its failure to exert national authority. Couve de Murville called for a "political solution" in Vietnam. (A spokesman later said this statement was, in effect, a plea for de Gaulle's neutralization proposal.)

U.S. support for Khanh and Saigon's war effort was expressed by State Secy. Dean Rusk at the Apr. 13 session. Conceding that the Viet Cong had captured large Vietnamese areas, Rusk said the U.S. was committed to supporting the war against the guerrillas. He said the U.S. did not rule out the possibility of extending the conflict to North Vietnam.

De Gaulle proposed July 23 an agreement among the U.S., France, USSR and Red China to end the struggle for control of Laos and South Vietnam. Declaring that "it does not appear there can be a military solution in South Vietnam," de Gaulle urged, at a Paris news conference, that the 4 powers agree to leave the Indochinese peninsula and guarantee its neutrality and future political independence. He suggested that the 4 powers supplement this agreement with massive economic and technical aid to the 4 Indochinese states—North and South Vietnam, Laos and Cambodia.

Pres. Johnson July 24 rejected de Gaulle's proposed Indochinese agreement. Mr. Johnson called North Vietnam a "danger and provocation" in the South Vietnamese guerrilla war. The U.S. did "not believe in conferences called to ratify terror, so our policy is unchanged," the President said. Mr. Johnson said U.S. policy was to "support the freedom and independence of South Vietnam" and "the legitimate government of Laos."

The French proposals were also rejected July 24 by South Vietnam. Such suggestions were "prejudicial to the fight that Vietnam leads . . . against aggression imposed upon it by the Communist International," a governmental statement said. "A new Geneva conference would not resolve the problem, for experience shows that the Communists . . . do not hesitate to promote . . . a false peace to continue their invasion movement toward the South."

Taylor Replaces Lodge as U.S. Ambassador

The resignation of Henry Cabot Lodge as U.S. ambassador to South Vietnam was announced June 23 by Pres. Johnson. In a statement issued simultaneously in Saigon, Lodge said he had resigned to return to the U.S. and join Republican Party moderates in their effort to deny the party's Presidential nomination to Sen. Barry M. Goldwater (Ariz.). The President appointed Gen. Taylor the same day as Lodge's successor.

Lodge returned to Washington June 29 and gave the Johnson Administration an optimistic report on the campaign against the Viet Cong. Lodge told the President that South Vietnam was "on the right track" in the war but that victory would require a long struggle. Lodge testified June 30 at a closed joint session of the Senate Foreign Relations and Armed Services Committees. In a statement after the hearing, Lodge rejected a June 29 report by 13 Republican Congressmen that suggested U.S. assumption of direct operational command of the anti-guerrilla war. "If we do that, we become a colonial power," Lodge said, and there would be "unfortunate results in the form of anti-American feelings."

Taylor arrived in Saigon July 7 to assume his ambassadorial duties. He met with Premier Khanh July 8 and urged him to press his program of political and administrative reforms designed to secure critical areas against Viet Cong attacks.

Lodge, as a personal emissary of Pres. Johnson, toured Western European capitals Aug. 16-Sept. 1 to explain the U.S.' policy on South Vietnam and seek support in the war against the Viet Cong. Lodge reported to the President Sept. 10. He said at a news conference later that all the Western leaders he had seen, including the French, had expressed willingness to help the South Vietnamese. Lodge had received pledges from West German, Dutch, Belgian, British and Spanish officials to provide South Vietnam with non-military technical assistance. (Lodge made his trip after the anti-Goldwater forces were defeated at the Republican National Convention.)

Diem's Brother Executed, Buddhist Rights Restored

Ngo Dinh Can, 53, younger brother of the late Pres. Diem, was convicted and sentenced to death Apr. 22 on charges of murder, extortion and misuse of power while governor of Central Vietnam. Can was executed by firing squad in Saigon May 9. He had been arrested after the coup that had overthrown Diem.

Maj. Dang Si, former commander of the Hué military district, was convicted and sentenced June 6 to life in prison for his role in the slaying of 8 Buddhist demonstrators in Hué May 8, 1963. The incident had led to nationwide Buddhist demonstrations and the overthrow of Diem.

(Mrs. Ngo Dinh Nhu, exiled widow of the late Pres. Diem's brother and adviser, applied in Paris June 11 for a 6-month visa to enter the U.S. The State Department was reported June 23 to have rejected the application under an Immigration Act clause that barred aliens who sought to enter the U.S. "to engage in activities which would be prejudicial to the public interest.")

State of Emergency Decreed

Premier Khanh declared a nationwide state of emergency Aug. 7 to cope with what he called increasing pressures from Communist China and North Vietnam following a clash between U.S. destroyers and North Vietnamese PT boats in the Gulf of Tonkin and a retaliatory U.S. air attack on North Vietnam. "All laws and regulations" were temporarily suspended, a curfew was imposed in Saigon, travel and food distribution were controlled, authority for house arrest and detention was widened, strikes and public meetings were banned and internal press censorship was imposed. Khanh said Chinese troops were "stationed—not infiltrated—in North Vietnam."

(A South Vietnamese draft law announced Apr. 5 had authorized the conscription of men into the Civil Guard and the Self-Defense Corps. The 2 paramilitary forces, which carried the burden of the fighting against the Viet Cong guerrillas, had been undermanned as a result of a drop-off in the volunteer rate and an increase in desertions. The Self-Defense Corps, which guarded villages and the countryside, reportedly was about 30% below its authorized strength of 72,000. The Civil Guard, stationed in each of South Vietnam's 43 provinces, was said to be about 15%-20% below its authorized strength of 80,000.)

Government Upheavals Continue

Premier Khanh became president of South Vietnam Aug. 16 under a new constitution approved at the conclusion of a 3-day meeting of the Military Revolutionary Council. Gen. Minh was ousted as chief of state, and the post was abolished. The new constitution, consolidating Khanh's powers, eliminated the offices of premier and chief of state, provided for a strong presidential system and established a 150-member advisory provisional National Assembly and a separate judicial branch.

However, Khanh and his new government resigned Aug. 25 following nationwide riots protesting his assumption of wider powers and the repressive Aug. 7 emergency decrees.

The Revolutionary Council voted to "repeal the constitution" and "to elect a new leader." The Council said that following the election it would "dissolve itself, and its members will return to their purely military functions" of fighting the Viet Cong. Khanh's régime was to remain in a caretaker capacity pending the formation of a new government. The anti-government demonstrations had erupted Aug. 19. They were carried out by students and Buddhists, who charged that Khanh's new régime was dictatorial and oppressive. The Buddhists further accused the government of anti-religious bias. They called for elimination of "anti-Buddhist elements" in government, many of whom, they charged, were holdovers from the Diem era. Police made no attempt to interfere with the riots, many of which caused widespread damage to government buildings and property in Saigon. The unrest was further heightened by communal clashes between Roman Catholics and Buddhists in Danang (where 9 persons were killed Aug. 24-25), Hué and Quinon.

In a move to solve the government crisis, Khanh and members of his hold-over régime, in constant negotiations since Aug. 25, agreed Aug. 27 to replace the ruling Council with a triumvirate of 3 generals. Its members were Khanh, Gen. Minh and Lt. Gen. Tran Thien Khiem, defense minister. All 3 were to have equal power. The negotiators upheld the defunct Council's Aug. 25 decision to repeal the Aug. 16 constitution. The triumvirate was to govern for no more than 2 months and then convene a national convention to elect a "provisional leader." The latter was to rule until a permanent government was formed following national elections in 1965. Khanh's arrangement with Minh and Khiem apparently was a tenuous one since the Council reportedly had refused to give him dominant powers. The agreement was further clouded when Khanh mysteriously left Saigon for Dalat, a resort city in the north. Former Deputy Premier Nguyen Xuan Oanh, designated as acting premier Aug. 29, said Khanh had gone to Dalat to recuperate from the physical and mental strain brought on by the crisis.

Khanh returned to Saigon Sept. 2 and renewed political discussions with Gens. Minh and Khiem. As a result of the talks, Khanh resumed his post as premier Sept. 3 and undertook a series of measures to provide the country with a stable régime. He immediately dissolved the triumvirate and renamed Minh to his former position as chief of state. Khanh reiterated Sept. 4 the intention of his interim government to serve for no more than 2 months and then turn "all powers" over to a civilian régime. The Sept. 3 directive dissolving the triumvirate apparently was rescinded and the military group was reinstated for the 2-month transitional period. Khanh announced the resignation of Khiem as defense minister and the resignation of all other army officers serving in ministerial posts. The withdrawal of the army officers reportedly was decided on to enable Khanh to attract wider civilian support in his efforts to form a new cabinet. Khiem retained his triumvirate seat, and Minh was appointed chairman of the triumvirate Sept. 8. A government spokesman said Minh would have the powers of chief of state but would not assume that title. He was to sign legislation and receive diplomatic credentials.

U.S. Amb. Taylor returned to Washington Sept. 7 to report on South Vietnam's government upheaval. At meetings with Pres. Johnson and other Administration officials, Taylor gave a cautiously optimistic assessment of the country's military and political situation. At a White House news conference Sept. 9, Taylor provided what he called a "very broad-brush description" of what had been discussed at the White House meetings. Taylor said Khanh "is very definitely head of the interim government. . . . By November, we hope there will be a provisional government which will have full powers, . . . taking as its ultimate goal a full representative government." Before flying back to Saigon Sept. 10, Taylor testified before the House Foreign Affairs Subcommittee on the Far East. According to excerpts of his testimony made public Sept. 11, Taylor warned that U.S. withdrawal from South Vietnam would result in a Communist country "almost all at once," and "the remainder of Southeast Asia would very shortly thereafter go neutralist, possibly Communist."

Dissident army officers attempted unsuccessfully to overthrow the Khanh government Sept. 13. The uprising, staged in Saigon, collapsed under a government display of military force. The rebels formally capitulated Sept. 14 at a meeting with government negotiators. The abortive coup was engineered by officers who had been opposed by Buddhist leaders during the government crisis the previous week. The coup leaders were Brig. Gen. Lam Van Phat, a Roman Catholic who had been dismissed as interior minister under the Sept. 3 directive ousting all military officers from the cabinet, and Brig. Gen. Duong Van Duc, 4th Corps commander. The rebels, numbering about 2,000, had moved into Saigon and seized the national radio station. They called their movement the People's Council for Salvation of the Nation and said its purpose was to combat communism by strengthening the government and armed forces. The rebels' main force, centered near Saigon's huge Tan Sonnhut military air base, withdrew after government troops were deployed there and loyalist planes flew threatening passes over the insurgents. The rebels then acceded to government demands to capitulate. Gens. Phat and Duc were arrested Sept. 16 along with 3 other rebel generals.

A communiqué signed by 8 army unit commanders Sept. 14 urged Khanh to oust and penalize "all corrupt and dishonest" military and civilian leaders who had served in the Diem regime. The communiqué warned that if this demand was not carried out "within 2 months," "the people and the armed forces will be compelled to make a 2d revolution."

The U.S. Sept. 13 strongly backed Khanh's government against the dissident officer faction. The U.S. position was made clear in a White House statement issued following a meeting of Pres. Johnson with top cabinet officials. State Secy. Rusk said Sept. 14 that the U.S. had appealed to South Vietnam's leaders to settle their differences.

The Viet Cong's political arm, the National Liberation Front, ordered Sept. 15 a general military drive to take advantage of Saigon's unsettled political situation resulting from the abortive coup.

Montagnards Rebel, U.S. Mediates

Montagnard tribesmen in South Vietnam's central plateau rebelled against the central government Sept. 20 and demanded self-rule. The revolt was brought to an end Sept. 28 by government military pressure and by negotiations directed by U.S. military advisers.

The first and most violent *montagnard* outbreak occurred Sept. 20 when about 500 tribesmen killed 50 Vietnamese soldiers at a U.S. Special Forces camp near Banmethout (160 miles northeast of Saigon). The camp was one of 5 centers used by the Americans to train the *montagnards* in fighting the Viet Cong guerrillas. The tribesmen then moved into Banmethout, capital of Darlac Province, and seized the city. The rebels withdrew from the city and surrendered the camp 9 hours later following appeals from Premier Khanh, who had flown to Banmethout, and from U.S. military advisers.

The *montagnards* also seized a Special Forces camp Sept. 20 at Bonsarpa, near the Cambodian border. The insurgents permitted U.S. helicopters Sept. 27 to evacuate 60 South Vietnamese hostages from the camp as a result of negotiations instituted by U.S. officers who had remained in Bonsarpa and attempted to persuade the rebels to surrender. About 1,000 government troops, who had surrounded the camp during the U.S.-rebel talks, marched in Sept. 28 as the *montagnards* formally capitulated.

Another major *montagnard* stronghold at Buonmoprong had surrendered Sept. 26 after U.S.-conducted mediation.

In addition to demanding tribal autonomy, the rebels also had insisted on: (a) representation in the central government; (b) the assignment of Americans to replace South Vietnamese officers in their training camps; (c) the teaching of tribal languages in local schools.

Opposition to Khanh Régime Continues

Premier Khanh's régime continued to be plagued by internal unrest during September-October. Reports of an impending coup led the government to station troops at key points in and around Saigon Sept. 25-26. The uprising never materialized, however, and the precautions were relaxed Sept. 27.

A group of young army officers demanded Sept. 26 that Khanh dismiss from the armed forces Gen. Khiem, a member of the ruling triumvirate, and 5 other generals for their alleged neutralist sympathies. Khanh yielded and announced the resignation of the 6 officers Sept. 30. Khiem was ordered to leave the country for fear that his presence would encourage military dissidents. His appointment as ambassador to the U.S. was announced Oct. 29.

Violent anti-government demonstrations erupted Sept. 26 in and around Quinhon, scene of Buddhist riots during the August crisis. 2 government battalions were flown to Quinhon Sept. 27 and restored order.

The Buddhists assumed a more aggressive rôle in public affairs, forming a new political party called the People's Council of National Salvation. The Council held its first formal session in Hué Oct. 3-4 in an effort to establish itself as a national political force. In a series of resolutions adopted at the Hué meeting, the Council denounced anti-U.S. demonstrations, opposed neutralism and communism, indorsed Khanh's régime and the war against the Viet Cong and urged that a civil government resume power on the departure of Khanh's interim régime. Hué University Prof. Le Khac Quyen, a member of the High National Council, was named temporary chairman of the Buddhist party Oct. 3.

Civilian Régime Established

The Saigon régime Sept. 26 formed a 17-member civilian High National Council to prepare for the installation of a provisional civilian government to replace Premier Khanh's caretaker rule. The Council was empowered to: (a) write a provisional constitution and set up the national institutions it entailed; (b) convene a national convention to draft a permanent constitution; (c) serve as a legislature pending the formation of a permanent government; (d) advise the Khanh government during its caretaker period. Council membership included Roman Catholic and Buddhist groups, opposition civil organizations and political leaders. Council chairman was Phan Khac Suu. Another member was Le Khac Quyen, the Buddhist leader.

The High National Council carried out a series of measures that led to the establishment of a civilian government Nov. 4. The Council proclaimed a new draft constitution for South Vietnam Oct. 20. In essence, the charter provided for a chief of state, a premier, a cabinet and a legislative assembly. The Council was to serve as the legislature until the assembly was elected and convened. A preamble to the constitution declared that "the armed forces have rightfully asserted that they would return to their purely military duties and gradually hand over the power to a civilian government." (Premier Khanh had objected to the draft Oct. 17 on the ground that it had not given the military "a place of honor" in government and that the chief of state was to have more power than the premier.) The Council Oct. 24 elected its chairman, Phan Khac Suu, as chief of state. Suu was sworn in Oct. 26 and accepted the resignations of Khanh as premier and of Gen. Duong Van Minh as chairman of the ruling triumvirate. Nguyen Xuan Chu replaced Suu as Council chairman. Suu Oct. 30 designated Tran Van Huong, 60, a former mayor of Saigon, to replace Khanh as premier. The council confirmed Huong's appointment Oct. 31, and the new premier and a 17-member civilian cabinet were installed Nov. 4. He assumed the additional post of defense minister, and Khanh was appointed commander-in-chief of the armed forces.

Huong Régime Opposed

Premier Huong's new régime was met by a storm of criticism on its assumption of office Nov. 5. Major opposition was spearheaded by the Buddhists, and this brought the sect into direct confrontation with the government.

The Buddhists, as well as Roman Catholics, politicians and newspapers, assailed Huong for having appointed civil servants and technicians to his cabinet rather than political leaders. Huong also was accused of having appointed many ministers who had served with the unpopular governments

of the late Pres. Ngo Dinh Diem and former Emperor Bao
Dai. The Buddhists were further incensed at Huong's in-
sistence that religion be kept out of politics.

Nguyen Xuan Chu resigned as chairman of the High
National Council Nov. 5, charging that Huong's "government
cannot win the confidence of the population." Le Van Thu
became Council chairman Nov. 18.

Discounting criticisms of his government, Huong warned
Nov. 5 that he would use force to suppress violent demonstrations. "The government is not going to be a prisoner of
any pressure groups," he said.

In a move to head off scheduled anti-government demonstrations and marches by Buddhist, Catholic and student groups,
Huong appealed Nov. 6 to dissident factions to cooperate with
his government. Acknowledging weaknesses of his régime,
Huong "urge[d] all persons of all classes . . . to help restore
authority and discipline in the building of the country against
communism." U.S. officials also urged opposition elements
to forego direct action against the government. As a result
of the pleas, Buddhist and Catholic groups agreed to postpone
for at least 2 weeks any public display of their grievances.

The High National Council met with Huong Nov. 13 and
criticized the premier for the composition of his cabinet.
Huong explained that he had selected technicians and civil
servants as ministers only after several political leaders had
rejected his invitations to serve.

The moratorium on violent demonstrations ended Nov.
22. Thousands of persons, armed with rocks and clubs, clashed
with police that day during a march from the National Buddhist Center on Saigon's outskirts into the city itself. The
march ended at Chief of State Suu's palace, where it was
broken up by combat police using tear gas.

Buddhist leaders publicly denounced the Huong régime
for the first time in a statement issued Nov. 22. The statement also assailed the government's "brutal suppression" of
the protest march. The Buddhist leadership met Nov. 23 and
decided to oppose the Huong régime openly. In a communiqué made public Nov. 24, the Buddhists called on Suu

and the High National Council to: (a) reject the government, "which does not command the sympathy of the population"; (b) halt the arrests of demonstrators; (c) order the army and police to "take no part in repressing the population." The communiqué declared that "there can be no order in the current confused and crumbling state of the nation, when the rights of the people—the majority of them Buddhists—are being ruthlessly denied."

Buddhist rioting continued in Saigon Nov. 24-25. As a result, the government Nov. 25 imposed a curfew from 10 p.m. to 5 a.m., closed city schools and ordered newspaper censorship. To cope with possible further violence, martial law was declared Nov. 26. Demonstrations were banned, and the military took control of police and other civilian security forces in Saigon. A campaign of non-violence through non-cooperation was announced Nov. 28 in a Buddhist Secular Institute statement.

The armed forces leaders, including Gen. Khanh, appealed to Buddhist and other opposition elements Dec. 4 "to sink your differences" and support the government. The plea was made in a communiqué that backed Huong's régime and said that the government should be "under no pressure, internally or externally, in its mission to fight the Communists."

The Buddhists defied the military's appeal and announced Dec. 10 a new drive to oust Huong. In a letter to Suu, the Buddhists Dec. 11 reiterated charges of anti-Buddhist bias and urged the chief of state to dismiss Huong. The letter accused U.S. Amb. Taylor of supporting the premier against the "just desires of the Vietnamese people and the Buddhist Church."

Asserting that the Buddhist complaints were unjustified, Huong said Dec. 12: "The Buddhists tried to impose ministers upon me when I was choosing my cabinet. I cannot admit a state within a state."

At a meeting with Suu Dec. 19, Thich Tam Chau reportedly insisted that Huong withdraw his charges that the

Buddhists were linked to the Viet Cong and that Huong say instead that Buddhist-government differences were due to "misunderstandings." Tam Chau also demanded the announcement of a specific date for convening a permanent legislature. Suu reportedly informed Tam Chau that Huong's condition for resolving the Buddhist-government dispute was the Buddhists' acceptance of government authority.

Military Dissidents Overthrow Council

Dissident military officers seized virtual control of the government by overthrowing the High National Council in a bloodless coup Dec. 19. The rebels arrested 7 of the Council's 9 active members and about 50 Buddhists, students and military officers opposed to the Huong régime. Among Council members seized were Buddhist leaders Mai Tho Tiryen and Le Khac Quyen.

The military dissidents explained that the Council had become a source of "dissension." The rebel officers said their actions were not aimed at Huong or Chief of State Suu. They offered "to act as a mediator to achieve national unity" among South Vietnam's feuding political groups. The rebels vowed to abide by the military's Aug. 27 pledge to support the maintenance of a civilian régime.

The dissident officers were members of the Armed Forces Council, whose formation had been announced Dec. 18. The purpose of the group, whose chairman was Gen. Khanh, was to advise on major military matters and help improve the army's morale. Their chief spokesman was Air Commodore Nguyen Cao Ky, air force commander. Other coup leaders included several corps commanders and the navy and marine commanders.

The Buddhists denounced the Council's ouster, but they suspended their anti-government campaign pending clarification of the political situation.

The Council's overthrow brought the military dissidents into direct conflict with the U.S. U.S. opposition to the coup was expressed Dec. 20 by Washington officials and by Amb. Taylor in talks with coup leaders in Saigon. Taylor reportedly had warned them that the U.S. would have to reconsider its close alliance with Saigon against the Viet Cong unless "the fabric of legal government" was quickly restored. Taylor also conferred with Gen. Khanh Dec. 21 in an effort to restore Huong's authority.

U.S. officials announced Dec. 21 the suspension of talks aimed at providing South Vietnam with more military aid pending restoration of a legal governmental system. A State Department statement declared Dec. 22 that "a duly constituted government, exercising full power on the basis of national unity and without improper interference from any group, is the essential condition for the successful prosecution of the effort to defeat the Viet Cong and is the basis of United States support for that effort." The department supported Taylor against criticism by Khanh.

In an interview with the *N.Y. Herald Tribune* Dec. 22, Khanh said: The Council "will not be reactivated" to please Washington; the U.S. "and their representatives in Vietnam, like Taylor, should work with decisive elements in the nation —those that have the power of decision—and not try to exert pressure"; Taylor's "attitude during the last 48 hours . . . and his activity have been beyond imagination as far as an ambassador is concerned."

Khanh further assailed U.S. policy in an order of the day issued Dec. 22 following a meeting of the Armed Forces Council. The military, he insisted, "still have the task of acting as an intermediary to settle all disputes and differences if they create a situation favorable to . . . communism and colonialism." "We make sacrifices for the country's independence . . . but not to carry out the policy of any foreign country." Khanh charged that the Council had been "exploited by counterrevolutionary elements who placed partisan considerations above the homeland's sacred interests."

Taylor conferred with Huong and other Vietnamese leaders Dec. 23 and again insisted on the restoration of constitutional government. A report from Saigon Dec. 26 said that Washington had taken retaliatory action against Saigon by suspending U.S. participation in advanced planning of all non-routine military and civilian operations pending clarification of American aid. A joint communiqué issued Dec. 28 by Huong and Suu charged that the Council's ouster "shook the solution of civilian government." The 2 leaders stated that "because of a lack of a legislative body constituting the legal basis for the present government, the executive agencies no longer fully represent the government by civilians."

As 1964 drew to an end, Huong, Suu and other civilian leaders began a series of negotiations with military leaders in an effort to resolve the political crisis.

EXPANSION OF WAR TO NORTH VIETNAM

U.S. Opposes Extension of Hostilities

The U.S. rejected persistent South Vietnamese demands in 1964 for expanding the war against the Viet Cong guerrillas by attacking Communist North Vietnam. The Saigon régime proposed extending the conflict to the north to deprive the Viet Cong of arms and men allegedly supplied from North Vietnam.

The Soviet Union warned the U.S. Feb. 25 that it would not stand idly by if the U.S. extended the war to North Vietnamese territory. Asserting that the USSR would provide "the necessary assistance and support" to the "national liberation struggle" in South Vietnam, the Soviet statement, issued through Tass, called for the withdrawal of U.S. military aid and a halt to "interference" in South Vietnam's affairs. The statement also said: The U.S. was increasing its war effort in Vietnam, thus making it "the biggest of all military operations now conducted in the world"; the situation was becoming "ever more acute" and posed a "serious threat to peace throughout the whole of Southeast Asia."

Broken line traces route of Ho Chi Minh Trail along which Communist troops, arms and supplies were passed from North Vietnam, through Laos, to South Vietnam. The U.S. in 1964 rejected proposals to attack North Vietnamese territory to deprive the Viet Cong of these supplies.   (Wide World map)

A full-scale military attack on North Vietnam was first publicly recommended by South Vietnamese Premier Nguyen Khanh July 19. He declared that a million refugees who had fled from North to South Vietnam nourished "the dream of

liberating their native land." Khanh spoke to an estimated
100,000 persons at a Saigon rally marking the 10th anniversary
of the 1954 Geneva accords freeing Indochina from French
rule and partitioning it into the separate and independent
countries of North and South Vietnam, Laos and Cambodia.

Khanh's demand for an invasion of the north was reiterated in a government statement July 20. The statement
charged that "over the last 10 years Communist China and
Communist North Vietnam never once implemented the cease-
fire and helped to restore peace, which was the only objective
of the Geneva agreement they themselves had signed. . . ."
If Peiping and Hanoi "obstinately continue their war of
aggression," the statement concluded, "the government . . .
will step up the war . . . until total victory liberates the whole
of our national territory."

American opposition to enlarging the war was expressed
by U.S. Amb. Maxwell D. Taylor at a meeting with Premier
Khanh in Saigon July 23. Taylor told Khanh that Saigon's
threats to carry the war beyond South Vietnam's borders
were contrary to U.S. policy. Taylor protested a statement
made by Vietnamese Air Commodore Nguyen Cao Ky July
22 that his planes were ready to bomb North Vietnam. Ky
also had said that for the past 3 years South Vietnamese
"combat teams" had carried out hit-and-run attacks inside
North Vietnam by "air, sea and land." Khanh reportedly
assured Taylor that the U.S.' and South Vietnam's war policies
conflicted only on timing and on what to announce publicly.

In a further explanation of his military policy, Khanh
said July 28: "We are already victims of North Vietnamese
aggression" and "any response from us would be a counter-
attack."

(Pres. Johnson had said Feb. 29 that plans for possible
expansion of the Vietnamese war "that have been discussed in
the papers are not plans . . . that I have approved." Mr. Johnson made a similar denial June 2.)

Warning the U.S. and South Vietnam against expanding
the conflict, North Vietnamese Pres. Ho Chi Minh said in an
interview made public May 10 that Hanoi had "powerful

friends ready to help." In a letter to Communist China and 13 other signers of the Geneva accords, North Vietnamese Foreign Min. Xuan Thuy June 25 urged them "to demand that the U.S. government give up its design of . . . provocation and sabotage against North Vietnam." Communist Chinese Foreign Min. Chen Yi replied July 6 that China would defend North Vietnam against any U.S. attack.

North Vietnamese Attack U.S. Warships

North Vietnamese PT boats attacked 2 U.S. destroyers in the Gulf of Tonkin Aug. 2 and 4. Neither of the U.S. ships was damaged.

In reporting the first clash, the U.S. Defense Department said Aug. 2 that 3 Communist vessels had fired torpedoes and shells at the *U.S.S. Maddox* that day while the destroyer was on routine patrol in the gulf in international waters 30 miles off the coast of North Vietnam. The *Maddox* fought off the attackers with the aid of 4 fighter planes that came to its assistance from the aircraft carrier *Ticonderoga,* also on patrol in the gulf. One PT boat was put out of action by the destroyer's guns; the 2 other Communist boats were damaged by U.S. aircraft fire.

After the incident, Pres. Johnson Aug. 2 ordered the Navy "to attack any force which attacks" its ships "in international waters and to attack with the objective of not only driving off the force but of destroying it." The President ordered a 2d destroyer, the *U.S.S. C. Turner Joy,* to join the *Maddox* on patrol and that both be provided with air cover. A U.S. protest note delivered Aug. 4 to North Vietnam warned "of grave consequences which would inevitably result from any further unprovoked offensive military action against United States forces."

North Vietnam had charged Aug. 2 that 4 U.S. planes, flying from northern Laos Aug. 1, had attacked the North Vietnamese border post of Nam Can and the village of Noong De. Hanoi warned that Laos "must bear heavy responsibility for having allowed the U.S. to use Laotian territory to encroach" on North Vietnam. The U.S. rejected Hanoi's protest Aug. 3.

In reporting the 2d North Vietnamese naval raid, the Defense Department announced Aug. 4 that an "undetermined number of North Vietnamese PT boats" had made a "deliberate attack" that day on the *Maddox* and *C. Turner Joy* about 65 miles from shore. The department said the destroyers, assisted by carrier-based planes, repelled the attackers and apparently sank 2 of them in a 3-hour clash.

U.S. Bombs North Vietnamese Bases

Retaliating for the attacks on the 2 American destroyers, U.S. Navy planes Aug. 4 bombed North Vietnamese coastal bases and an oil installation. The 5-hour raid, over a 100-mile area, was ordered by Pres. Johnson earlier Aug. 4 following the 2d North Vietnamese PT boat attack on the *U.S.S. Maddox.*

Publicly announcing the U.S. action in a nationwide TV broadcast, Mr. Johnson said that "repeated acts of violence against the armed forces of the United States must be met not only with alert defense but with positive reply." "That reply," Mr. Johnson said, "is being given as I speak to you tonight. Air action is now in execution against North Vietnamese gunboats and certain supporting facilities which have been used in these hostile operations." The President said that although the U.S.' "full commitment" to South Vietnam "will be redoubled by this outrage," "our response for the present will be limited and fitting." Asserting that "we still seek no wider war," the President stated that he had instructed State Secy. Dean Rusk "to make this position totally clear . . . to all." The President said he had spoken to Sen. Barry Goldwater just before his speech and that the Republican Presidential candidate had "expressed his support of the statement that I am making to you tonight." After hearing Mr. Johnson's speech, Goldwater said: "I am sure every American will subscribe to the President's statement. . . . We cannot allow the American flag to be shot at." Mr. Johnson had discussed the crisis prior to his speech at separate meetings with 16 Democratic and Republican Congressional leaders and with the National Security Council.

Details of the U.S. raid were disclosed by Defense Secy. Robert S. McNamara Aug. 5. McNamara said that U.S.

planes, flying 64 sorties from the 7th Fleet's aircraft carriers *Constellation* and *Ticonderoga* in the Gulf of Tonkin, had destroyed or damaged 25 PT boats (about ½ of the North Vietnamese navy) in attacks on naval bases at Hongay, Loc Ghao, Phuc Loi and Quang Khe. He said the attackers virtually destroyed an oil storage depot near Phuc Loi that accounted for about 10% of the country's oil storage facilities. The depot, McNamara said, was used by the North Vietnamese navy's Soviet-built Swatow-type torpedo boats. 2 U.S. planes, according to McNamara, had failed to return and 2 others had been damaged. He said that the U.S., bracing for possible Communist counter-action, was reinforcing its military position in Southeast Asia. Among moves undertaken: an anti-submarine force was assigned to the South China Sea; Army and Marine units had been alerted "for movement"; warplanes from the Philippines were flown to South Vietnam and Thailand.

North Vietnam provided a different version of the clash Aug. 5. A Hanoi communiqué said its anti-aircraft had shot down 5 U.S. planes and had damaged 3 others and that one pilot had been captured. It charged that Washington's report of the North Vietnamese PT-boat attacks on the destroyers had been falsified to cover up U.S. aggression in Southeast Asia. North Vietnam had admitted the Aug. 2 attack on the *Maddox* but declared that it took place in North Vietnamese waters. Hanoi charged that the *Maddox* had been part of a U.S.-South Vietnamese naval force that had bombed the North Vietnamese islands of Hon Me and Hon Ngu July 20. The U.S. denied the attacks on the islands. The Hanoi government Aug. 6 denounced the U.S. raid as "premeditated warlike acts." It said the attack "exposes even more clearly the design to invade North Vietnam and extend the war here as declared many times by the U.S." A Hanoi note to the International Control Commission (ICC) Aug. 8 called the U.S.' raid an act of aggression. (A North Vietnamese note to the ICC Aug. 7 had charged that U.S. planes that day had flown illegally over Nghean Province. The U.S. denied the charge.)

McNamara said at a news conference Aug. 6 that reconnaissance-flight pictures showed that 7 anti-aircraft installations had been destroyed at the North Vietnamese base at Vinh. He also stated that the U.S.' routine Tonkin Gulf patrol, suspended during the attack, had been resumed (the patrol ended Aug. 9, according to a Defense Department announcement Aug. 13). The U.S. was seeking the release of Lt. (jg.) Everett Alvarez Jr., one of the downed pilots captured by the North Vietnamese. "We have no indication that there have been any substantial movements of Communist Chinese forces, either land or air," in the past "few days" or, "for that matter, during the past several months."

Pres. Johnson Aug. 5 warned the Communists in Southeast Asia not to "be tempted to support or widen the present aggression." Speaking at Syracuse (N.Y.) University, Mr. Johnson said: "There is no threat to any peaceful power from the United States. . . . But there can be no immunity from reply. And that is what is meant by the actions we took yesterday."

Asst. Defense Secy. Arthur Sylvester announced Aug. 11 that the U.S. had "indications that a number of Chinese Communist" jet planes "have been introduced into North Vietnam." Sylvester said this had "been expected for some time because of known preparations such as lengthening of runways of airfields in the Hanoi area."

Response to the U.S. attack ranged from Communist denunciation to full support from pro-U.S. powers. Among reactions reported:

• Communist China warned Aug. 5 that it would not "sit idly by" while the U.S. committed "deliberate armed aggression" against Hanoi. Peiping accused the U.S. of going "over the brink of war." Repeating this charge Aug. 6, a Chinese statement asserted that the U.S. had taken "the first step in extending the war in Indochina" and that Peiping "fully supports the just stand" of North Vietnam. The USSR Aug. 7 assured North Vietnam of Moscow's support. A Soviet note charged that U.S. "intrusion into the airspace" of North Vietnam posed "a threat to the security of the peoples of other countries" and "can entail dangerous consequences." Soviet Premier Nikita S. Khrushchev warned Aug. 8 that the USSR would "stand up for . . . other Socialist countries if the imperialists impose war on them." An Aug. 6 Cuban communiqué, signed by Premier Fidel Castro and Pres. Osvaldo Dorticos Torrado, assailed the U.S. raids as "criminal." Prince Norodom Sihanouk, Cambodian chief of state, said Aug. 8 that the attack was "a [U.S.] pretext to extend the war to North Vietnam" and that it also was directed at Cambodia.

● British Foreign Secy. R. A. Butler said Aug. 5 that U.S. naval ships had been "gratuitously attacked" and had "every right on the high seas to defend themselves." British Prime Min. Sir Alec Douglas-Home described the U.S. action Aug. 6 as "in accordance with the inherent right of self-defense recognized" by the UN Charter. A statement issued by South Vietnamese Premier Nguyen Khanh's office Aug. 5 said: North Vietnam's "2d attack confirms . . . the provocative attitude of the Communists of North Vietnam and Red China"; South Vietnam "supports the [U.S.'] firm reaction." Laotian Premier Souvanna Phouma Aug. 7 upheld the U.S. air strikes. (Souvanna also denied North Vietnam's Aug. 2 protest that U.S. planes had taken off from Laotian territory to bomb 2 North Vietnamese villages. A formal Laotian denial was sent to Hanoi Aug. 11.)

● France and India made noncommittal comment Aug. 5. Paris officials said the latest crisis pointed to the necessity of accepting Pres. Charles de Gaulle's repeated calls for an international conference on Southeast Asia. India said it was "distressed" over the Gulf of Tonkin clashes and expressed "hope that the explosive situation" "will not be further aggravated."

Congress Gives Johnson Powers

In a message to Congress Aug. 5 Pres. Johnson requested advance approval of any actions he might have to take in the Southeast Asian crisis. Congress approved the requested resolution Aug. 7, the House by 416-0 vote, the Senate by 88-2 vote. The resolution permitted the President to take "all necessary measures" "to repel any armed attack" on U.S. forces and "to prevent further aggression." It authorized him to undertake "all necessary steps, including the use of armed forces," to assist any nation that requested aid "in defense of its freedom" under the Southeast Asia Collective Defense Treaty. Mr. Johnson said Aug. 7 that Congress' action "prove[d] our determination to defend our forces, to prevent aggression and to work . . . for peace and security in the area." In signing the resolution Aug. 10, the President said: "There can be no mistake—no miscalculation—of where America stands or what this generation of Americans stands for. The unanimity of the Congress reflects the unanimity of the country."

The 2 dissenting votes against the resolution were cast by Sens. Wayne L. Morse (D., Ore.) and Ernest Gruening (D., Alaska), who contended in Senate debate that the resolution was unconstitutional as "a predated declaration of war power." Morse charged Aug. 5 that the U.S. was as responsible as North Vietnam for the latest crisis.

In debate Aug. 6, Senate majority leader Mike Mansfield (D., Mont.) asserted that the President had "weighed the degree of military response to the degree of military provocation" and that "what needs to be done to defend ourselves will be done." Sen. Richard B. Russell (D., Ga.) said it was "not our purpose to escalate the war, but if events require more vigorous response, I believe our nation has the will to use that power." Sen. John C. Stennis (D., Miss.) called the resolution a "firm course [that] may be our last and only chance to avoid what could quickly develop into a full-scale war." Sen. George D. Aiken (R., Vt.) stated Aug. 7 that he supported the resolution "with misgivings" but felt that prompt action was required to defend U.S. interests.

In House debate Aug. 7, Rep. Ed Foreman (R., Tex.) questioned the timing of Pres. Johnson's announcement of the U.S. retaliatory attack on North Vietnam. "What kind of responsibility is this," he asked, "when the President goes on radio and TV and tells them [the Communists] one hour and a half in advance that the air strike is coming?" (Mr. Johnson had delivered his announcement at 11:40 p.m.; the first North Vietnamese base had been hit by U.S. planes at 1:15 a.m.) McNamara explained Aug. 7 that he had suggested the timing of Mr. Johnson's announcement because "by that time U.S. naval aircraft had been in the air on their way to the targets approximately one hour." Despite North Vietnamese radar warnings of the approaching attack, the Communists did not have sufficient time "to move their boats to sea or to alert their forces," McNamara said. In defense of his announcement, Mr. Johnson said at his news conference in Austin, Tex., Aug. 8: "When the strike got off the carrier they were in their [North Vietnamese] radar, and it was very important that we say to the American people what was happening before Hanoi said it to them and that we say to all people what kind of an attack it was without any description."

UN Debates U.S.-North Vietnamese Clashes

The UN Security Council met in emergency session Aug. 5 to consider Washington's charges of North Vietnamese aggression in attacking the U.S. destroyers in the Gulf of Tonkin. U.S. Amb. Adlai E. Stevenson, who had requested the meeting, defended the retaliatory air attack on North Vietnam as a "defensive measure" to counter Hanoi's "deliberate and repeated attacks" on U.S. naval vessels. Stevenson said the U.S. was in Southeast Asia "to help our friends" against "imported terror" "managed" by North Vietnam and "backed" by Communist China.

Soviet delegate Platon D. Morozov condemned the U.S. for what he termed "acts of aggression" against North Vietnam. Morozov submitted a resolution to permit a North Vietnamese delegate to participate in Council debate. On Stevenson's request, the resolution was amended to extend the invitation to a South Vietnamese representative also. Both Vietnams were asked Aug. 7 to join the debate, but Hanoi rejected the invitation Aug. 9. A North Vietnamese Foreign Ministry statement said: "The U.S. imperialists have more than once used UN as a tool to carry out their aggressive policy, but the Vietnamese people . . . were determined not to let the U.S. imperialists realize their perfidious schemes." The ministry's statement instead urged Britain and the USSR, as Geneva co-chairmen, to get the U.S. to adhere to the Geneva conference agreements "and stop . . . its aggressive war in South Vietnam and its provocative acts against North

Vietnam." The Council took no further action in the dispute after North Vietnam's refusal to attend the debates.

The U.S. charges of North Vietnamese aggression were again denied by Hanoi in a note sent to the Security Council Aug. 19. The Council took no further action on the matter.

(North Vietnam announced Sept. 1 that its airspace and territorial limits extended 12 miles offshore and that it would defend this area against any U.S. incursions. U.S. Deputy Defense Secy. Cyrus R. Vance had announced that the U.S. recognized only a 3-mile limit.)

Fresh Clash in Gulf of Tonkin

2 U.S. destroyers were reported to have sunk at least one and possibly 3 unidentified vessels Sept. 18 in the Gulf of Tonkin. The vessels, presumed to be North Vietnamese, were observed only on the destroyers' radar screens during the night-time clash.

In reporting the incident, Defense Secy. McNamara said Sept. 19 that the 2 destroyers—later identified as the *Richard S. Edwards* and the *Morton*—were "on a routine patrol 42 miles from land . . . [and] were menaced by 4 unidentified vessels, which, because of their disposition, courses and speed, indicated hostile intent." McNamara said the vessels continued to approach despite warning shots but fled when the destroyers fired.

North Vietnam reported on the incident Sept. 19 but did not say whether any of its ships had been hit or sunk. A Foreign Ministry statement said 2 U.S. destroyers "had sailed to a point near [North Vietnam's] Nghean [Province], heavy explosions were heard, and flashes of light and aircraft circling over the spot were seen from the shore." The statement assailed the U.S. Defense Department for having "scurrilously accused Vietnamese patrol boats of attacking United States warships." Hanoi charged that as in the case of the Aug. 4 Tonkin Gulf incident, the U.S. was "circulating another such myth as an excuse for attacking" North Vietnam.

North Vietnam Sept. 19 filed separate complaints with the International Control Commission and with Britain and the USSR, as co-chairmen of the 1954 Geneva Conference on Indochina. Hanoi urged an immediate ICC meeting on the incident and appealed to London and Moscow to "check the United States scheme for renewed war acts."

Pres. Johnson was reported Sept. 26 to have ordered "hot pursuit" by U.S. fighters of Communist planes, across the Chinese Communist border if necessary, if they attacked U.S. warships off the Vietnamese coast. The decision reportedly was in response to the sending of Chinese planes to North Vietnam as a result of the Aug. 4 U.S. retaliatory air raid on North Vietnam.

U.S. Increases Aid, Denies Planning to Expand War

Increased U.S. military and economic aid to expand South Vietnam's armed forces and joint U.S.-Vietnamese plans to interdict North Vietnamese supplies to the Viet Cong were announced in a communiqué issued in Saigon Dec. 11. The communiqué was based on talks Amb. Taylor had held with Premier Huong in Saigon Dec. 7-11. The American assistance and military plans outlined in the communiqué had been decided on by Pres. Johnson following conferences with Taylor in Washington Dec. 1-3. Taylor had been recalled to Washington Nov. 26 to report to Administration officials who were becoming increasingly concerned over Saigon's unstable government and lack of progress against the Viet Cong.

The Saigon communiqué, approved by Huong and Taylor, said: South Vietnam had accepted the U.S. offer of "additional . . . assistance to improve the execution of the government's program to restrain the mounting infiltration of men and equipment by the Hanoi régime in support of the Viet Cong"; the government and the U.S. mission were "making joint plans to achieve greater effectiveness against the infiltration threat"; the U.S. aid offer provided "for increased . . . military, paramilitary and police forces, the strengthening of the air defense . . . and further economic assistance for a variety of reforms of industrial, urban and rural development [the U.S. had urged South Vietnam to increase its 650,000-man force by an additional 100,000 men]."

Washington officials insisted that the increase in U.S. aid did not mean plans were being made to expand the war to North Vietnam. The State Department Nov. 23 had issued a similar denial about possible plans for air strikes against Communist supply routes in Laos and North Vietnam. The denial was prompted by a statement Taylor made in a *Life* magazine interview, whose transcript had been released Nov. 23 by the U.S. embassy in Saigon. Taylor said victory over the Viet Cong could possibly be helped by air attacks against the Communist supply routes. He stressed, however, that "military action outside the country [South Vietnam], just as pure military action inside the country, will not win in itself." Taylor said the war's outcome remained "very much in doubt."

Sen. Wayne Morse (D., Ore.) charged Nov. 27 that Taylor was the "key leader among United States military and State Department warmongers who are seeking to extend the war in Asia in the absence of a declaration of war." Morse, an opponent of the intervention in Vietnam, demanded Taylor's dismissal.

CIVIL WAR

Fighting Increases in Intensity

South Vietnam's war against the Communist-led Viet Cong guerrillas continued during 1964 with increased ferocity. Vietnamese casualties suffered on both sides were greater than in each of the 3 previous years of renewed fighting. U.S. losses also mounted as American military advisers and U.S. helicopters became further involved in the combat.

Capitalizing on the continued political instability in Saigon, the guerrillas carried out more intensified assaults, expanded their areas of operation, captured greater quantities of U.S.-made weapons from South Vietnamese troops, and at the year's end appeared to be in control of $2/3$ to $3/4$ of the country. The fighting also was marked by a change in Viet Cong tactics. Heretofore, the rebels had confined their activities largely to hit-and-run attacks. But in 1964 they turned more and more to the classic infantry strategy of coordinated frontal assaults and fought longer-sustained battles, some lasting 5 days. U.S. personnel and installations came under heavy attack by Viet Cong units and individual terrorist bombings, even in Saigon itself. In February alone 6 U.S. servicemen were killed in terrorist bombing and grenade attacks in the capital. (The *U.S.N.S. Card*, a World War II escort carrier used as an aircraft and helicopter ferry, was sunk at its dock in Saigon harbor May 2 by the explosion of a charge believed

South Vietnamese troops with U.S. patrol leader, S/Sgt. Howard Stevens, 31, of Army's Special Forces, wade along stream in South Vietnam's Central Highlands in search of Viet Cong.
(Wide World photo)

to have been placed by Viet Cong terrorists. No one was injured. The *Card* had arrived in Saigon Apr. 30 with helicopters and fighter planes for U.S. forces in South Vietnam. The ship, under charter to the government's Military Sea Transportation Service, was manned by a civilian crew.)

According to figures reported by the U.S. Military Assistance Command in South Vietnam and confirmed by the Defense Department in Washington, 140 Americans were killed in combat in 1964 (compared with 76 in 1963), 1,138 were wounded and 11 were listed as missing. Defense Department figures for Vietnamese casualties in 1964: 7,000 government troops killed, 16,700 wounded, 5,000 missing or captured; 17,000 Viet Cong guerrillas killed, 4,200 captured.

The Defense Department estimated that despite their heavy casualties, at the end of 1964 the Viet Cong had from 28,000 to 34,000 full-time guerrilla troops in action, plus 60,000 to 80,000 armed supporters fighting part-time. South Vietnam's regular armed forces totalled 265,000 men (Army 240,000, Air Force 10,000, Navy 8,000, Marines 7,000), supported by paramilitary and militia forces of 290,000 men and a National Police force of 30,000. By the year's end, the government's forces were assisted by 23,000 U.S. servicemen: Army 15,000, Air Force 6,000, Navy 1,150, and Marines 850.

The Year's Major Military Operations

Among the major engagements fought by Viet Cong and U.S.-assisted South Vietnamese government forces in 1964:

● A 500-man Viet Cong battalion escaped from a South Vietnamese encircling movement in a clash Jan. 5 in Long An Province, 25 miles southwest of Saigon. 9 of the 1,500 attacking government troops were killed. Guerrilla ground fire hit 15 U.S. planes participating in the attack; 5 Americans were wounded. Viet Cong casualties were estimated at 60-70.

● U.S. military advisers Jan. 5 branded as a failure a Dec. 31, 1963-Jan. 4 offensive by 10 South Vietnamese battalions that sought to crush a Viet Cong force of 2 battalions in the Bensuc region, about 40 miles west of Saigon. The battle started as the South Vietnamese sent reinforcements to rescue a ranger battalion under heavy Viet Cong attack. But the Communist force had disappeared by the time the reinforcements arrived. 15 government troops and 2 Viet Cong were killed.

• About 500 Viet Cong reportedly crossed from a base in neighboring Cambodia Feb. 6 and seized 3 strategic hamlets at Bencau. The guerrillas killed 114 government troops before withdrawing after a 14-hour battle. The attackers were believed to have lost 100 men.

• The first engagement in which the Viet Cong employed the tactic of frontal assault took place near Long Dinh Feb. 26. Encircled by 2 government lines of 2,500 troops, 600 men of the Viet Cong's 514th Battalion successfully smashed their way through the trap. More than 40 Viet Cong were killed in the 8-hour battle, most of them by air strikes. 16 government troops were slain.

• South Vietnamese forces killed at least 75 Viet Cong in capturing a guerrilla base in Kontum Province 300 miles north of Saigon Apr. 8. The base was in the Viet Cong's so-called 5th Interzone Area, reportedly a vital distribution point for arms and men arriving via Laos from North Vietnam along the guerrillas' Ho Chi Minh Trail.

• Viet Cong and government forces Apr. 11-15 fought the longest and severest battle to date at Kien Long, 135 miles south of Saigon. It was the first time that Viet Cong forces of such size—3 battalions—had fought so long under unified command from fixed positions. The attack began Apr. 11-12 with a guerrilla assault on Kien Long's civil guard post; 70 of its defenders were killed. The fighting widened and intensified as U.S. helicopters airlifted government reinforcements into the area. Government units retained the Kien Long positions when the fighting ended Apr. 15. In addition to the 70 guardsmen killed, 55 South Vietnamese troops were slain and 17 were missing in the 5-day battle. 175 Viet Cong were killed.

• The Viet Cong's major stronghold in the Do Xa region in the central highlands was the successful target of a one-month government drive launched Apr. 27 by 5,000 government troops. The men were landed in the zone by 20 U.S. helicopters. 18 of the aircraft were damaged by Viet Cong ground fire; 4 of them were shot down but were recovered. Highlight of the campaign was the capture (reported May 22) of the guerrillas' Do Xa headquarters. Vietnamese authorities said that Viet Cong Gen. Don had escaped from his command post but that its capture had set back guerrilla attacks in the area by at least 6 months. Casualties in the one-month operation were relatively light: 21 Viet Cong and 26 government troops killed.

● Viet Cong forces attacked 2 U.S. Special Forces camps in the northern highland regions July 4 and 6. In the first raid, a guerrilla battalion killed 45 Vietnamese trainees at a camp at Polei Krong and fled with stocks of arms and ammunition. In the July 6 attack, the Viet Cong killed 60 defenders, including 2 Americans and an Australian military adviser, at a camp at Nam Dong. The 500-man guerrilla force withdrew after fighting a bitter 5-hour battle with the camp's 300 defenders. An estimated 49 Viet Cong were killed.

● Government forces Aug. 12 launched an unsuccessful effort to capture a large Viet Cong base near Ap Bo Cang, 29 miles northwest of Saigon. In one of the largest airborne operations of the war, 90 U.S. and 12 South Vietnamese helicopters ferried the government troops into the area while Vietnamese ground forces converged simultaneously on the enemy. However, by the time the first paratrooper had landed, the 2,000-man guerrilla force had disappeared into the jungle. The government force found only 2 burned and abandoned Viet Cong camps and 4 dead guerrillas. A U.S. helicopter pilot was killed in the action.

● Viet Cong forces Nov. 1 struck a heavy blow at the U.S. air base at Bienhoa, 12 miles north of Saigon. The raiders infiltrated onto the airfield in the early morning hours, killed 5 Americans and 2 South Vietnamese with mortar fire, destroyed 5 U.S. jet bombers and damaged 22 other U.S. and South Vietnamese planes. The guerrillas, numbering about 100 men, then fled without losses. A 10-hour search of the area by 800 Vietnamese soldiers, assisted by U.S. helicopters, failed to find a trace of the attackers. Pres. Johnson ordered immediate replacement of the destroyed and damaged planes. The aircraft had been sent to Bien Hoa in August following the Gulf of Tonkin naval clashes as a precaution against possible reprisals by Hanoi for the subsequent retaliatory U.S. air raids on North Vietnam.

• Another massive U.S.-South Vietnamese air and ground search for a supposed Viet Cong stronghold near Saigon proved futile Nov. 18. More than 1,100 government troops were flown into Bing Duong and Tayninh Provinces by 116 U.S. and South Vietnamese helicopters but made only light contact with the enemy.

• The government district headquarters of Anlao and most of the surrounding Anlao valley, 300 miles northeast of Saigon, were captured by the Viet Cong in a 3-day battle Dec. 7-9 against regular Vietnamese soldiers and paramilitary forces. At least 300 Vietnamese troops were missing. 6,000-7,000 civilians in the valley's 16 villages reportedly abandoned their homes.

• Binh Gia, 40 miles southeast of Saigon, was the scene of bitter fighting Dec. 28-Jan. 4, 1965. An estimated 1,500 guerrillas captured the town in an initial assault Dec. 28. The Viet Cong were forced to withdraw Dec. 30 after U.S. helicopters had flown reinforcements into the village. The fighting, however, continued on a heavy scale outside Binh Gia and finally ended with government forces in complete control.

1965

U.S. planes began regular bombing of North Vietnamese targets in retaliation for Viet Cong ground attacks on U.S. military installations. The air raids stirred both international and U.S. domestic controversy as further "escalation" of the war and of U.S. involvement in it. The air strikes on North Vietnam were suspended during a Christmas truce, and they were not resumed when ground fighting was renewed after the holiday. A U.S. white paper cited "massive evidence" that Communist forces fighting in South Vietnam were largely trained, led and supplied by North Vietnam and that thousands of North Vietnamese regulars were among them. The build-up of U.S. military forces—and the expansion of U.S. involvement in the ground fighting—continued during 1965. Both developments provoked additional controversy and domestic U.S. demonstrations such as peace marches and "teach-ins." Fresh efforts were made by U.S. and international leaders during 1965 to find a way to end the war. South Vietnam's shaky governments continued to falter, and the military were in command throughout the year.

130

AIR WAR EXTENDED TO NORTH VIETNAM

U.S. Planes Pound Northern Targets

The Vietnamese war assumed a new, disquieting aspect Feb. 7 when U.S. planes launched heavy air attacks on North Vietnamese territory. Carrier-based planes bombed and strafed the southern military base of Donghoi. South Vietnamese planes, escorted by U.S. jets, carried out a follow-up attack Feb. 8 against the North Vietnamese military communications center in the Vinhlinh area. One U.S. plane was downed in the Feb. 7 raid, and in the 2d attack a South Vietnamese pilot parachuted safely after his plane was hit by ground fire.

Both air strikes were in retaliation for a Viet Cong ground attack earlier Feb. 7 on the U.S.' Camp Holloway airbase at Pleiku, 240 miles northeast of Saigon. 8 Americans were killed and 126 others wounded when a barracks was blown up in the Communist attack. The Viet Cong also destroyed 9 helicopters and a transport plane and damaged at least 9 helicopters and 6 light observation planes.

A White House statement revealing the air attacks Feb. 7 said that North Vietnamese "barracks and staging areas" hit by the U.S. planes had been "actively used by Hanoi for training and infiltration of Viet Cong personnel into South Vietnam." U.S. Presidential aide McGeorge Bundy said Feb. 8 that the air strikes against North Vietnam were "right and

necessary" but that "the primary contest is in South Vietnam."
Bundy made the statement at a news conference after report-
ing to Pres. Lyndon B. Johnson and the National Security
Council on a fact-finding mission he had conducted in South
Vietnam Feb. 4-6. Bundy said the air-strike decision was
made "after the Pleiku incident."

About 160 U.S. and South Vietnamese land-based and
carrier-based planes carried out a 3d retaliatory strike against
North Vietnamese targets Feb. 11. A U.S. Navy spokesman
said 3 Navy planes had been lost in the operation (the pilot of
one was rescued). The planes hit barracks and staging points
in 2 separate areas—Chan Hoa and Chaple, 160 miles and 40
miles, respectively, north of the 17th Parallel, which divided
North and South Vietnam. The attack was in reprisal for
Viet Cong terrorist assaults that had followed the first 2 air
raids on North Vietnam. In one terrorist attack, the Viet
Cong Feb. 10 blew up a U.S. barracks at Quinhon, killing at
least 23 Americans. The White House Feb. 11 said the air
strikes "were in response to further direct provocations by
the Hanoi régime" since Feb. 8.

The National Liberation Front, the Viet Cong's political
arm, pledged Feb. 12 that its forces would launch an all-out
attack on U.S. military installations in South Vietnam in retaliation for the raids on North Vietnam. Hanoi announced
Feb. 14 that it had asked the ICC (International Control
Commission) to withdraw its observers from their 5 posts in
North Vietnam because it could not guarantee their safety
in view of the air strikes.

The air strikes against North Vietnam evoked sharp
criticism and threats from Communist nations and precipitated
violent anti-U.S. demonstrations in various parts of the world:

● Communist China Feb. 8 called the first air strike an "extremely serious provocation by United States imperialism to
extend the war to" North Vietnam "in an effort to avert total
defeat in South Vietnam." A Peiping statement Feb. 9 said
that China "will definitely not stand idly by." Peiping Feb. 13
reiterated its assertions that "aggression" against North Vietnam "means aggression against China, and . . . the Chinese

people . . . know how to aid the people of Vietnam in driving out U.S. aggressors."

• A Soviet government statement Feb. 9 warned that in view of U.S. "military actions" against North Vietnam and the massing of "armed forces and weapons in South Vietnam," Moscow "will be forced, together with its friends and allies, to take further measures to safeguard the security and strengthen the defense capability" of North Vietnam. The U.S. embassy in Moscow was subjected to a pre-arranged one-hour attack Feb. 9 by 2,000 anti-American demonstrators led by Vietnamese and Chinese Communist students.

• Anti-U.S. demonstrations protesting the U.S. air strikes and Washington's Vietnamese policy in general were staged Feb. 13-16 in Budapest, London, Sofia, Jakarta and Caracas.

(North Vietnam had charged that U.S. and South Vietnamese naval vessels had carried out a series of attacks on North Vietnamese territory Jan. 20-25. The accusations were made in protest notes to the International Control Commission. According to Hanoi: U.S. and South Vietnamese warships Jan. 20 had shelled the North Vietnamese village of Vinthai near the North-South Vietnam demilitarized zone; 2 U.S. and South Vietnamese ships had shelled Conco Island Jan. 21; 2 persons were killed and 3 wounded Jan. 23 when 6 warships under U.S.-South Vietnamese command shelled a North Vietnamese village; 3 warships under U.S.-South Vietnamese command shelled a North Vietnamese village near the demilitarized zone Jan. 25, and one of the ships was set afire by North Vietnamese forces.)

New U.S. Raids Arouse Reds

Another powerful U.S.-South Vietnamese air strike against North Vietnam Mar. 2 evoked further sharp reaction from the Communists. The attack was the first that was not in direct retaliation for Viet Cong guerrilla assaults on U.S. installations in South Vietnam. It was the forerunner of similar raids that continued through 1965. In the Mar. 2 attack, 160 planes bombed an ammunition depot at Xombang, 10 miles inside North Vietnam, and the Quangkhe naval base, about 65 miles north of the 17th Parallel. Reconnaissance photos showed heavy damage.

A denunciation of the air attack was issued Mar. 3 by 19 Communist parties holding an international conference in Moscow. They accused the U.S. of "open aggression" and "barbarous acts." A mob of nearly 2,000 students, led by Asians, attacked the U.S. embassy in Moscow Mar. 4. The incident elicited a sharp complaint from Communist China to Moscow Mar. 6. Peiping denounced Soviet suppression of the anti-U.S. riot, and the Soviet embassy in Peiping was the scene of an unusual anti-Soviet demonstration that day.

U.S. and South Vietnamese planes attacked North Vietnamese targets again Mar. 14-15. The first raid was directed against military and naval installations on Conco (Tiger) Island, 20 miles off the coast of North Vietnam, and was led by Air Vice Marshal Nguyen Cao Ky, commander of South Vietnam's Air Force. The attacking pilots reported the near-total destruction of the island's facilities, used by junks carrying military supplies southward to Viet Cong coastal units. More than 100 U.S. Air Force jets and carrier-based Navy bombers were said to have flown in the Mar. 15 raid, against an ammunition depot at Phuqui, 100 miles south of Hanoi.

Further attacks were carried out Mar. 19, 26 and 29 and Apr. 3-5. One of the Apr. 4 missions—against the Hamrong Bridge, 70 miles south of Hanoi—provoked the first reported response from the North Vietnamese Air Force. 4 North Vietnamese MiG jet fighters intercepted the attacking U.S. F-105 jets and shot 2 of them down. 2 other U.S. jets were destroyed during the day's action, one by ground fire and one by the guns of a Communist ship.

The continued raids led Apr. 9 to the first reported clash between U.S. and Communist Chinese aircraft. Communist China asserted that MiGs of its Air Force had exchanged fire that day with U.S. jets over the Chinese island of Hainan. U.S. authorities acknowledged an American aerial engagement with MiGs over the South China Sea but said they did not know whether the planes were North Vietnamese or Chinese. According to Peiping's version of the incident, Chinese

MiGs intercepted 2 flights of 8 U.S. jets over Hainan. The Chinese said that the U.S. planes "fired 2 guided missiles at random," striking one of their own jets and causing it to crash. The U.S. mission in Saigon said Apr. 9 that 4 U.S. carrier-based F-4 Phantom jets had clashed with MiGs off Hainan and that a Communist plane was hit and set afire. Insisting that the planes had not invaded Hainan air space, a U.S. Defense Department spokesman said the jets were at least 35 miles from the island. U.S. military officials in Saigon admitted Apr. 12 that one F-4 Phantom and its 2 pilots had been lost in the clash, but they would not tell how the plane was downed.

Johnson Opposes Halting Air Strikes

Pres. Johnson asserted Apr. 17 that the U.S. would continue its air strikes against North Vietnam despite appeals from many persons who expressed hope that a halt in the raids might increase the prospects of peace negotiations. In a statement made at his ranch near Johnson City, Tex., the President reaffirmed the U.S.' willingness to participate in "unconditional discussion" with "any government willing to talk," "next week, tomorrow or tonight."

Deploring Communist rejection of his peace offers, Mr. Johnson said: "It has been a week of disappointment, because we tried to open a window to peace, only to be met with tired names and slogans—and a refusal to talk." The President insisted that the U.S.' aims in Vietnam remained "an independent South Vietnam, tied to no alliance, free to shape its relation and association with all other nations." He warned that until Saigon's independence was guaranteed, "there is no human power capable of forcing us from Vietnam."

State Secy. Rusk Apr. 17 also opposed suspending U.S. air attacks on North Vietnam. He said the U.S. "had tried publicly and privately to find out if" a suspension would "end aggression from the north," "but there has been no response." A halt in the aerial strikes "would only encourage the aggressor and dishearten our friends who bear the brunt of battle," Rusk predicted. Defense Secy. Robert S. McNamara said

Apr. 18 that "we have no indications that a cessation of the bombing would move the North Vietnamese to discussion leading to termination of their aggression in the south."

Senate Foreign Relations Committee Chrmn. J. W. Fulbright (D., Ark.) said Apr. 18 that if a truce in Vietnam could not be achieved, "then I believe there might be some value in stopping the bombings temporarily." The current raids were "inclined to keep the atmosphere very tense," encourage the North Vietnamese to "dig in" and discourage Soviet participation in peace talks, Fulbright said.

Canadian Prime Min. Lester B. Pearson had suggested Apr. 2 a "pause" in U.S. air strikes on North Vietnam. In an address in Philadelphia, where he accepted Temple University's 2d annual World Peace Award, Pearson said that if the raids were halted it "might provide the Hanoi authorities with an opportunity . . . to inject some flexibility into [their] policy without appearing to do so as the direct result of military pressure," and thus "the stalemate might be broken." Pearson discussed his proposal with Pres. Johnson at Camp David, Md. Apr. 3. In a report to the Canadian House of Commons, Pearson said Apr. 6 that Mr. Johnson had been "very interested" in his suggestions for a pause in the air strikes.

Pres. Johnson Apr. 27 reiterated his offer of "unconditional discussions" "with any government concerned." He said: "This offer may be rejected, as it has been in the past, but it will remain open, waiting for the day when it becomes clear to all that armed attack will not" lead to "domination over others." Reviewing the period after the Aug. 1964 incident in which U.S. planes first bombed North Vietnam in retaliation for an attack on U.S. warships in the Gulf of Tonkin, the President said: "For the next 6 months we took no action against North Vietnam. We warned of danger. . . . Their answer was attack and explosion and indiscriminate murder. So, it soon became clear that our restraint was viewed as weakness. . . . We could no longer stand by while attack mounted and while the bases of the attackers were immune from reply. And, therefore, we began to strike back."

(The air strikes against North Vietnam were continued intermittently but with mounting intensity during the last week of April and beginning of May. In one of these assaults, more than 200 U.S. and South Vietnamese planes roamed the skies of North Vietnam Apr. 24, destroying bridges and ferries in a coordinated effort to wreck Communist supply routes to the south.)

U.S. Halts, Resumes Raids

The U.S. suspended air attacks on North Vietnam May 13 but resumed them May 18. A report from Washington said that the U.S., through the International Control Commission's Canadian delegate, had informed the North Vietnamese government that the U.S. had suspended the bombings for an indefinite period. The North Vietnamese were said to have displayed no interest in peace talks.

State Department press chief Robert J. McCloskey said May 18 that the Administration was "disappointed at the fact that there was no reaction" by Hanoi to the suspension of the bombings. He said "we must assume that the other side was aware that the strikes had not been carried out for a number of days, and we have seen no reaction to that fact."

The North Vietnamese Foreign Ministry charged May 18 that the air strike halt was "an effort to camouflage American intensification of the war and deceive world opinion." The Chinese Communist news agency Hsinhua contended May 18 that the U.S. had not halted its air attacks at all. Hsinhua claimed that during the weekend "many waves of reconnaissance and fighter aircraft" from Thailand bases had attacked North Vietnam.

Hanoi radio charged Dec. 10 that the May suspension of U.S. air strikes against North Vietnam "was only a maneuver to pave the way for further escalation of the war of aggression." The broadcast claimed that a U.S. message sent by State Secy. Rusk May 12 to the North Vietnamese embassy in Moscow, "announcing a halt in the bombing," "in its essence . . . was an ultimatum . . . urging the South Vietnamese to abandon their patriotic struggle as a condition for a halt in the bombing. . . ." The Hanoi broadcast claimed that the U.S. actually had not stopped the raids during the supposed suspension period; it said North Vietnamese forces had downed 2 U.S. F-105 jet fighters during that period. The text of the U.S. message on the raid pause was made public for the first time by the Hanoi broadcast. According to Hanoi, State Secy. Rusk had said in the U.S. note: The U.S. had "taken account of repeated suggestions from various quarters, including Hanoi . . ., that there can be no progress toward peace while there are air attacks on North Vietnam. . . . The United States will be very watchful to see whether in this period of pause there are significant reductions in . . . armed actions [against South Vietnam]. . . . [The U.S.] is very hopeful . . . that this first pause in air attacks may meet with a response which will permit further and more extended suspension[s] . . . in expectation of equal constructive actions by the other side in the future."

A U.S. State Department spokesman Dec. 11 confirmed the accuracy of Hanoi radio's text of Rusk's message. But the spokesman added: The broadcast "reaffirms without the slightest ambiguity its rejection of the May pause."

Missile Sites Attacked

With the resumption of U.S. air raids on targets in North Vietnam, the Communists initiated measures to provide a more effective air defense system. The U.S. State Department announced July 6 that air reconnaissance had shown that 2 Soviet-type anti-aircraft missile sites had been built and were combat-ready in the Hanoi-Haiphong area and that at least 2 others were under construction in the same area. The sites were said to be similar to the SAM-2 rocket installations set up by the Russians in Cuba in 1962.

Anti-aircraft missiles were used against attacking U.S. planes for the first time July 24, when rockets fired from a new launching complex destroyed one and damaged the remaining 3 craft of a flight of 4 U.S. F-4C Phantom jets flying west of Hanoi. The F-4Cs were escorting a formation of bombers raiding munitions manufacturing and storage facilities at Langchi, 55 miles northwest of Hanoi. The attack occurred when the planes were flying at an altitude of 20,000 to 30,000 feet at a point outside the effective range of the known Hanoi missile sites. U.S. spokesmen in Saigon reported July 25 that there were "indications" the jet had been downed by a missile from a hitherto unknown anti-aircraft installation.

The new missile installation and another located in the same area, 40 miles northwest of Hanoi, were attacked by a force of 46 U.S. F-105 fighter-bombers July 27. One missile launcher was destroyed and the other heavily damaged, but 5 U.S. planes were lost in the attack. 3 of the planes destroyed were shot down by conventional anti-aircraft guns; press reports said that 2 other jets were lost when a damaged jet rammed another plane in its formation while returning to its base in South Vietnam.

(U.S. missiles—of the Sidewinder air-to-air type—were credited with the destruction of 2 North Vietnamese MiG-17 jets July 10. The MiGs had attacked U.S. Phantom jets escorting a fighter-bomber formation in an attack on the Yen Sen ammunition depot, 65 miles northwest of Hanoi. The Phantoms fired their Sidewinders and downed both Communist planes.)

A Navy A-4 Skyhawk was the 2d U.S. plane downed by a missile over North Vietnam. It was hit Aug. 12 by a rocket fired from a previously unknown launching site 50 miles southwest of Hanoi. Adm. U.S. Grant Sharp Jr., U.S. commander in the Pacific, confirmed the incident and said that the site would be destroyed when it was located.

Heavy U.S. Air Losses Reported

The U.S. suffered unusually heavy air losses in attacks on North Vietnam between Sept. 20 and Oct. 5.

6 U.S. aircraft were destroyed Sept. 20: A helicopter was shot down while trying to rescue the pilot of an F-105 jet shot down over North Vietnam. Another F-105 pilot was killed when his plane crashed into a bridge he was bombing southeast of Dienbienphu. A Navy Skyhawk was downed southeast of Hanoi, but the pilot was rescued at sea. 2 F-104

planes collided over the sea near Danang after completing a support mission; the pilots were rescued.*

2 U.S. Air Force planes were shot down over North Vietnam Sept. 30 during a bombing raid against the Minhbinh bridge, 55 miles southeast of Hanoi. One of the planes was believed to have been downed by a surface-to-air missile.

A Peiping broadcast Oct. 5 claimed that Communist Chinese ground fire that day had downed one of 4 U.S. planes intruding into Kwangsi Province, which bordered North Vietnam. The U.S. Defense Department acknowledged that a U.S. plane had been missing as a result of a bombing mission about 50 miles northeast of Hanoi; it said it was investigating Peiping's claim that the aircraft was lost over Kwangsi.

4 U.S. planes were lost Oct. 5: 3 of them were downed in separate missions over a 40-50 mile area northeast of Hanoi; all crew-members were listed as missing. The 4th plane also was lost over North Vietnam but the pilot was rescued.

Communist China had reported Sept. 20 that its planes that day had intercepted another U.S. F-104 jet over Hainan Island and had shot it down. Peiping radio said that the pilot, identified as Capt. Philips Smith, parachuted and was captured as he tried to flee. A Chinese Defense Ministry official called the "intrusion another and still more serious war provocation by a U.S. military aircraft." A U.S. spokesman in Saigon said Sept. 20 that Smith had parachuted into the Gulf of Tonkin because of mechanical trouble and fuel shortage during a routine patrol. (Peiping had charged in a broadcast July 11 that 4 U.S. jets had crossed its frontier into the province of Yunnan, in southwest China. The report also charged that the planes had attacked the North Vietnamese town of Laokay. A U.S. spokesman at the Pentagon in Washington denied that U.S. planes had participated in a raid close to the Chinese border.)

U.S. jets carried out a series of successful air strikes on North Vietnamese missile sites in October and November. The strikes were intended to prevent North Vietnam from developing more than a minimal anti-aircraft missile defense.

U.S. plane losses remained heavy, however, due to the effectiveness of North Vietnam's conventional anti-aircraft artillery. One Communist missile site about 50 miles northeast of Hanoi was destroyed Oct. 17 in a raid by 5 U.S. Navy planes from the carrier *Independence*. The pilots reported that 8 tons of bombs exploded the surface-to-air missiles, set fire to 10 transport vehicles and heavily damaged radar guidance vans. The 5 jets returned safely to the carrier despite heavy anti-aircraft fire. U.S. planes Oct. 31 destroyed 3 anti-aircraft missile sites and a highway bridge defended by the missiles about 35 miles northeast of Hanoi, a spokesman in Saigon reported Nov. 1. The pilots reported that about 10 missiles had been fired at them before they bombed the site. (The North Vietnamese news agency reported Oct. 31 that 15 U.S. planes had been shot down over North Vietnam that day: 14 over Habac and Langson Provinces and one over Bachlong Island.)

15 fighter-bombers from the aircraft carrier *Oriskany* bombed a mobile missile site 35 miles east of Hanoi Nov. 5. The planes raided the installation after 5 missiles had been fired at the aircraft during a strike against the Haiduong bridge. Pilots reported the destruction of one missile launcher and an anti-aircraft gun position. One plane was downed by conventional anti-aircraft fire. Jets from the *Oriskany,* accompanied by land-based U.S. Air Force jets, Nov. 7 struck 2 missile installations, about 25 miles and 40 miles from Thanhhoa, respectively, destroying 2 sites and heavily damaging 2 others. One plane was downed by conventional anti-aircraft fire; the pilot bailed out and was rescued in the Gulf of Tonkin. A flight of jets from the *Oriskany* Nov. 8 struck more missile sites in the Hanoi area. Pilots reported inflicting heavy damage on 4 missiles, 4 launchers and several support buildings.

Haiphong Area Bombed

U.S. Air Force planes Dec. 15 bombed and destroyed a North Vietnamese thermal power plant at Uongbi, 14 miles north of the country's chief port of Haiphong. This was the first American air raid on a major North Vietnamese industrial target. A flight of 4 to 6 F-105 Thunderchief jet fighter-bombers dropped 12 tons of bombs on the installation, which reportedly supplied a significant amount of power for the Hanoi-Haiphong area. The plant had a 24,000-kilowatt capacity, about 15% of North Vietnam's total electric-power production. Pilots reported observing several secondary explosions on the ground following the bomb drop. Heavy antiaircraft fire forced one pilot to abandon his damaged plane over the Gulf of Tonkin. The pilot parachuted and was rescued by a helicopter.

Defense Secy. McNamara said Dec. 16 that the Uongbi raid was "appropriate to the increased terrorist activity in Vietnam." He said the raid was "representative of the type of attacks we . . . will continue to carry out." The Uongbi power plant was attacked again Dec. 20 in one of the last major raids to be carried out before the Johnson Administration suspended the bombing of North Vietnam in a new effort to stimulate Vietnamese peace talks.

One of the heaviest air attacks of the war against North Vietnamese targets had been carried out by U.S. planes Dec. 8-9. 150 Air Force and Navy aircraft launched what Saigon sources described as a major assault to reduce the infiltration of North Vietnamese troops into South Vietnam. Pilots reported they had severed transport routes at 117 points.

The *N.Y. Times* reported Dec. 10 that after 10 months of U.S. air attacks against North Vietnam, the country's economic and military machine remained essentially intact. According to the report: The raids had failed to halt appreciably the flow of North Vietnamese troop infiltrators into South Vietnam (estimated current rate 1,500 a month). Economic life had been disrupted by the air strikes but not enough to impede North Vietnam's will to continue the struggle. To compensate for the severance of road and rail traffic in many parts of the country, the North Vietnamese concealed bridges under water, employed boats and every type of vehicle to substitute for truck traffic.

Christmas Truce Suspends Air Raids

The fighting in Vietnam was largely suspended for 30 hours Dec. 24-25 by a Christmas truce originally proposed by the Communist side. Although ground fighting in South Vietnam was resumed Dec. 26, the pause in air strikes against North Vietnam continued on into 1966. U.S. reconnaissance flights over North Vietnam, however, were still made. The latter flights were designed to determine whether the North Vietnamese were taking advantage of the lull to regroup their forces or to continue to infiltrate South Vietnam. The *N.Y. Times* reported Dec. 29 that the U.S. had informed Hanoi that the pause in the air raids was designed to give North Vietnam an opportunity to display an interest in peace talks.

The National Liberation Front had said in a Dec. 7 broadcast that the Viet Cong would halt attacks from 7 p.m. Christmas Eve until 7 a.m. "to allow people on the other side to celebrate Christmas in peace" provided U.S. and South Vietnamese troops carried no arms. A U.S. State Department response Dec. 8 said "the real Christmas present for the world would be a readiness to make peace and to accept any of the suggestions made by ourselves and others to move to the conference table." Gen. William C. Westmoreland, commander of U.S. forces in Vietnam, said Dec. 10: "The prospect of fighting is prevalent on any day. Christmas Day is no exception."

The U.S. and its allies Dec. 23 accepted the Viet Cong offer and made a counter-offer to extend the 12-hour halt in fighting for an additional 18 hours, from 6 p.m. Dec. 24 to midnight Dec. 25. Such an extension order, announced on behalf of Westmoreland, said that U.S., South Vietnamese, Australian, New Zealand and South Korean troops would "not fire on the enemy except in self-defense" during the 30-hour period. The order also announced the decision to suspend the air strikes on North Vietnam.

On the expiration of the 30 hours, during which some small-scale ground clashes were reported, Westmoreland Dec. 25 issued another order to U.S. and allied troops to retain their defensive posture and not to fire unless attacked. South Vietnamese troops got a similar directive. This attempted extension of the truce was canceled by U.S. military authorities Dec. 26 in the face of heavy Viet Cong attacks; U.S. and Vietnamese forces then launched offensive operations. U.S. officials claimed that the Viet Cong had initiated 84 attacks, all but 24 of them begun during the 30-hour truce period. Communist attacks immediately after the truce were

U.S. Skyraider comes down low to drop 500-pound bombs on presumed Viet Cong target in South Vietnamese jungle. Smoke rises from previous pass at same target.   (Wide World photo)

described as "low-level," but they eventually increased to the pre-cease-fire intensity.

(The Viet Cong Dec. 28 proposed a 4-day cease fire for Jan. 20-23, 1966 to mark the Vietnamese lunar new year. The proposal, broadcast by the guerrillas' clandestine radio, said: During Jan. 20-23 the Viet Cong would fire only if attacked; South Vietnamese soldiers and officials would be permitted to visit their relatives in the battle zone, even in Viet Cong-held areas, to attend the holiday rites, provided they did not carry weapons. South Vietnamese government sources reported Dec. 29 that the Saigon régime had been planning a lunar new year truce before the Viet Cong had made their proposal.)

WIDESPREAD SEARCH FOR PEACE

Thant Proposes 'Dialogues'

The "escalation" of the Vietnamese war and its possible threat to world peace prompted UN Secy. Gen. U Thant Feb. 24 to propose an informal 7-government conference as a preliminary attempt to end the conflict. Thant called for "dialogues" among the U.S., Communist China, North and South Vietnam, France, the USSR and Britain. He suggested that the conferees concentrate on providing South Vietnam with a stable government and that U.S. forces be withdrawn "from that part of the world." Such meetings, with Thant or someone else acting as intermediary, could pave the way for a formal conference, he declared. (Thant had appealed Feb. 12 to all sides in the Vietnamese conflict "to refrain from any new acts which may lead to an escalation of the present conflict." Asserting that "means must be found, . . . within or outside the United Nations, of shifting the quest for a solution away from the field of battle to the conference table," Thant suggested "a revival of the Geneva conference" on Indochina.)

North Vietnam was reported Feb. 25 to have informed Thant that it was sympathetic to his peace plan.

State Secy. Dean Rusk said Feb. 25 that the U.S. would not enter negotiations until North Vietnam gave some "indication" that it was "prepared to stop what it is doing . . .

against its neighbors." He ruled out U.S. participation in a negotiation aimed at the "acceptance or confirmation of aggression." Formal U.S. rejection of the Thant plan was announced by the State Department Mar. 9. The department said it had informed Thant that it opposed his plan or similar proposals until North Vietnam indicated a desire to halt its "aggression."

Thant's proposal was rejected by Communist Chinese Premier Chou En-lai, it was reported Apr. 6. Chou's views were delivered to Thant by Tewfik Bouattoura, Algeria's chief representative to the UN. Chou said that the Viet Cong, and not Peiping or North Vietnam, must be a direct party in any peace conference.

Britain, France and the Soviet Union also were active in February in efforts to end the conflict.

A French government statement issued Feb. 10 said Paris desired an international accord that would end outside intervention in North and South Vietnam, Laos and Cambodia and bring independence and neutrality to those areas. The statement followed a conference of French Pres. Charles de Gaulle with his cabinet on the Vietnam situation. De Gaulle suggested that the 1954 Geneva conference on Indochina be reconvened to negotiate peace in South Vietnam.

Soviet Amb.-to-France Sergei A. Vinogradov Feb. 23 handed de Gaulle a Moscow memo that supported the French leader's proposal. The Soviet statement expressed concern over the critical situation, especially "the United States bombing of North Vietnam." French Information Min. Alain Peyrefitte said Feb. 24 that as a result of the de Gaulle-Vinogradov talks, France and the USSR had decided to press for an international meeting on South Vietnam.

50 Labor members of the British Parliament Feb. 10 signed a motion urging Britain to initiate moves for a cease-fire and negotiated political settlement in Vietnam. But the Labor government held firm in supporting U.S. policy, and the British Foreign Office declared that "the basis" for reconvening the Geneva conference "does not at this moment exist." The

British government backed the U.S. view that there could be no negotiations while Communist attacks continued in South Vietnam.

British Press Peace Efforts

The British government took a series of steps in February and March in the search for a peaceful settlement of the Vietnamese war.

In a note sent to Moscow Feb. 20 London urged that Britain and the USSR, as co-chairmen of the 1954 Geneva conference on Indochina, pool their efforts to help end the conflict. A Soviet reply Mar. 17 called on the U.S. to cease its air raids on North Vietnam and withdraw its troops and arms from South Vietnam. The Soviet message attributed the war to "the gross violation of the Geneva agreements on Indochina by the United States and its armed interference in the affairs of the Vietnamese people."

Britain Mar. 8 published an ICC (International Control Commission) report that had called on London and Moscow to issue an "immediate appeal" for measures to "stem the deteriorating situation in Vietnam." Britain issued the report despite Soviet objections. The report, written by the ICC's Polish and Indian delegates, had been submitted Feb. 13. It dealt with the U.S.' Feb. 7 and 8 air strikes on North Vietnam. The ICC document suggested that the raids on North Vietnam violated the Geneva agreements. A minority report filed by the ICC's Canadian delegate, J. Blair Seaborn, said the Vietnamese crisis was a result of "the deliberate and persistent pursuit of aggressive but largely covert policies by North Vietnam directed against South Vietnam."

British officials failed Mar. 16-19 to persuade the Soviet Union to join in a major effort to encourage the convening of Vietnam peace talks. The failure took place during discussions in London Mar. 16-19 with Soviet Foreign Min. Andrei Gromyko. Gromyko held separate meetings with British Foreign Min. Michael Stewart and Prime Min. Harold Wilson. A British communiqué Mar. 19 said only that in the discussions particular attention was "devoted to the dangerous situation in Indochina, and the 2 sides explained their respective views as to what action should be taken to remove the dangers."

British Foreign Secy. Stewart conferred with U.S. officials in Washington Mar. 22-23 and expressed support for American policy in Vietnam. Following Stewart's talks with State Secy. Rusk Mar. 22, a U.S. official said "the public attitudes of the 2 governments make it clear that there is no divergence in our views." Stewart met Mar. 23 with Pres. Johnson, Rusk, Defense Secy. Robert S. McNamara and other U.S. officials. In support of the U.S. raids on North Vietnam, Stewart said that "whatever the right answer to the world's problems may be, it is certainly the wrong answer to yield invariably to the aggressor." Stewart informed the U.S. officials that the Soviet Union had "made clear" that currently it was not interested in proposals by Britain and others for peace negotiations on Vietnam. Stewart said North Vietnam and Communist China had been equally unresponsive.

South Vietnam Lists Peace Terms

South Vietnam Mar. 1 stated for the first time its conditions for ending the conflict in South Vietnam. In a formal statement, the South Vietnamese government declared that "the Communists [must] end the war they have provoked," stop their infiltration, subversion and sabotage and offer "concrete, efficient and appropriate means" to guarantee South Vietnam's security. A South Vietnamese cabinet communiqué Apr. 11 further stated that withdrawal of Viet Cong troops and cadres from South Vietnam was one of Saigon's preconditions for participation in peace talks with North Vietnam. The cabinet also said the government would refuse to recognize the National Liberation Front and would agree only to "qualified representatives" of the other side in any future negotiations.

South Vietnam's terms were listed in greater detail Oct. 13 by Nguyen Duy Lien, Saigon's observer at the UN. Speaking at a news conference at UN headquarters in New York, Lien said his government's 4-point peace formula differed from the U.S. position since Washington was "disposed to enter negotiations without prior conditions while we . . .

think some conditions are necessary." Saigon's peace plan:
(1) There must be a halt to all foreign-directed military action
and subversion and a guarantee that foreigners would not
interfere in the internal affairs of North and South Vietnam.
(2) South Vietnam "must be left alone, to choose . . . its own
destiny . . . without any intervention of whatever form and
whatever source." (3) Saigon reserved the right to request
the withdrawal from South Vietnam of military forces of
"friendly countries" and "to call again for foreign assistance
in case of renewed aggression or threat of aggression." (4)
The Vietnamese should be given stronger guarantees of independence and liberty than the 1954 Geneva agreements had
provided.

Lien said South Vietnam's terms would mean the dissolu-
tion of the NLF and all other Communist-organized groups.
Denying that these groups were native to South Vietnam,
Lien said a majority of the guerrillas had been trained in
North Vietnam and remained under Hanoi's orders. Lien
said he had submitted South Vietnam's formula to UN Secy.
Gen. U Thant.

South Vietnamese Premier Nguyen Cao Ky declared in
Seoul, South Korea Nov. 11 that "as an anti-Communist," he
would never participate in peace talks with the Communists.
Ky made the statement at a news conference at the conclu-
sion of 3 days of talks held with South Korean Premier
Chung Il Kwon.

Non-Aligned Nations Propose Talks

The heads of state of 17 non-aligned nations Apr. 1
urged a "peaceful solution through negotiations" of the Vietnamese war "without posing preconditions." The appeal was
made to UN Secy. Gen. U Thant, the U.S., Britain, the Soviet
Union, France, Communist China, North and South Vietnam, the
National Liberation Front, Poland and Canada. The statement was drawn up at a conference of the 17 nations in
Belgrade Mar. 14-15. It asserted that the current fighting
"can only lead to . . . a more generalized war with catastrophic
consequences." The statement contended that the situation in
Vietnam was aggravated by "foreign intervention in various

forms, including military intervention. . . ." The non-aligned group said "a political solution" should be sought "in accordance with the legitimate aspirations of the Vietnamese people and in the spirit of the Geneva agreements." (The 17 non-aligned nations were: Afghanistan, Algeria, Cyprus, Ceylon, Ethiopia, Ghana, Guinea, India, Iraq, Kenya, Nepal, Syria, Tunisia, Uganda, the United Arab Republic, Yugoslavia and Zambia.)

Pres. Johnson replied Apr. 8. He said the U.S. was "ready to withdraw its forces from South Vietnam" "when conditions have been created in which the people . . . can determine their own future free from external interference." Mr. Johnson asserted that the U.S. supported the neutral nations' position that all people were entitled to the right to self-determination and "that recourse to force is contrary to the rights of the people of Vietnam to peace, freedom and independence." The President, however, reiterated the U.S. view that "the basic cause of the conflict in Vietnam is the attack by North Vietnam on . . . South Vietnam. The object of that attack is total conquest." "We believe," the President said, "that peace can be achieved in Southeast Asia the moment that aggression from North Vietnam is eliminated."

North Vietnam rejected the non-aligned nations' appeal Apr. 20. Hanoi claimed that some of the 17 nations attending the conference at which the peace plea had been drawn up "did not sign the appeal." North Vietnam added that those nations that did sign "were not accurately informed about the bloody war provoked in South Vietnam by the U.S. imperialists. . . ."

Johnson Offers Talks & Aid

Pres. Johnson announced Apr. 7 that the U.S. was ready to participate in "unconditional discussions" toward a Vietnamese settlement. He also proposed a massive international program to promote the economic development of Southeast Asia. The President made the proposals in a speech delivered at Johns Hopkins University in Baltimore, Md.

The President said the talks could be "discussion or negotiation with the governments concerned, in large groups or in small ones, in the reaffirmation of old agreements or their strengthening with new ones. . . ." The "essentials of any final settlement," he declared, were "an independent South Vietnam—securely guaranteed and able to shape its own relationships to all others, free from outside interference, tied to no alliance, a military base for no country." In reaffirming the U.S. commitment in Vietnam, the President said: "We fight because we must fight if we are to live in a world where every country can shape its own destiny. . . ." Although some South Vietnamese were fighting their own government, the flow of men, supplies and others "from north to south" was "the heartbeat of the war."

"Over this war and all Asia is another reality: the deepening shadow of Communist China," Mr. Johnson charged. "The rulers in Hanoi are urged on by Peiping," which "is helping the forces of violence in almost every continent." The U.S.' "stepped up" air attacks on North Vietnam, Mr. Johnson said, were "not a change of purpose" but "a change in what we believe that purpose requires" in order to "slow down aggression," "increase the confidence" of the South Vietnamese and "convince the leaders of North Vietnam, and all who seek to share their conquest, of a very simple fact: We will not be defeated."

(Administration sources told reporters after the President's speech that the U.S.' readiness for "unconditional discussions" included willingness to hold talks with Communist China or North Vietnam even while the fighting continued but did not include engaging in talks with the National Liberation Front.)

Mr. Johnson appealed for UN Secy. Gen. U Thant to "use the prestige of his great office and his deep knowledge of Asia" to start the Southeast Asian aid plan he was proposing. The President said that he himself would name a "special team" of Americans, headed by ex-World Bank Pres. Eugene Black, "to inaugurate our participation in these programs." He urged all Southeast Asian nations, including North Vietnam, to take part in the aid plan. Mr. Johnson suggested that the plan be financed by the U.S. and all other industrialized countries, including the Soviet Union. He said he would ask Congress to approve "a billion-dollar American investment in this effort as soon as it is under way."

Pres. Johnson's proposals were rejected Apr. 9-12 by Communist China, North Vietnam and the Soviet Union.

Peiping radio charged Apr. 9 that Pres. Johnson's offer was "full of lies and deceptions." "While the United States trumpets peace by word of mouth," the Chinese statement said, "it is actually pushing on with preparations for expansion of the war." Scorning the proposed Southeast Asian development program as "pursuance of 'the stick and the carrot tactics,'" the Chinese statement said "that Washington's dream to strike a political bargain with a billion dollars . . . could not possibly soften the Vietnamese people's resistance. . . ."

Pres. Johnson's proposals were denounced by the USSR Apr. 10 as "noisy propaganda" that "cannot change the fact that the United States aggression in Vietnam is . . . endangering peace in Southeast Asia and elsewhere in the world." The Soviet statement, published in the Communist Party newspaper *Pravda,* asserted that Mr. Johnson's offer to negotiate was far from "unconditional," that his address had not mentioned "a word about the United States' intention to halt its aggression."

North Vietnam's rejection appeared Apr. 12 in its Communist Party newspaper, *Nhan Dan.* The newspaper described the proposed Southeast Asian regional aid program as "bait" of "stupid pirates." *Nhan Dan* reiterated Pres. Ho Chi Minh's declaration that the U.S. must halt its raids on North Vietnam and withdraw from South Vietnam if peace talks were to be held. Ho's position had been stated in an interview in the Japanese Communist Party newspaper, *Akahata,* prior to Mr. Johnson's Apr. 7 address; it had been made public Apr. 9 by the North Vietnam Press Agency.

Thant Apr. 8 praised the President's development-plan proposal as "positive, forward-looking and generous." In a letter to Mr. Johnson he asserted that the plan reflected "my

recent thinking . . . along similar lines." Thant described
Mr. Johnson's proposals on negotiations "as both constructive
and statesmanlike."

South Vietnamese Premier Phan Huy Quat Apr. 8 praised
Pres. Johnson's speech. But privately some Vietnam government officials expressed apprehension about the President's
endorsement of "unconditional discussions." In an effort to
assure the apprehensive officials in his government, Quat said
in his statement that Pres. Johnson "simply wanted to make
it clear that the United States is not attaching any conditions
to discussions that would lead to an end to the aggression
against free Vietnam."

(An indirect offer of "economic and social cooperation"
had been made by Pres. Johnson Mar. 25 to North Vietnam
and other Southeast Asian nations. Mr. Johnson's main condition: restoration of peace in the region. The offer was made
by the President in a statement issued following a 2-hour
cabinet meeting on Vietnam. He said: The U.S. "looks for-
ward to the day when the people and governments of all
Southeast Asia may be free from terror, subversion and assassination—when they will need not military support . . .
against aggression, but only economic and social cooperation
for progress in peace." Citing U.S.-aided economic programs
in Vietnam and elsewhere, Mr. Johnson said the U.S. "would
want to help" in "wider and bolder programs [that] can be
expected in the future from Asian leaders and Asian councils.")

Hanoi States Peace Terms

A formal North Vietnamese proposal for peace talks was
made in a 4-point policy statement delivered Apr. 8 by Premier Pham Van Dong at a meeting of the National Assembly.
Hanoi's proposals, as made public Apr. 13 by the Chinese
Communist news agency, Hsinhua:

1. "Recognition of the basic national rights of the Vietnamese people—peace, independence, sovereignty, unity and
territorial integrity." The U.S. must, in accordance with the
1954 Geneva agreements, withdraw its forces from South
Vietnam, end its "military alliance" with Saigon, halt its

"intervention and aggression in South Vietnam," and "stop its acts of war" against North Vietnam.

2. "Pending the peaceful reunification of Vietnam," the country's "2 zones [North and South Vietnam] must refrain from joining any military alliance with any foreign countries. There must be no foreign military bases, troops or military personnel in their respective territories."

3. South Vietnam's "internal affairs" "must be settled by the South Vietnamese people themselves, in accordance with the program" of the National Liberation Front, "without any foreign interference."

4. Vietnam's reunification must be settled by the Vietnamese people themselves "without any foreign interference."

France & USSR Issue Joint Plea

France and the Soviet Union Apr. 29 urged reaffirmation of the 1954 and 1962 Geneva agreements. Their call was issued in a communiqué based on talks Soviet Foreign Min. Gromyko had held in Paris Apr. 26-29 with Foreign Min. Maurice Couve de Murville and other French officials. The joint statement declared that "the situation in the Indochinese Peninsula and, in particular, Vietnam, has worsened . . . and creates dangers for peace."

Gromyko had expressed continued Soviet interest in an international conference on Cambodia, according to a French statement issued Apr. 28. But Communist China Apr. 29 expressed opposition to a Cambodian conference that would be used as a forum to discuss Vietnam. Communist Chinese Premier Chou En-lai said his government supported Cambodian Prince Norodom Sihanouk's position that any international parley on Cambodia be confined to discussion of his country's neutrality and independence. As for a possible conference on Vietnam, Chou insisted that South Vietnam could be represented only by the National Liberation Front.

British Advance New Plan

A new British proposal for ending the Vietnamese war was outlined in the House of Commons June 3 by Foreign

Secy. Michael Stewart. Under the proposal: A conference would be called for the purpose of ending the fighting and removing all foreign troops from South Vietnam. A cease-fire either would precede the talks or would be discussed as the first topic at the conference. It was reported that the British plan also called for granting North and South Vietnam a free hand in deciding on their future relationship and their form of government.

Stewart also disclosed that the Soviet Union continued to oppose the Wilson government's suggestion that Moscow join London in reconvening the Geneva conference. Stewart said that at a meeting May 15 with Soviet Foreign Min. Gromyko in Vienna, Gromyko had responded negatively to the British proposal.

Johnson Restates Offer; Intermediaries Busy

Pres. Johnson appealed again for world peace in a commencement speech at Catholic University in Washington June 6. "Peace is still a stranger knocking at the door," Mr. Johnson said. But he emphasized that "we of America—we of the free world—are ready, as we are always, to open the door and invite peace to enter, to dwell in the house of all nations forever." In apparent reference to the Communists' reputed lack of response to his proposal for unconditional talks, Mr. Johnson declared June 8 that the Administration was straining "to hear with every antenna at our command that word from other lands which will signify willingness to talk of peace and willingness to work for justice."

Pres. Johnson revealed at his news conference in Washington June 17 that foreign intermediaries "negotiating for" the U.S. had held a series of meetings with North Vietnamese officials but that the latter had expressed no interest in peace talks. Mr. Johnson refused to identify the intermediaries, but one of them was believed to have been J. Blair Seaborn, Canada's representative on the ICC, whose May 31 discussions in Hanoi had been made public June 7. Mr. Johnson disclosed that an intermediary (apparently Seaborn) had said in his report Feb. 15 on a meeting with Hanoi's leaders: The North Vietnamese government "considers it holds all the trump cards; that world opinion is becoming more sympathetic; that the United States retaliation is limited; that South Vietnam is having its difficulties, and they are not the slightest interested" in talks.

Mr. Johnson declassified part of a June 7 intermediary report (apparently also made by Seaborn) to further illustrate what he called Hanoi's intrasigence. The President said the negotiator was "completely persuaded from his conversations with the [North Vietnamese] officials they are not now interested in any negotiations of any kind." Mr. Johnson said that in response to the intermediary's request for elaboration "on any proposal they would consider," one high-ranking North Vietnamese official with whom he had met "remained deliberately vague and gave no clear answer."

The President also recalled that "when we asked them to come into the United Nations last August, after we said you bring these people in and let's try to work through the UN, they weren't the slightest interested—the North Vietnamese were not."

State Secy. Rusk July 4 shed further light on North Vietnam's response to intermediaries sounding out Hanoi on behalf of the U.S. In a Voice of America broadcast (taped 10 days previously), Rusk said: On several occasions the U.S., acting through an unnamed intermediary, had asked Hanoi "what would be stopped if we stopped the [aerial] bombing [of North Vietnam]. . . . Are you going to stop sending those tens of thousands of men from North Vietnam into South Vietnam? Are you going to stop attacking these villages and killing off thousands of innocent civilians? And we've never had a reply." Asserting that the U.S. would be willing to hold discussions with the Viet Cong, Rusk said "their voices undoubtedly would be heard as the voices of other groups in Vietnam are heard." But Rusk insisted that the Viet Cong could not be a "primary party" in negotiations on the Vietnamese war.

Senate majority leader Mike Mansfield (D., Mont.) Sept. 1 listed in a Senate speech 5 conditions that he said he believed constituted the Administration's basic prerequisite for a peaceful settlement of the war. White House Press Secy. Moyers said after the address that it "reflect[ed] the sentiment of the Johnson Administration." Disclosing that Mansfield had informed the President of the speech prior to its delivery, Moyers said Mr. Johnson's "feeling is that the Senator touched on 5 very vital points."

The conditions, as summarized by Mansfield: (1) South Vietnam must have the right to choose its own government —"a verified choice free of terrorism, violence and coercion from any quarter." (2) "There can be a future for South Vietnam either in independence or as part of a unified Vietnam on the basis of a peaceful, free and verified expression of the wish of the people . . . in general accord with the Geneva agreements." (3) All foreign forces and bases should be withdrawn from North and South Vietnam, "provided peace can be reestablished" and such arrangements "include adequate international guarantees of non-interference, not only for Vietnam but for Cambodia and Laos as well." (4) An amnesty must be provided for all persons involved in the Vietnamese war on all sides "as an essential block to an extension of barbarism and atrocities of the struggle into the subsequent peace. . . ." (5) There must be "a willingness to accept, on all sides, a cease-fire and stand-fast throughout all Vietnam which might well coincide with the initiation of negotiations."

Mansfield pointed out that the above conditions, when juxtaposed with North Vietnam's "4 points," could lead to "the unconditional discussions" that Pres. Johnson had "properly and urgently" sought. Mansfield complained, however, that the U.S. had not yet stated its conditions clearly enough and that "there may still be confusion both at home and abroad" about them.

(Mansfield reported to Pres. Johnson Dec. 19 on an international fact-finding mission he had conducted for the President. After delivering an oral assessment of the trip to the President, Mansfield submitted a written report that, he said Dec. 20, was "to a large extent . . . dominated by the Vietnam issue." Mansfield said he strongly urged the President to seek a negotiated peace. Mansfield had returned to

Washington Dec. 18 after a tour of Europe and Asia with 4 other Senators: Daniel K. Inouye [D., Hawaii], Edmund S. Muskie [D., Me.], George D. Aiken [R., Vt.] and J. Caleb Boggs [R., Del.]. After meeting with Soviet officials and other East European leaders in November, Mansfield and his party had traveled to the Middle East, Southeast Asia and the Far East. The Mansfield mission had met with South Vietnamese leaders in Saigon Dec. 2-4.)

British Commonwealth Mission Fails

A 4-nation British Commonwealth mission was formed at the opening session of a 21-nation Commonwealth conference in London June 17 in an effort to find a way to end the war in Vietnam. The Commonwealth's peace effort collapsed immediately, however, when Communist China, North Vietnam and the USSR refused to accept the mission's projected visits to their respective capitals. (The mission also was to visit Washington and Saigon.)

Prime Min. Wilson sent leftwing Labor MP Harold Davies to Hanoi July 8-13 to persuade the North Vietnamese to withdraw their rejection, but this effort, too, proved unavailing. (Wilson had been named chairman of the mission. Its other members were Pres. Kwame Nkrumah of Ghana, Prime Min. Sir Abubakar Tafawa Balewa of Nigeria and Prime Min. Eric E. Williams of Trinidad & Tobago.)

A communiqué issued at the conclusion of the Commonwealth conference June 25 stated the mission's "ultimate objectives" to be: (1) "A suspension of all United States air attacks on North Vietnam." (2) A North Vietnamese halt in "the movement of any military forces or assistance or matériel to South Vietnam." (3) "A total cease-fire on all sides to enable a conference to seek a peaceful solution."

The first rejection of the Commonwealth mission came from the Soviet Union June 23. A Moscow statement said the USSR was "not authorized" to conduct talks with the peace group.

Communist China rejected the mission's proposed visit to Peiping in a note handed June 25 to the British *chargé d'affaires.* A Foreign Ministry message assailed Britain for "siding with U.S. aggressors against the Vietnamese people" and for having "actively supported the 'unconditional discussions swindle' of the United States." The Chinese Communist news agency Hsinhua reported June 27 that the National Liberation Front had refused to meet with the mission. The NLF statement charged that the Commonwealth group was "aimed at peddling the 'peaceful negotiation' swindle" of Pres. Johnson.

North Vietnam turned down the proposed visit of the Commonwealth peace group to Hanoi July 1. In a broadcast from Hanoi, the official North Vietnamese press agency said: "We do not receive [Prime Min.] Wilson's mission because we have every reason for doubting Mr. Wilson's 'goodwill' for peace." The broadcast said North Vietnam regarded the mission as "only a repetition of Lyndon Johnson's 'peace negotiations' swindle." North Vietnam announced its rejection of Davies' mediation efforts July 10. In a speech to the House of Commons July 15, Wilson said that Davies had conferred with subordinate North Vietnamese officials during a July 8-13 stay in Hanoi but was rebuffed in his attempts to see North Vietnamese Pres. Ho Chi Minh or Premier Phan Van Dong. Davies, Wilson explained, "had to struggle against the evident conviction on the part of his North Vietnam hearers that their prospects of victory were too imminent for it to be worth their while to forsake the battlefield for the conference table."

UN Gets U.S. Peace Plea

The U.S. July 30 formally called on the UN Security Council to help settle the Vietnamese war. In a letter sent to Council Pres. Platon D. Morozov of the USSR, U.S. Amb.-to-UN Arthur J. Goldberg expressed hope that the Council "will somehow find the means to respond effectively to the challenge raised by the present state of affairs in Southeast Asia." Goldberg pledged that the U.S. would "collaborate unconditionally with members of the Security Council in the search for an acceptable formula to restore peace and security to that area of the world."

(Goldberg's note did not specifically ask for a Council meeting. Heretofore, the U.S. had been averse to having the Vietnamese situation debated by the Council on the ground that North Vietnam did not recognize UN authority. In suggesting Council action, the U.S. sought to use a possible meeting to explain its own actions in Vietnam.)

A Presidential appeal delivered to Thant by Goldberg July 28 had requested vigorous UN efforts to bring about peace talks on Vietnam. Thant's reply, handed to Goldberg July 29, lauded Mr. Johnson for his "reassurance that your government attaches highest importance to the work" of the UN.

A North Vietnamese policy statement issued Aug. 2 by Deputy Foreign Min. Nguyen Co Thach rejected UN intercession in Vietnam. The statement reiterated Hanoi's conditions for ending the conflict: an immediate halt in U.S. air attacks on North Vietnam and withdrawal of U.S. troops from South Vietnam. North Vietnamese Pres. Ho Chi Minh said in an interview published Aug. 13 in the Paris newspaper *Le Monde* that North Vietnam's conditions for participating in negotiations still required the U.S. to give "tangible proof of its acceptance" of Hanoi's 4-point peace formula. (Ho had promised July 20 that his people would fight another 20 years or longer to achieve victory in Vietnam. The statement was issued on the 11th anniversary of the Geneva accords on Vietnam.)

A Chinese Communist government statement Sept. 1 said Peiping opposed UN "intervention in the Vietnamese question." The Vietnamese situation, the statement insisted, had "nothing to do with the United Nations," and the UN had "absolutely no say on that question." The statement said the U.S. was "seeking to make use of the United Nations" in promoting its own "peace-talk scheme," which had "met with rebuffs everywhere." Peiping's opposition to UN intervention was restated by Premier Chou En-lai in an interview made public Sept. 12.

Johnson Rejects Ghanaian Peace Plea

Pres. Johnson Aug. 6 rejected a request of Ghanaian Pres. Kwame Nkrumah that air strikes against North Vietnam be temporarily "halted so that it would be safe for him [Nkrumah] to go to Hanoi" to discuss possible peace moves with North Vietnamese officials. Nkrumah's request was made in a letter handed to the President in Washington Aug. 6 by Ghanaian Foreign Min. Alex Quaison-Sackey. White House Press Secy. Bill D. Moyers disclosed Aug. 7 that in reply, Mr. Johnson had "asked Pres. Nkrumah to tell Hanoi that our military resistance would end when the aggression ends." Moyers reported that the President had told Quaison-Sackey that if Nkrumah "visits Hanoi and arrives at an arrangement which would open the way to peace, he, Pres. Johnson, would, of course, be prepared to add his full weight to initiatives arising out of that visit."

Nkrumah's letter to Mr. Johnson was prompted by a reply of North Vietnamese Pres. Ho Chi Minh to a mission to Hanoi July 26-29 led by Ghanaian Amb.-to-Britain Kwesi Armah. Armah had sought to arrange a meeting of Ho and Nkrumah in the North Vietnamese capital. Ho had said he could not guarantee Nkrumah's safety because of the U.S. air raids on North Vietnam.

Pres. Johnson Aug. 3 had reiterated that the U.S. would neither extend the war nor withdraw American troops from South Vietnam. In a White House address to the International Platform Association, the President called advocates of either policy misguided and insensitive to the U.S.' rôle in Southeast Asia.

Chrmn. J. W. Fulbright (D., Ark.) of the Senate Foreign Relations Committee suggested Oct. 24 that U.S. air strikes against North Vietnam be halted for a longer period than the May suspension to encourage peace talks. In a reply made through Presidential Press Secy. Moyers, Mr. Johnson said Oct. 25 that the U.S. would suspend the air strikes if there were indications that such action would lead to negotiations.

U.S. Rejected Hanoi Peace Overture?

Correspondent Eric Sevareid reported in a *Look* magazine article published Nov. 15 that the U.S. had rejected a Hanoi proposal in the fall of 1964 that U.S. and North Vietnamese representatives meet in Rangoon, Burma to discuss a possible means of ending the Vietnam war.

Sevareid wrote that in an interview in London July 12 with U.S. Amb.-to-UN Adlai E. Stevenson, 2 days before Stevenson's death, the ambassador had said that the North Vietnamese offer had been relayed to him by UN Secy. Gen. Thant. According to Sevareid: "Someone in Washington insisted that this attempt be postponed until after the Presidential election. When the election was over, U Thant again pursued the matter; Hanoi was still willing to send its man. But Defense Secy. Robert S. McNamara, Adlai went on, flatly opposed the attempt: He said the South Vietnamese government would have to be informed and that this would have a demoralizing effect on them; that government was shaky enough as it was. Stevenson told me that U Thant was furious over the failure of his patient efforts but said nothing publicly."

Sevareid said Thant had proposed to Stevenson "an outright cease-fire, with a truce line to be drawn across not only Vietnam but neighboring Laos." Thant's proposal, Sevareid said, was coupled with a suggestion that "U.S. officials could write the terms of the cease-fire offer, exactly as they saw fit, and he, U Thant, would announce it in exactly these words." McNamara "turned this down, and from Secy. Rusk there was no response, to Stevenson's knowledge," Sevareid reported.

State Department spokesman Robert J. McCloskey Nov. 15 confirmed the North Vietnamese peace feeler. But McCloskey denied that McNamara had any rôle in proposed peace talks or that Thant had made the cease-fire proposals as reported by Sevareid. McCloskey said: "We saw nothing to indicate that Hanoi was prepared for peace talks, and the Secretary of State said he would recognize it when it came. His antenna is sensitive."

McNamara said Nov. 16 that the report that he had opposed peace talks with North Vietnam in 1964 was "totally false."

The State Department Nov. 17 confirmed another North Vietnamese peace feeler that had been made May 20, 1965 in talks held in Paris by a Hanoi representative and French officials. The department pointed out, however, that the North Vietnamese had merely restated Hanoi's 4 points, which had been rejected by Washington. The department said that since April Hanoi had not indicated "modifications" of its peace terms in contacts made by 3d parties.

In apparent reply to the Sevareid article, Rusk Nov. 26 further clarified the U.S.' position on North Vietnam's 1964 peace feelers. Rusk said that at the time it had appeared "beyond a . . . doubt that Hanoi was not prepared to discuss peace in Southeast Asia based upon" the Geneva accords. "Indeed, in the latter part of 1964 Hanoi increased its infiltration, including units of its regular army. They undoubtedly felt they were on the threshold of victory. Just yesterday Hanoi denied that they had made any proposals for negotiations." Rusk's latter reference was to a report by *Nhan Dan,* North Vietnam's Communist Party newspaper, that Hanoi had not proposed negotiations to end the Vietnam war. *Nhan Dan* said: "An American newspaper even fabricated the legend that since last fall Hanoi has 2 or 3 times proposed negotiations."

In an address at a fund-raising luncheon for the Dag Hammarskjöld Memorial Scholarship Fund in New York Nov. 16, Thant called on nations involved in the Vietnamese conflict to make "major concessions" to help pave the way for peace talks. Alluding to the U.S.' alleged rejection of North Vietnam's peace feeler in 1964, Thant said that if "bold steps" had been taken that year the current crisis could have been averted.

USSR Rejects British Bid

British Foreign Secy. Michael Stewart conferred with Soviet Premier Aleksei N. Kosygin and other Soviet officials in Moscow Nov. 30-Dec. 2 in a fruitless effort to persuade the USSR to join Britain in reconvening the Geneva conference on Indochina to negotiate an end to the Vietnamese fighting. At a meeting with Stewart Dec. 1, Soviet Foreign Min. Andrei Gromyko said peace talks were conditioned on the halting of U.S. air strikes against North Vietnam and the withdrawal of U.S. troops from South Vietnam.

Stewart used Moscow TV Dec. 2 to appeal for an international conference. Stewart suggested that the proposed parley "arrange a cease-fire" and "then make arrangements whereby both North and South Vietnam could be left in peace, assured they would not be attacked by each other or anyone else."

A Soviet note handed to the British embassy in Moscow Dec. 6 proposed that Britain and the USSR jointly condemn U.S. military action in Vietnam. London diplomatic sources said Dec. 8 that a British reply to the Soviet message expressed strong disagreement with it.

New North Vietnam Bid Reported

The U.S. government disclosed Dec. 17 that North Vietnamese Pres. Ho Chi Minh had relayed through 2 private Italian intermediaries an offer of talks with the U.S. to negotiate an end of the Vietnamese war. A North Vietnamese statement Dec. 18 called the reports of Hanoi peace feelers "sheer groundless fabrications."

The reputed North Vietnamese offer was aired publicly when the U.S. State Department Dec. 17 published an exchange of letters between Italian Foreign Min. Amintore Fanfani, in his capacity as president of the UN General Assembly, and State Secy. Rusk. Fanfani, in a letter written to Pres. Johnson Nov. 20 and relayed through U.S. Amb.-to-UN Goldberg, said that the 2 Italian go-betweens, later identified as ex-Florence Mayor Giorgio La Pira, 61, and Mario Primicerio, 25, both University of Florence professors, had informed him that they had conferred in Hanoi Nov. 11 with Ho and Premier Pham Van Dong. Fanfani said that Ho and Dong had expressed "the strong desire to find a peaceful solution to the conflict in Vietnam."

Fanfani gave this summary of Hanoi's peace terms contained in a letter sent him by La Pira and handed him Nov. 19 in New York by Primicerio: A cease-fire in all of Vietnam, North as well as South; a halt in the further debarkation of U.S. troops in South Vietnam; a declaration that Hanoi's 4-point peace formula was "in reality the explanation" of the 1954 Geneva agreements on Vietnam.

Fanfani quoted the 2 intermediaries as saying that Hanoi was "prepared to initiate negotiations without first requiring actual withdrawal of the American troops" from South Vietnam.

In a reply handed by Goldberg to Fanfani Dec. 4, Rusk said that Washington did not agree with North Vietnam's contention that its 4-point formula "constitute[d] an authentic interpretation" of the Geneva accords. Rusk added: "Elements in the 4 points, notably in the political program of the so-called National Liberation Front, have no basis in the Geneva agreements. . . ." Rusk said, however, that the U.S. was willing to "include these 4 points for consideration in any peace talks. . . ."

Rusk also questioned Hanoi's truce proposals. He said any cease-fire would have to be on "an equitable and reciprocal basis." Hanoi's formula, Rusk contended, "does not appear to meet this test."

Fanfani replied to Rusk Dec. 13 that he had documented the points raised by Rusk and had been informed Dec. 8 that they had been sent to North Vietnamese officials.

Hanoi's Dec. 18 statement disavowing the peace feelers conceded that Ho and Dong had conferred with La Pira and Primicerio. But the statement said that the State Department's publication of the Fanfani-Rusk exchange was "part" of the U.S.' "peace hoax."

The story of Hanoi's reported peace feeler was first reported Dec. 17 in the *St. Louis Post-Dispatch*. It was written by the newspaper's Washington correspondent, Richard Dudman. It was then that U.S. officials decided to publish the

Fanfani-Rusk exchange to counter what was believed the implication of Dudman's story that Washington had ignored a North Vietnamese peace overture and that Washington's repeated offers to negotiate were insincere.

Amb. Goldberg said Dec. 19 that the U.S.' disclosure of the Fanfani-Rusk exchange was premature. But he said it was necessary because "there has been great concern as to whether we . . . really are pursuing what has been said is a path to peace . . . and the credibility of our government has been assailed."

Other U.S. attempts to contact Hanoi had been reported Dec. 1 by Goldberg and Rusk. Goldberg said that the U.S.' UN mission had asked Communist delegations "whether there is willingness to enter into an equitable arrangement for a cease-fire that would call for a diminution of military activities on both sides." The North Vietnamese, Goldberg said, had not responded.

Rusk, in a speech before the White House Conference on International Cooperation, said: "We have been trying to find out" from "the other side" "regularly every week," whether the halting of U.S. air strikes against North Vietnam would hasten peace talks. Hanoi, Rusk said, had been "unwilling to give an answer."

The *N.Y. Times* reported Dec. 2 that UN Secy. Gen. U Thant, acting through intermediaries, had recently inquired of North Vietnam whether it was interested in peace negotiations but that Hanoi rejected his overture. A *Times* report Dec. 3 said that in July Hanoi had refused to accept 2 letters in which Thant had proposed arrangements for peace talks.

U.S. Starts Massive Peace Drive

As 1965 drew to a close, the U.S. launched a concerted peace drive to seek an end to the Vietnamese war. High-ranking emissaries, personally representing Pres. Johnson, began to leave Washington Dec. 27 for world capitals to restate the U.S.' Vietnam policy and to sound out the possibilities of achieving a negotiated settlement. The diplomatic moves were preceded Dec. 24-25 by a one-day Christmas truce agreed to by the U.S. and the Viet Cong and by a U.S. decision to suspend air strikes against North Vietnam as an extension of the short-lived cease-fire. The bombing pause continued through Dec. 31.

The international missions were conducted by Amb. Goldberg, Amb.-at-Large W. Averell Harriman, Vice Pres. Humphrey and Presidential Asst. McGeorge Bundy.

Humphrey left Washington Dec. 27 for a 5-day tour of Japan, Nationalist China, South Korea and the Philippines. He arrived in Tokyo Dec. 28 and conferred the following day with Japanese Premier Eisaku Sato. He left later Dec. 29 for Manila, where he attended the inauguration of Philippine Pres. Ferdinand Marcos Dec. 30. Humphrey met later in Manila with Thai Foreign Min. Thant Khoman and conferred with Marcos Dec. 31.

On the first leg of his mission, Goldberg conferred with Pope Paul VI in Rome Dec. 29. Goldberg transmitted a message from Pres. Johnson describing the pontiff's pleas Dec. 19 and 24 for a cease-fire as "helpful in bringing about a Christmas truce." (The pope was reported to have sent messages Dec. 24 thanking Pres. Johnson, North Vietnamese Pres. Ho Chi Minh and South Vietnamese Chief of State Nguyen Van Thieu for accepting the Christmas truce. In a reply to the pope, sent Dec. 28 and made public Dec. 29, Ho thanked him "for the interest you show in the problem of peace in Vietnam." The remainder of Ho's reply was largely a reiteration of Hanoi's accusation against the U.S.)

Goldberg Dec. 30 discussed Vietnam with Premier Aldo Moro and other Italian leaders. Goldberg then flew to Paris and met with French Pres. Charles de Gaulle Dec. 31. Goldberg said at a news briefing later that he had told de Gaulle of Pres. Johnson's conviction that the conflict "can only be settled at the conference table without prior conditions." (In a year-end message, de Gaulle criticized the U.S. and the USSR for creating "painful tension in numerous countries.")

The U.S.' position on Vietnam was explained by Harriman in Warsaw Dec. 29 in talks with Polish Foreign Min. Adam Rapacki. Harriman flew to Yugoslavia Dec. 30 to confer with Pres. Tito. Harriman's itinerary provided for stopovers in several Asian and Southeast Asian capitals.

Bundy met with Canadian Prime Min. Lester B. Pearson in Ottawa Dec. 29. A statement issued by Pearson Dec. 30 expressed "appreciation and support for the latest American effort to find a peaceful solution to the conflict in Vietnam."

AGGRESSION FROM THE NORTH

U.S. White Paper Accuses Hanoi

In a white paper released Feb. 27, the U.S. State Department charged that "massive evidence" established "beyond question that North Vietnam is carrying out a carefully conceived plan of aggression against" South Vietnam. The 14,000-word document was entitled "Aggression from the North—the Record of North Vietnam's Campaign to Conquer South Vietnam." It charged that Hanoi's military assistance to the Viet Cong was in violation of the UN Charter and the 1954 Geneva conference agreements on Indochina and was "a fundamental threat to the freedom and security of South Vietnam." The report cited testimony of North Vietnamese soldiers who either had defected or had been captured after being sent South by Hanoi.

Among major accusations made in the white paper:

● "The hard core of the Communist forces attacking South Vietnam were trained in the North. . . . They are ordered into the South [by Hanoi] and remain under the military discipline of the military command in Hanoi. Special training camps operated by the North Vietnamese army give political and military training to the infiltrators."

● "Since 1959 nearly 20,000 Viet Cong officers, soldiers and technicians are known to have entered South Vietnam" through Hanoi's "infiltration pipeline" "under orders from Hanoi." These infiltrators were "well-trained officers, cadres and specialists." Viet Cong forces had increased from less than 20,000 in 1961 to 35,000.

(It was reported in Saigon Mar. 28 that 12 destroyers and minesweepers of the U.S. 7th Fleet had started 2 weeks previously to patrol the Vietnamese coast from the 17th Parallel to the Cambodian border in the Gulf of Siam to keep North Vietnamese supply boats from reaching the Viet Cong. Navy planes also patrolled the area. The U.S. planes and ships were under instruction to shoot back if fired on.)

Kosygin Visits Hanoi, Signs Defense Pact

Soviet Premier Aleksei N. Kosygin had conferred with Pres. Ho Chi Minh and other North Vietnamese leaders during a visit to Hanoi Feb. 6-10. Principal topics of discussion were Soviet military and economic aid to North Vietnam and the Sino-Soviet dispute. In a speech at a Hanoi rally Feb. 7, Kosygin said Moscow "was ready to give" North Vietnam "all necessary assistance if aggressors dare to encroach upon" its "independence and sovereignty." He said the USSR "severely warns the United States against its schemes to provoke acts of war against North Vietnam." (Kosygin's remarks were made prior to the announcement later Feb. 7 of the first U.S. air strikes.)

A joint Soviet-North Vietnamese communiqué signed by Kosygin Feb. 10 said agreement had been reached "on steps that should be taken to strengthen the defense potential" of North Vietnam. The communiqué said the 2 nations would conduct regular defense discussions. The defense pact was ratified Mar. 26 by the Soviet Communist Party's Central Committee.

Red China Threatens to Send Troops

As air and ground fighting intensified in Vietnam, Communist China sounded several warnings in March and April of possible military intervention on the side of the Viet Cong guerrillas.

A Peiping statement, appearing Mar. 25 in the Communist Party newspaper *Jenmin Jih Pao,* said: "We Chinese people . . . will join the people of the whole world in sending . . . material aid, including arms and other war materials, to the heroic South Vietnamese people who are battling fearlessly." China was "ready to send" its "own men whenever the South Vietnamese people want them, to fight together with the South Vietnamese people to annihilate the United States aggressors." "All negotiations with the United States imperialists at this moment are utterly useless if they still refuse to withdraw from South Vietnam. . . ."

The Chinese statement was made in support of an appeal that had been issued Mar. 24 by the National Liberation Front (NLF), the Viet Cong's political arm. The NLF had declared itself "ready to receive all assistance, including weapons and all other war materials, from their friends in the 5 continents." The front warned that if the U.S. "imperialists continue to commit . . . combat troops and those of their satellites to South Vietnam and continue to extend the war to North Vietnam and Laos, the . . . front will call on the people of various countries" for troops.

Communist Chinese Premier Chou En-lai predicted that "the Chinese and Russian people will close ranks" and fight side by side in the event the U.S. precipitated a major war in Southeast Asia. In a Peiping interview published Mar. 25 by the Paris weekly *Nouvel Observateur,* Chou warned that Pres. Johnson, "who is dancing on the tightrope of war and doesn't know how to turn around, is risking some surprises." Chou said that China supported demands by the NLF and North Vietnam for withdrawal of U.S. forces from South Vietnam. Chou declared Mar. 28, during a visit to Tirana, Albania, that his country was "ready to give all help at any time to the Vietnamese people."

Chinese Foreign Min. Chen Yi Mar. 28 said China would "exert every effort" to send military matériel to the Viet Cong, and troops also, if they were needed. Chen's statement was made in reply to a letter from North Vietnamese Foreign Min. Xuan Thuy, who had accused the U.S. of aggression in Vietnam.

A further threat to send troops was made in a resolution adopted Apr. 20 by the Chinese National People's Congress. The congress' standing committee urged "the people's organizations and the people throughout the country" "to make full preparations to send their own people to fight together with the Vietnamese people and drive out the United States aggressors in the event the United States imperialism continues to escalate its war of aggression and the Vietnamese people need them."

McNamara Reports Hanoi Troop Rôle

U.S. Defense Secy. Robert S. McNamara reported Apr. 26 that North Vietnamese "infiltration both of arms and personnel into South Vietnam" had increased despite the air raids on Communist supply routes in the north.

McNamara said: This infiltration "continues to play a vital rôle in providing the Communist Viet Cong" with the means "to carry on their insurgency." "Recent evidence both from captured prisoners and . . . documents has increased our estimate of the number of infiltrators to a total of 39,000." At least 5,000-8,000 and possibly 10,000 Communist soldiers had been brought clandestinely into South Vietnam from North Vietnam during 1964. The presence of a regular 400-500-man North Vietnamese army battalion in South Vietnam had definitely been established, and the unit had been identified as the 2d Battalion of the 101st Regiment, 325th Division, based in Kontum Province, in the north central highlands area around Pleiku. The air strikes against North Vietnam had "slowed down the movement of men and matériel."

In a further report on Communist strength in South Vietnam, McNamara said June 16 that there were indications that 8 other North Vietnamese battalions were in position in the Pleiku-Kontum area. McNamara estimated the Viet Cong force at 65,000 regular combat and combat-support troops and 80,000-100,000 part-time guerrillas. In addition, he said, there were 30,000 Viet Cong "serving in political and propaganda activities in South Vietnam." McMamara conceded that the air strikes against North Vietnam, whose basic objective was to disrupt the southward flow of arms and men from North Vietnam, had failed to stop the infiltration. Mc-Namara said that with South Vietnam's entire force totaling 574,000 men, the government had less than a 4-1 advantage and "less than the force required to deal effectively with the type of military and terrorist threat" posed by the Viet Cong.

Viet Cong Holds 'Congress'

North Vietnam's official news agency reported May 13 that the Viet Cong had held its first "congress" May 2-6 in a "liberated area" of South Vietnam. The news agency said the meeting had been attended by National Liberation Front Pres. Nguyen Huu Tho and the Viet Cong's 150 "outstanding cadres and fighters." The news agency quoted Tho as having declared in an address that "this congress is an expression of the determination of our entire army and people to fight and defeat the United States aggressors."

(Maj. Gen. Song Hao, political commissar of North Vietnam's armed forces, was reported May 16 to have declared that North Vietnam was "in a state of war." In an article written for the armed forces, Song exhorted the country's soldiers to "make a mighty and timely change in their thought, organization . . . and daily activities to fulfill the task of struggling to protect North Vietnam and support . . . the liberation revolution in South Vietnam.")

Johnson Says War Aids Chinese Plan

Pres. Johnson declared May 13 that Communist China "apparently" wanted to continue the Vietnamese war despite the fact that "it would clearly be in the interest of North Vietnam to now come to the conference table." For North Vietnam, he said, "continuation of war without talks means only damage without conquest." However, he said, Communist China's target, "whatever the cost to their allies," was "not merely South Vietnam" nor "fulfillment of Vietnamese nationalism" but the domination of "all of Asia." "In this domination they shall never succeed," Mr. Johnson asserted.

The remarks were made in a nationally televised address before the Association of American Editorial Cartoonists. The

President said that "there is no purely military solution in sight for either side" and that the U.S. was "ready for unconditional discussions."

Chinese Criticize Soviet Aid

Soviet assistance to North Vietnam became the subject of a new feud between Peiping and Moscow. Communist China charged Dec. 22 that "so far a great part of the Soviet military equipment supplied to [North] Vietnam consisted of

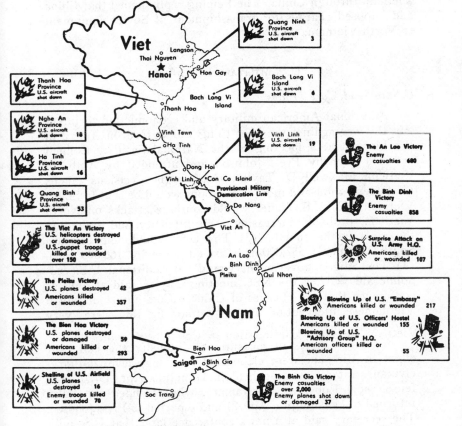

A Communist view. Headlines on map in Chinese Communist propaganda booklet read: "Victories Won by the Vietnamese People in Their Struggle Against U. S. Aggression (From Aug. 5, 1964 to Apr. 5, 1965)"

obsolete equipment discarded by the Soviet armed forces or damaged weapons cleaned out from the warehouse." The statement, carried in *Jenmin Jih Pao,* contended that the USSR matériel was "not only far from commensurate with the strength of the Soviet Union but also far below the aid the Soviet Union has given the Indian reactionaries."

The Chinese statement was in response to a report in the *N.Y. Times* Dec. 3 that Peiping was insisting that the USSR pay China in dollars for Soviet goods shipped to North Vietnam through China. The Peiping reply denied that China had imposed charges for transshipment of Soviet equipment to North Vietnam.

U.S. MILITARY BUILD-UP

U.S. to Send More Troops

Additional American military and economic aid to intensify the war against the Viet Cong was agreed on Apr. 2 in Washington at a meeting of the National Security Council presided over by Pres. Johnson and attended by Amb.-to-Vietnam Maxwell D. Taylor. Among the decisions taken: (1) Several thousand more U.S. troops would be sent to South Vietnam. (2) U.S. planes would continue attacks on North Vietnam, probably increasing their intensity and extending the raids further north. (3) The U.S. would help increase South Vietnam's 557,000-man armed force by 160,000 men. (4) The Saigon government would get additional U.S. economic aid. (After the NSC meeting Taylor said at a news conference that the chances of Chinese Communist or North Vietnamese intervention in the Vietnam fighting were "very slight at the present time.")

The new series of measures to intensify the U.S. war effort in Vietnam were elaborated at a high-level military-civilian strategy meeting held in Honolulu Apr. 19-20. Defense Secy. Robert S. McNamara, who attended the talks, returned to Washington Apr. 21 and reported to Pres. Johnson. The secretary said at a news conference later that U.S. military aid to South Vietnam would be increased from $207 million to $330 million a year. He said U.S. air and logistical support for the Vietnamese forces also would be raised. More helicopter and air support would be provided to help the South Vietnamese troops counter greater infiltration from North Vietnam, McNamara said.

The Administration confirmed publicly in July that it was considering a limited mobilization of U.S. military manpower to cope with increasing Communist guerrilla pressure in Vietnam. The disclosure was made by Pres. Johnson at his news conference July 9. (The major measures under study by the Administration: an increase in defense expenditures; the call-up of armed forces reservists; larger draft quotas; the extension of enlistments of men currently on active military service.) Replying to a reporter's request for his assessment of the current situation in Vietnam, the President said he expected "that it will get worse before it gets better" and that an enlarged military effort would be needed to face mounting Communist attacks. (The Defense Department revealed Aug. 3 that it had increased the monthly draft quotas to 27,400 men in September—up 10,400 over August—and to 33,600 men in October. It also announced that for the first time since 1956 the Navy would get draftees—4,600 men.)

McNamara headed a U.S. fact-finding mission to South Vietnam July 16-21. McNamara and his party conferred with South Vietnamese government leaders, were briefed by U.S. military officers and toured the battle areas. Summarizing the findings of his mission, McNamara said at a news conference in Saigon July 21 before departing for Washington: "The over-all situation continues to be serious. . . . There has been deterioration since I was here last, 15 months ago. The size of the Viet Cong forces has increased; their rate of operations and the intensity of their attacks has been expanded; their disruption of the lines of communications, both rail and sea and road, is much more extensive; and they have intensified their campaign of terror against the civilian population." "But the picture is not all black. . . . The Vietnamese people continue to be willing to fight and . . . die in their own defense. The Viet Cong . . . are suffering increasingly heavy losses, and the U.S. combat forces are adding substantially to the military power of the government."

Johnson Orders Troop Expansion

Pres. Johnson announced July 28 that he had ordered U.S. military forces in Vietnam increased from 75,000 men to 125,-000. In a prepared statement read at his White House news conference and broadcast to a nationwide radio-TV audience, Mr. Johnson added that he would order further military increases if such action were dictated by the course of the war.

The President's decision followed 8 days of almost daily conferences held in the White House to discuss U.S. strategy in the light of Defense Secy. McNamara's report that the Vietnamese military situation had deteriorated. The White House meetings had been attended by McNamara, State Secy. Rusk, Gen. Earle G. Wheeler, chairman of the Joint Chiefs of Staff, McGeorge Bundy, special Presidential assistant for national security affairs, and other top officials. The President had discussed his decision with Congressional leaders of both parties at a White House meeting July 27.

Mr. Johnson said in his July 28 announcement that he had ordered several military units dispatched to Vietnam, among them the Airmobile (First Cavalry) Division. This action "almost immediately" would raise U.S. military manpower in that country by 50,000. He said that to fill the envisaged increase in current and future manpower needs for Vietnam, military draft calls would be raised from 17,000 monthly to a rate of 35,000 and the campaign for voluntary enlistments in the armed forces would be intensified.

Mr. Johnson coupled his announcement with a reaffirmation of the U.S.' readiness to seek a negotiated end to the Vietnam conflict. He said that several attempts had been made to win agreement to such negotiations but that all had been rejected by Communist China and North Vietnam. The U.S.' aim, he declared, was not to expand the struggle but to frustrate Communist aggression to the point where the instigators of the war would be forced to the negotiating table. The U.S., he said, would persist until "death and desolation" had brought the same peaceful solution that currently could be had at much lower cost. He appealed for the intercession of the UN and any of its 114 member states to bring about

peace talks and announced that the U.S. had begun a major
initiative to stimulate UN action in this direction.

The U.S. decision to expand its military forces in Vietnam evoked violent denunciations from the Communists and
elicited renewed pledges to aid the Viet Cong and North Vietnam military effort:

● Moscow radio warned July 28 that Pres. Johnson was taking "a colossal risk" in causing "an escalation of the war." The
statement said that the "accumulation of military potential
. . . can easily reach a critical point beyond which it will not
be possible to control events." Soviet Premier Aleksei N.
Kosygin said Aug. 6 that Moscow "regards the new [U.S.]
step . . . as aggressive acts tending to widen the war in Vietnam." (Kosygin had declared July 17 that "every new aggressive act in Vietnam undertaken by the Americans . . . will be
followed by an appropriate rebuff from the Communist camp."
The USSR, he asserted, would render "all the aid necessary
to repel the aggression. . . ." The Soviet news agency Tass
had announced July 11 that the USSR had signed an agreement July 10 with a North Vietnamese delegation to provide
for aid "over and above that already being rendered.")

● A Chinese Communist statement Aug. 7 reminded the U.S.
that Peiping already had "pledged to the Vietnamese people
our all-out support . . . up to and including the sending of our
men to fight . . . with them." The statement condemned Pres.
Johnson for "announcing the sending of large reinforcements
to South Vietnam [while] he hypocritically talked about
America's willingness to begin unconditional discussions with any
government at any place at any time." (The N.Y. Times reported from Hong Kong Nov. 30 that Communist China was
providing North Vietnam with increased military and industrial equipment and that China had assigned service troops
to help maintain Chinese-North Vietnamese railroad links.
The N.Y. Times said that Chinese engineer troops were in North
Vietnam helping repair bridges destroyed by U.S. air raids.
China granted North Vietnam a series of loans [amount un-
disclosed] under an agreement signed in Peiping Dec. 5. The
2 nations also signed a "protocol on mutual supply of com-
modities and payments for 1966." The Chinese were reportedly

sending North Vietnam trucks, steel for bombed-out bridges and other material.)

• A Viet Cong statement issued Aug. 3 and made public by Hanoi radio Aug. 7 urged "the North Vietnamese people to actively assist the South Vietnamese people in all fields in order to increase our forces and step up the resistance of the war 10 times more vigorously with a view to winning back and preserving the independence of the fatherland."

(In a military assessment of the situation in Vietnam, Adm. U. S. Grant Sharp Jr., U.S. Commander in Chief, Pacific, said at his headquarters in Honolulu Oct. 21 that U.S. and South Vietnamese forces had "stopped losing" the war and that "there's no doubt we can stay in there until we've got it cleared up." Sharp, back from a trip to Southeast Asia, including South Vietnam, said: "Today, the Vietnamese can see a possibility of winning, whereas they didn't a few months ago"; he thought it unlikely that Communist China would intervene in the war since "they have plenty to lose" by such action; China was "actually holding Hanoi's coat while encouraging the North Vietnamese to do the fighting.")

McNamara announced Nov. 11 that the Administration "believe[d] it will be necessary to add further to the strength of United States combat forces in Vietnam." McNamara disclosed the decision after discussing the matter earlier in the day with Pres. Johnson, State Secy. Rusk and other Administration officials at the President's Texas ranch. McNamara said that in the previous 4 weeks he had received requests from U.S. commanders in Vietnam for more men. McNamara said U.S. and South Vietnamese forces had defeated the Viet Cong's monsoon offensive, intended to cut South Vietnam in half at its narrow waist and to destroy the South Vietnamese force. The guerrillas, McNamara said, thus far this year had suffered 100% higher losses than for a comparable period in 1964. Despite the rising casualties, McNamara said, Viet Cong forces had continued to increase.

It was reported in Saigon Dec. 4 that U.S. military leaders had asked McNamara, during a visit to South Vietnam Nov. 28-29, to increase U.S. military forces in Vietnam to 350,000-

400,000 men. Current U.S. military strength there had reached 170,000 men. A U.S. official was quoted as saying that "a significant increase in [U.S.] troop numbers is necessary just to keep up with the game." U.S. military authorities cited the need to reinforce the First Cavalry Division (Airmobile) with another division or 2 to secure the Central Highlands area, scene of fierce fighting in the previous 3 months.

McNamara, addressing reporters in Saigon Nov. 29, had asserted that the "decision by the Viet Cong to stand and fight" despite powerful U.S. attacks "expressed a determination to carry on the conflict which can lead to only one conclusion—that it will be a long war." McNamara added that the recent fighting in the Central Highlands and the killing of thousands of Viet Cong and North Vietnamese troops there represented a "clear decision on the part of Hanoi to escalate the level of infiltration and to raise the level of the conflict."

Advance elements of the U.S. 25th Infantry Division arrived in Pleiku by plane Dec. 29 from their base in Hawaii. U.S. officials described the 14-hour 7,000-mile flight as the longest combat airlift in history. The rest of the division's 20,000 troops were scheduled to reach South Vietnam in 1966. The division's arrival would bring to more than 200,000 the number of U.S. military personnel in Vietnam, exclusive of 7th Fleet units stationed in the South China Sea.

Australian Troops Arrive

The first contingent of Australian troops to be sent to fight in Vietnam—111 infantrymen—arrived by plane in Saigon June 2 to join U.S. 173d Airborne Brigade troops in protecting the Bienhoa airbase 12 miles from Saigon. An additional 400 Australian soldiers arrived in Bienhoa June 8 after having landed earlier that day in troopships. Australia had earmarked the 800-man First Battalion of the Royal Australian Regiment for service in Vietnam, but Defense Min. Shane D. Paltridge had disclosed May 26 that logistical support units would bring his country's force there to about 1,000 men. Australia already had about 80 military advisers serving with the South Vietnamese army. Prime Min. Sir Robert Gordon Menzies had announced Apr. 29 that the troops were being sent on the request of the South Vietnamese government and in consultation with the U.S.

Menzies June 7 supported U.S. Vietnam policy in a statement made at the White House in Washington after a meeting with Pres. Johnson, State Secy. Dean Rusk and other U.S. officials. Menzies declared that most Australians were "overwhelmingly in favor of what's being done" by the U.S. in Vietnam because they feared if the Communist won in Vietnam the whole world would be endangered. The Soviet Union had joined North Vietnam May 15 in protesting Australia's decision to send troops to South Vietnam. An Australian reply handed Moscow June 1 rejected the Soviet protest and suggested that the USSR instead prevail upon Hanoi and Communist China to end the war in Vietnam.

Lodge Returns as Ambassador

The resignation of Gen. Maxwell D. Taylor as U.S. ambassador to South Vietnam was announced July 8 by the White House. Henry Cabot Lodge, Taylor's predecessor, was

U.S. 173d Airborne Brigade troops after landing by helicopter northwest of Bienhoa May 20 in search of Viet Cong.
(Wide World photo)

renamed to the post. (Lodge had served as ambassador to South Vietnam from June 27, 1963 until his resignation in June 1964 to take part in the campaign for the GOP Presidential nomination.) Lodge arrived in Saigon Aug. 20 to assume his ambassadorial duties. In an exchange of letters between Taylor and Pres. Johnson, Taylor said that "at the time of my acceptance of this post I asked that for personal reasons the duration of the assignment be limited to one year. That year is now past and I feel obliged to request relief. . . ." Johnson replied: "It is with great regret that I accept your resignation. . . . I do so only because I am bound to honor the understanding we had at the time of your appointment."

WAR AGAINST VIET CONG

The bloody fighting of U.S. and South Vietnamese forces against the Viet Cong grew in intensity during 1965.

U.S. Planes Bomb Viet Cong

U.S.-piloted jet planes carried out direct attacks on Viet Cong guerrillas Feb. 18. The beginning of this new phase of U.S. involvement (the Feb. 18 strikes were the first in which no participation by South Vietnamese airmen was reported) was disclosed by the U.S. embassy in Saigon Feb. 24. The embassy revealed that the attacks took place in Binhdinh Province, on the request of the South Vietnamese government, to support government troops. Another attack by U.S. B-57 bombers and F-100 fighter-bombers, from the Bienhoa and Danang air bases, was carried out Feb. 24 in Binhdinh Province, the embassy announced.

The air attacks constituted a departure from previous U.S. policy that American military personnel merely "advise and assist" Vietnamese government troops and fight only in self-defense. In reporting this new development, the State Department said Feb. 24 that the air raids were "carried out because of the concentration of Viet Cong in this area [Binhdinh Province] as a result of increased infiltration of men and equipment in recent months." The department said that "this is consistent with the [Aug. 7, 1964] Congressional resolution

approving and supporting the determination of the President
. . . to prevent any further aggression. . . ."

U.S. military spokesmen in Saigon said the jet attacks
were made possible because for the first time the Viet Cong
were assembling in large formations away from villages.

(2 U.S. Navy nuclear-powered vessels joined the 7th
Fleet in the South China Sea Nov. 26 to take part in the
Vietnam campaign. The ships—the aircraft carrier *Enterprise*
and the guided-missile frigate *Bainbridge*—took up positions
off Saigon, and the *Enterprise's* planes carried out air strikes
against the Viet Cong in South Vietnam.)

(27 U.S. servicemen and 4 South Vietnamese were killed
May 16 when a row of bomb-laden planes exploded at the
Bienhoa air base. 102 men, including 95 Americans, were
injured. More than 40 U.S. and South Vietnamese planes,
including 10 B-57s, were destroyed by explosions and fire.
Maj. Gen. Joseph H. Moore, U.S. Air Force 2d Division commander, described the incident as "an accidental explosion
of a bomb on one aircraft which spread to others." The base's
landing field was reported back to normal operation May 18.)

The expansion of U.S. military action in Vietnam was
heightened June 17 when, for the first time, an attack was
mounted by B-52 heavy jet bombers from the U.S. Strategic
Air Command in Guam, 4,300 miles away. 27 of the planes
bombed a suspected Viet Cong concentration north of the
Binhduong Province town of Bencat, 30 miles north of Saigon.
30 B-52s originally had started out on the raid, but 2 were
destroyed in a collision 40 miles west of the Philippines. (8
crewmen were lost.) A 3d plane returned to Guam with
mechanical trouble.

The B-52s carried out intermittent raids against Viet
Cong targets through July and August. Starting in September
and through the remainder of 1965 the heavy jet bombers
carried out the strike missions at the rate of about one a day.

Americans in Direct Ground Combat

The State Department reported June 8 that Pres. Johnson
had authorized Gen. William C. Westmoreland, commander

of U.S. forces in South Vietnam, to commit his ground troops to direct combat against Viet Cong guerrillas if the South Vietnamese army requested such assistance. Department spokesman Robert J. McCloskey made the disclosure after newsmen asked him what the U.S. response would be if Saigon requested combat aid. McCloskey replied: U.S. commanders had advised the Saigon government that "American forces would be available for combat support with Vietnamese forces when and if necessary." Although the Vietnamese army had not yet asked for such help, U.S. and Vietnamese commanders were working out "coordinating" arrangements. If U.S. troops joined Vietnamese soldiers, they would fight as units under U.S. officers. McCloskey had confirmed June 5 that troops sent to South Vietnam to guard American installations against Viet Cong attacks were engaged in direct combat against the guerrillas. Heretofore, the U.S. had contended that American military personnel were acting solely in an advisory and defensive capacity. But newspaper reports had described the Marines guarding the Danang airbase as conducting "search and clear" operations against the Viet Cong several miles from the base's defense perimeter.

U.S. Army soldiers participated in their first major attack of the Vietnamese war June 28 by joining South Vietnamese and Australian troops in what turned out to be a futile assault against the Viet Cong's Zone D area 20 miles northeast of Saigon. The zone was long regarded as the guerrillas' major stronghold in South Vietnam. In the Zone D operation, about 3,000 U.S. 173d Airborne Division troops teamed up with Vietnamese airborne units and a battalion of 800 Australian soldiers in a probing attack in a jungle area 18 miles wide and 36 miles long. The operation was called off June 30 after the attackers failed to make substantial contact with the enemy. During the 3-day operation, one American was killed and 9 other Americans and 4 Australians were wounded. A U.S. military statement said June 29 that Westmoreland had ordered the U.S. troops from their defensive positions at the nearby Bienhoa air base into Zone D "under the authority previously granted him" and "at the request of the government of Vietnam." The State Department said

June 29 that the operation took place in accordance with the Johnson Administration's policy statement outlining the expanded rôle of U.S. troops. The department said "U.S. and Vietnamese commanders are in charge of their own troops in their respective areas of responsibility."

Ground Fighting Intensified

Among other developments reported during 1965:

Binh Gia battle—South Vietnamese troops remained in possession of Binh Gia after fighting the longest and one of the costliest battles of the Vietnamese conflict. The struggle for the village, 40 miles southeast of Saigon, had started with a guerrilla assault Dec. 28, 1964 and finally ended Jan. 4. The guerrillas' decision to fight a sustained battle against superior ground and air fire-power appeared to be a reversal of their previous tactics. Normally, Viet Cong attacks followed a hit-and-run pattern. A South Vietnamese Defense Ministry report, issued Jan. 5, listed 158 South Vietnamese and 5 Americans killed, 11 Americans and 188 South Vietnamese wounded, 3 Americans and 77 South Vietnamese missing. All of the missing Americans were said to have been taken prisoner by the Viet Cong. U.S. authorities said they had counted the bodies of 102 guerrillas and had seen 20 other Viet Cong dead removed from the battlefield.

South Koreans attacked—South Korean troops who had arrived in South Vietnam Feb. 26 for non-combat duties came under fire for the first time Apr. 3. Guerrillas attacked an ROK engineer camp in Bienhoa Province, about 10 miles northeast of Saigon, wounding 11 Koreans. The defenders returned fire and killed at least one Viet Cong.

Dongxoai battle—U.S.-supported South Vietnamese troops fought off a Viet Cong attack in a fierce 4-day battle June 10-13 in the Phuoclong Province town of Dongxoai, 60 miles northeast of Saigon. An estimated 800-900 government troops were killed or reported missing. U.S. casualties were reported as 7 known killed, 12 missing and presumed dead and 15 wounded. South Vietnamese military sources estimated that 300 Viet Cong had been killed in the ground fighting and

that 400 others had been slain in air strikes on outlying positions. The battle had been started June 10 by 1,500 Viet
Cong who smashed their way into several buildings of the
town's district military headquarters and into an adjoining
militia compound. The guerrillas simultaneously raided a
U.S. Special Forces camp a mile away. The Viet Cong were
beaten off in a see-saw battle with the aid of reinforcements
airlifted to the scene aboard 100 U.S. helicopters and with
the assistance of heavy U.S. air strikes.

Ducco battle—A 3,000-man Viet Cong force Aug. 2 launched
a major drive to capture a South Vietnamese Special Forces
camp at Ducco. The camp, which had been under Communist
siege for more than 2 months, was located 7 miles east of
the Cambodian border on strategic Highway 19 and was 30
miles southwest of the military base at Pleiku. The siege was
finally lifted by a combined U.S.-South Vietnamese force Aug. 11.

In a first attempt to relieve the surrounded garrison, 2
South Vietnamese paratroop battalions of about 1,000 men
were flown in by helicopter Aug. 3 from Pleiku. But guerrilla counterattacks drove the reinforcements back into the camp.
Another government relief force was flown from Pleiku to
Ducco Aug. 9 to facilitate the paratroopers' withdrawal. The
2d relief force failed to reach the camp; it came under sharp
Viet Cong attack and suffered heavy casualties. U.S. advisers
Aug. 9 counted the bodies of 152 Viet Cong killed in the day's
fighting. At least 67 other guerrillas had been slain in the first
week around Ducco. During the early part of the siege, 60 of
the camp's 400 militiamen had been killed or wounded. 2 of
the garrison's 12 U.S. advisers also were slain, and a 3d was
wounded. U.S. troops of the First Infantry Division and the
173d Airborne Brigade were flown Aug. 11 from the Bienhoa
air base to Pleiku. From Pleiku the U.S. troops headed toward
Ducco on Highway 19 and prevented possible Viet Cong
attacks on a 3d South Vietnamese relief force. At this point
the enemy troops withdrew and the U.S. and South Vietnamese units moved into Special Forces camp.

Reds escape Binhdinh trap—A U.S.-South Vietnamese force
of more than 10,000 men opened a major drive in Binhdinh
Province Oct. 10 against an estimated 2,000 Communist troops

—elements of the North Vietnamese 325th Infantry (Song Lo) Division and Viet Cong guerrillas. But the North Vietnamese troops apparently eluded the trap by Oct. 12 and fled. The action—labeled "Operation Shiny Bayonet"—took place in the Suaica River Valley, 275 miles northeast of Saigon. The allied force consisted of (a) more than 5,000 troops of the U.S. First Cavalry Division (participating in their first operation since arriving in September), who were flown into the area by 176 helicopters, and (b) South Vietnamese marines, who moved in by foot.

The offensive was launched following reports that 5 Communist battalions had massed in the Central Highlands region about 25 miles from the First Cavalry's base at Ankhe. The target area was first pounded by U.S. planes based on Guam. Little contact was made with the enemy the first day. But by nightfall Oct. 11 U.S. authorities reported that First Cavalry troops had killed 70 Viet Cong and captured 100. A U.S. battalion guarding a possible escape exit at the western slope of the valley came under attack Oct. 12 by about 100 Viet Cong. It was believed that this action screened the North Vietnamese troops' escape from the allied entrapment. They left behind a 50-bed hospital equipped with U.S. medical supplies, a workshop with 4 new U.S. sewing machines and 10 tons of rice.

Vantuong battle—A force of 5,000-6,000 U.S. Marines Aug. 18-19 destroyed a major Viet Cong guerrilla stronghold near Vantuong on a small peninsula 16 miles south of the U.S. air base at Chulai. 599 Viet Cong of a 2,000-man force were reported killed and 122 captured in the 2-day battle and in a mopping-up operation that was conducted through Aug. 21. Marine casualties were described as substantial. This was the first major ground action fought solely by U.S. troops in Vietnam. (In addition to being pounded by ground forces, the Viet Cong were attacked by Marine jet planes and shelled by 3 U.S. warships.)

Pleime battle—A Viet Cong force of about 1,600 men launched a heavy attack Oct. 19 against a U.S. Special Forces camp at Pleime in the Central Highlands about 215 miles north of Saigon. Repeated guerrilla attacks through Oct. 27 brought some Viet Cong units only 20 yards from the besieged stronghold. Strong resistance by the defenders, supported by several hundred South Vietnamese troop reinforcements and hundreds of air strikes carried out by U.S. and South Vietnamese planes, took a heavy toll of the attackers and prevented the camp from being overrun. South Vietnamese army sources reported Oct. 25 that the air strikes had killed 153 Viet Cong and that an estimated 100 other guerrillas had been slain in the ground fighting. At least 4 U.S. planes were lost in the support action.

A U.S. spokesman in Saigon claimed Oct. 25 that the North Vietnamese army's 32d Regiment had fought alongside the Viet Cong.

The Pleime garrison was defended by 400 *montagnard* tribesmen and 12 U.S. Special Forces advisers and South Vietnamese guerrilla specialists when it first came under attack. 2,000 First Cavalry Division troops brought into the Pleime sector after Oct. 27 were reported to have killed about 106 Communist troops in a mop-up operation west of the camp. A U.S. spokesman reported Nov. 7 that an additional 72 Communist soldiers were slain Nov. 6-7 in a clash with 300 First Cavalry troops 8 miles west of the camp.

Iadrang Valley battle—The bloodiest battle of the war so far was fought Nov. 14-21 by U.S. and North Vietnamese troops against Viet Cong forces in the Iadrang Valley between the Cambodian border and Pleime. The fighting was an extension of the bitter engagement that had been waged around the U.S. Special Forces camp at Pleime since Oct. 19. North Vietnamese units that had sought to elude the search-and-destroy operation of the First Cavalry Division had decided to hold their ground in the Iadrang Valley; they offered stiff resistance. U.S. intelligence officers speculated that the North Vietnamese had halted their withdrawal to protect a possible major staging and supply base in the valley. About 2,000 troops of the North Vietnamese 66th Regiment were reportedly involved in the engagement. U.S. military authorities had identified the presence of 7 other North Vietnamese regiments in the Central Highlands.

First Cavalry troops suffered their heaviest casualties following a 500-man North Vietnamese ambush Nov. 17. Sharp hand-to-hand fighting followed the surprise attack. The Communists broke off the fight after being pounded by U.S. planes. U.S. military authorities said 300 North Vietnamese had been slain, but the effectiveness of the U.S. battalion as a fighting unit was said to have been destroyed.

B-52s from Guam flew missions against the Communists throughout the Iadrang fighting.

A U.S. military spokesman in Saigon reported Nov. 20 that 1,186 North Vietnamese troops had been killed in the Iadrang Valley. North Vietnamese losses since the launching of the attack on the Pleime garrison Oct. 19 were said to total 1,869 killed and 139 captured.

(The conflict in the Iadrang Valley plus other battles fought in the Central Highlands accounted for a record number of U.S. and Communist troops killed and wounded, U.S. authorities reported Nov. 24. The report said that during the week ended Nov. 20 240 U.S. troops had been killed and 470 wounded and that 6 were missing or captured. U.S. and South Vietnamese losses suffered in Central Highlands fighting the previous 7 weeks had totaled more than 2,300 killed; of this number, 678 were Americans. 1,400 U.S. soldiers had been killed or wounded during the previous 3 weeks. This represented 41% of the total allied casualties during that period. During the week ended Nov. 20 a record 2,262 Viet Cong and North Vietnamese troops had been killed. More than 7,000 Viet Cong were reported killed during the previous 7 weeks.)

U.S. Airbases Attacked

Viet Cong demolition units Oct. 27 destroyed or damaged 40 helicopters and 7 jet planes in 2 separate attacks on U.S. Marine Corps airbases near Danang and at Chulai.

In the first raid, guerrillas rowed up the Danang River in sampans, dug in near the heliport runway and launched a mortar attack. Others ran onto the runway and hurled explosive charges into open helicopter cockpits. A Navy medical corpsman asleep in a helicopter was killed. The attackers destroyed 18 helicopters and damaged 22 others. 9 of 11 Viet Cong of the first group were killed. Of the estimated 20 Viet

Cong in the 2d group, 8 bodies were found the following day, and 2 were wounded. Another Viet Cong unit operating near Danang, apparently in conjunction with the heliport assault, was ambushed by Marines, and 15 of the guerrillas were killed. In the Chulai attack, guerrilla mortar fire destroyed 2 jet fighter planes and damaged 5 others. Marine defenders killed 2 guerrillas and captured 3 others of a 2d group of bomb-carrying infiltrators who attempted to penetrate the base's outer defenses to get to the airstrip.

The U.S. airbase at Danang had come under Viet Cong attack for the first time July 1. The guerrillas, using mortars and small arms, killed a U.S. military policeman. They destroyed 3 U.S. Air Force planes and damaged 3 others.

Viet Cong Terrorist Attacks

The Viet Cong virtually turned Saigon itself into a battle zone by carrying out isolated but persistent and bloody attacks in the South Vietnamese capital with bombs and grenades. The principal targets were U.S. military personnel and installations. Many South Vietnamese civilians who happened to be in the vicinity were killed or wounded. The stealthy assaults were carried out by small groups of Viet Cong, rarely numbering more than 5 or 6. On most occasions the attackers escaped. The boldest raid occurred Mar. 30 when the U.S. embassy was struck.

(A U.S. spokesman reported in Saigon Aug. 16 that Viet Cong terrorists during Jan.-May had slain 225 South Vietnamese government officials in the provinces and had kidnaped 451 others. In similar terrorist actions in 1964, 479 government officials had been killed and 663 had been abducted.)

Among Viet Cong terrorist incidents reported in Saigon during 1965:

• A terrorist bomb Mar. 30 heavily damaged the U.S. embassy and killed 2 Americans inside the building and 15 Vietnamese on the street outside. The State Department said 183 persons were injured, including 54 Americans, 6 of them seriously. The dead Americans were a woman embassy secretary and a Navy petty officer. Deputy Amb. U. Alexis Johnson, who was in the building, suffered slight cuts. The blast, set off in a car that had been parked in front of the embassy only minutes earlier, wrecked the U.S. consulate's ground floor, shattered windows and shutters and destroyed 15-20 cars in the street.

● Viet Cong terrorists blew up a riverboat restaurant June 25, killing 44 persons, including 12 Americans. The riverboat, located near the U.S. embassy, was first struck by a grenade explosion. As the patrons rushed for the gangplank a 2d blast, apparently a land mine, was set off on the riverbank. Of the 12 Americans killed, 5 were civilians. Those killed included 27 Vietnamese and 5 French, Swiss and Filipinos. 80 other persons, including 15 Americans, were injured.

● 5 South Vietnamese policemen were killed and 17 wounded Aug. 16 in a bomb attack on the South Vietnamese National Police Headquarters. Several of the terrorists had driven 2 bomb-ladened cars into the compound of the building and had fled before the vehicles exploded. At the same time other terrorists machinegunned to death 2 policemen outside the compound gate. The explosion killed 3 other policemen and damaged the administrative building. 4 suspects were arrested Aug. 17. A Viet Cong broadcast the same day said Communist terrorists had carried out the attack.

● 2 separate Viet Cong bomb blasts Oct. 2 killed 11 South Vietnamese civilians and wounded 42 persons, including 3 U.S. servicemen. The first blast, set off near a stadium where police officers were trained, killed 9 persons, including 4 children and 5 police officers. The 2d, 6 hours later at a theater, killed 2 Vietnamese and wounded the 3 U.S. servicemen.

● Terrorists Dec. 4 set off a bomb at a U.S. servicemen's hotel (the Metropole). The blast killed a U.S. Marine, a New Zealand artilleryman and 6 South Vietnamese civilians. 137 persons were injured—72 Americans, 3 New Zealanders and 62 South Vietnamese civilians. A Viet Cong statement, broadcast over Hanoi radio Dec. 5, claimed that more than 200 U.S. pilots had been killed or wounded by the blast. Warning of "punishing new blows" against U.S. installations in Saigon, the broadcast urged South Vietnamese to stay away from "places frequented by the United States aggressors."

Increased Viet Cong terrorist attacks in Saigon prompted U.S. military authorities to impose a daily 7 p.m.-6 a.m. curfew for American servicemen there, effective Dec. 19.

Prisoners & Executions

With the spread and intensification of U.S. military operations in Vietnam, an increasing number of Americans—particularly pilots shot down on bombing raids against the north—fell into Communist hands. North Vietnam claimed Oct. 6 that it had shot down 15 U.S. planes and captured "a number of pilots in recent weeks." Hanoi had warned in a letter sent to the International Red Cross in August (and made public Sept. 29) that U.S. pilots captured while bombing North Vietnam would be regarded as "war criminals liable to go before tribunals." Although North Vietnam had signed the 1949 Geneva agreement on protection of war prisoners, the Hanoi statement said the convention did not apply to captives convicted under principles established by the Nuremberg war crimes trials. The U.S. State Department Sept. 29 protested Hanoi's position on U.S. captives. It said North Vietnamese trials of U.S. captives would be merely a "smokescreen for reprisals" for U.S. air strikes against North Vietnam. The department said such trials also would violate the Geneva convention.

North Vietnam's official journal, *Nham Dan,* published Sept. 29 a Viet Cong warning that U.S. military personnel captured by the guerrillas in South Vietnam would be executed.

At least 3 American prisoners were executed by the Viet Cong in June and September in retaliation for South Vietnam's execution of Communist terrorists. Hanoi radio announced June 24 that the Viet Cong had shot to death Army Sgt. Harold G. Bennett, 25, of Perryville, Ark. in retaliation for South Vietnam's June 22 execution of Tran Van Dong, a convicted Viet Cong terrorist. Bennett had been reported missing Dec. 29, 1964 after the South Vietnamese Ranger battalion, to which he had been attached as an adviser, was mauled by a guerrilla force at Binhgia. The execution of 2 more captive U.S. soldiers was announced Sept. 26 by a clandestine Viet Cong radio. A North Vietnamese broadcast said the slayings were in retaliation for South Vietnam's execution in Danang Sept. 23 of 3 Viet Cong agents. The 2 executed soldiers were identified as Capt. Humbert R. Versace, 28, of Baltimore and Sgt. Kenneth M. Roraback, 32, of Fayeteville, N.C. Both were members of Special Forces units and had been captives since 1963.

2 Special Forces soldiers who had been captured with Roraback Nov. 24, 1963, during a battle at Hiephoa, 40 miles southwest of Saigon, were released by the Viet Cong Nov. 27. A National Liberation Front communiqué broadcast by Hanoi radio Nov. 27 said Sgt. George E. Smith of Chester, W. Va. and Sp. 5/c Claude D. McClure of Chattanooga were being freed in appreciation of anti-war demonstrations in the U.S. The 2 Americans were taken to the Cambodian border Nov. 28 by a Viet Cong representative. At a news conference arranged by the Cambodian government in Pnompenh Nov. 30, Smith and McClure said they were against U.S. troops in South Vietnam and would campaign for their withdrawal. Smith later denied having made the statement, but U.S. authorities on Okinawa, where the 2 were taken after their return to U.S. control, said Dec. 27 that they faced trial for cooperating with the Viet Cong.

U.S. Supplies Combat Gas

The State Department disclosed Mar. 22 that the U.S. was supplying South Vietnamese armed forces with a "non-lethal gas which disables temporarily" for use against Viet Cong guerrillas. The gas was said to have been used 3 times with little effect—twice in Dec. 1964 and the 3d time Jan. 27, 1965. The department's disclosure touched off a furor of criticism and expressions of concern in U.S. and other Western political circles. Communist comment uniformly condemned the U.S. action. The department confirmed the use of the gas after it was first reported by official sources in Saigon. The U.S. statement explained that "in tactical situations in which the Viet Cong intermingle with or take refuge among noncombatants, rather than use artillery or aerial bombardment, Vietnamese troops have used a type of tear gas." The department said that it merely made "the enemy incapable of fighting" and that "its use in such situations is no different than the use of disabling gas in riot control."

In an effort to assuage widespread criticism and concern, State Secy. Rusk declared at a news conference in Washington Mar. 24 that the U.S. was "not embarking upon gas warfare in Vietnam." Acknowledging "the concern around the world and in this country about the spectre of gas warfare," Rusk pointed out that in South Vietnam "we are talking about a gas which has been commonly adopted by the police forces of the world as riot control agents."

In an address to the National Press Club in Washington Mar. 23 visiting British Foreign Secy. Michael Stewart said that at a meeting with Rusk he had expressed "the very grave concern" felt in Britain and other countries about the use of gas in Vietnam.

South Vietnamese seen in reflection in flooded rice paddy as they patrol Long An Province.   (Wide World photo)

North Vietnamese Information Department head Le Trang contended Mar. 23 that the U.S. was using "poison gas" in violation of international law. He "appealed to all progressive people of the world to rouse public opinion everywhere to stay the bloody hands of United States imperialism."

The U.S. embassy in Moscow Mar. 26 rejected as "unacceptable" a Soviet note received that day protesting the use of U.S.-supplied "poisonous gases" in South Vietnam. The embassy's reply said the Russian memo was "based on a completely false allegation that poisonous gases are being used in Vietnam."

SOUTH VIETNAMESE RÉGIME IN TURMOIL

Civilian Government Restored

The government crisis resulting from the 1964 ouster of South Vietnam's High National Council was resolved temporarily Jan. 9 with the restoration of a civilian régime. A compromise agreement was reached in Saigon after 3 weeks of negotiations by Vietnamese civilians and military leaders and U.S. officials, including U.S. Deputy Amb. U. Alexis Johnson.

The government accord was announced in a communiqué signed by Premier Tran Van Huong, Chief of State Phan Khac Suu and Lt. Gen. Nguyen Khanh, armed forces commander. Khanh headed an Armed Forces Council (created to advise the National Council on military matters). His council had seized the legislative body and had removed the civilian régime from office but had permitted Huong and Suu to retain their posts.

Under the agreement: (1) Huong, appointed premier Nov. 5, 1964, retained his position as head of government. (2) Armed forces leaders pledged to confine their activities to the military sphere and to leave affairs of state to the civilians. (3) A national convention, representing "all sectors of the population," was to be convened to "assume legislative powers" and to draw up a permanent constitution; Suu was to handle legislative powers pending the convention. (4) The 5 Council members and about 50 politicians, students and military officers arrested Dec. 20 were to be released. They were freed Jan. 10.

U.S. Ambassador Maxwell D. Taylor said the American mission in Saigon welcomed the agreement "as a promising step." The U.S. had suspended advanced planning for assistance to the Saigon government in its war against the Viet Cong as a protest against the Dec. 1964 military takeover. Washington had insisted on restoration of a civilian régime as its price for renewing such aid.

Despite the reemergence of civilian rule, the Huong régime continued to provoke the wrath of South Vietnam's Buddhists. Anti-government strikes by Buddhists were held Jan. 11-13 in the northern cities of Hué, Quangtri and Danang. Thich Tam Chau, head of the Buddhist Institute of Secular Affairs, charged Jan. 11 that the Huong government was following a policy of criminal activities against his sect. He demanded the lifting of anti-Buddhist restrictions.

New Cabinet Includes 4 Generals

A revised cabinet that included 4 generals assumed office Jan. 20. The appointments of the officers were designed to provide greater government stability and to give the military more influence in the régime.

The new cabinet ministers were Air Vice Marshal Nguyen Cao Ky, air force commander, who became youth and sports minister; Maj. Gen. Tran Van Minh, armed forces chief of staff, who became armed forces minister, a post previously held by Huong; Maj. Gen. Nguyen Van Thieu, IV Corps commander, appointed 2d deputy premier, replacing Nguyen Xuan Oanh, who was demoted to 3d deputy premier; Brig. Gen. Linh Quang Vien, armed forces security chief, named to head the newly-established Ministry of Psychological Warfare, replacing Le Van Tuan, who had been information minister; Huynh Van Dao, chief of cabinet of the minister of the armed forces, who replaced Luu Van Tinh as finance minister. The ouster of Tuan and Tinh followed sharp criticism of the 2 ministers by the Buddhists.

In a move to accelerate war mobilization, the government Jan. 17 had empowered the cabinet to draft personnel into the armed forces for up to a year. The ministers also were authorized to requisition movable property for up to 6 months and real estate for up to 3 years.

Military Leaders Depose Huong

The Armed Forces Council overthrew Premier Huong and his civilian government in a bloodless coup Jan. 27. Huong formally resigned Jan. 28. Gen. Nguyen Khanh was given all powers deemed necessary to establish a stable government. 3d Deputy Premier Oanh was named acting premier.

An Armed Forces Council statement broadcast by Khanh said the generals were forced to seize power and to withdraw their support of Huong and Chief of State Suu because Huong and Suu were "unable to cope with the present critical situation"—the unrest caused by intensification of nationwide violent Buddhist demonstrations Jan. 17-27. The Buddhists had continued to clamor for Huong's resignation and had assailed the U.S. and Amb. Taylor for supporting Huong.

The council's statement also said:

● The council would observe the Oct. 1964 constitution, which provided for the convening of a national congress to serve as an interim legislature and draw up a new constitution. The October constitution's "clauses that are contrary to the spirit of this document" were no longer in effect.

● An electoral law, proclaimed earlier in the week, which provided for elections and the meeting of a national congress Mar. 21, would be honored by the council.

● Khanh "would immediately convene an Army-Peoples Council, consisting of 20 representatives of the religions, of the armed forces and personalities from various parts of the country," to "advise the government in all its important decisions."

Suu resigned but agreed to stay on as a caretaker chief of state during the transitional period. The Armed Forces Council designated Nguyen Luu Vien to remain as a caretaker first deputy premier to supervise the operation of a cabinet in the interim.

The coup came as no surprise to U.S. authorities in Saigon. As the Buddhist riots intensified, the Armed Forces Council had decided Jan. 24 that it would seize power, and Khanh later informed U. S. Deputy Amb. Johnson of the council's decision. Amb. Taylor had continued to express support for the "duly constituted government" of Huong in 3 days of talks with military and civilian leaders prior to the coup.

Hundreds of Buddhists had been arrested and many others were injured in clashes with police and troops attempting to quell the unrest. The riots quickly assumed an anti-U.S. character, and the worst of these disturbances flared in Saigon Jan. 22-23 and in the Buddhist stronghold of Hué Jan. 23. In Saigon more than 200 Buddhists were arrested in day-long clashes with police after youthful demonstrators stoned the U.S. Information Service's Abraham Lincoln Library and smashed the building's doors and windows. A Buddhist delegation earlier Jan. 22 had delivered a petition to Taylor demanding withdrawal of U.S. support of Huong.

In the Hué demonstration, 5,000 student-led Buddhists marched on the U.S. consulate Jan. 23. About 40 demonstrators broke into the ground floor, which housed a library, set fire to 6,000 books and smashed windows and furniture. Police stood by and did not interfere. Earlier Jan. 23 about 90 monks and nuns had marched to the consulate and presented a petition urging Pres. Johnson and Taylor not to support Huong. Other Buddhists demanded Taylor's removal from Saigon and warned Hué's shops and restaurants not to serve Americans. The Armed Forces Council imposed martial law in Hué Jan. 25. In discussing the action, Khanh said in an interview that "something must be done to check the growing upsurge of anti-Americanism" among the Buddhists. "If it goes on," he warned, "it will slow down our war against the Communists." Khanh insisted that the Armed Forces Council supported Huong's régime. He added: "The military will not seize power from the civilian government. However, if the civilian government collapses and asks the military to assume power, the military would accept."

Quat Becomes Premier

The Armed Forces Council took its first step in establishing a stable government by appointing Dr. Phan Huy Quat, 56, as premier Feb. 16. Phan Khac Suu was reappointed chief of state.

Quat, a physician, had served as foreign minister in 1964. He was sworn in with a 21-member council-approved cabinet that included 3 military officers. The cabinet was composed of 4 Roman Catholics, one Cao Dai adherent and one Hoa Hao sect member; the remaining members, including Quat, were nominally Buddhists. 8 of the ministers, including Quat, were originally from areas that had become part of North Vietnam. In a statement at the oath-taking ceremony, Quat said his "chief objective will be to bring about unity among all the religions."

A council statement said that the military would withdraw from politics following the formation of the new government and the establishment of a military-civilian council that was to act as an interim legislature. In the meantime, the council said, it would continue to "act as mediator until the government is popularly elected." Quat's régime was to remain in office until a popularly-elected national assembly drafted a permanent constitution.

The new cabinet included Nguyen Hoa Hiep, a Catholic and leader of the nationalistic Vietnam Quoc Dan Dang, as interior minister and Gen. Thieu as deputy premier.

The Armed Forces Council Feb. 17 announced the promised formation of a 20-member National Legislative Council. It replaced the defunct High National Council. The new legislative body included 2 members each of the Roman Catholic, Buddhist, Cao Dai and Hoa Hao groupings, 2 each from Vietnam's 3 geographical divisions—South, Central and North—and armed forces representatives.

Anti-Khanh Coup Attempt Fails

Dissident military officers failed Feb. 19-20 in an attempt to overthrow Gen. Nguyen Khanh. The bloodless *coup d'état* was suppressed by Khanh and his supporters.

The dissidents, backed by troops of 5 battalions, moved into Saigon Feb. 19 and encountered no resistance in seizing the radio station and the Joint General Staff's headquarters. They also closed Saigon's Tansonnhut Airport and the post office and surrounded the residences of Khanh and Chief of State Suu. The leader of the dissidents was Col. Pham Ngoc Thao, 43, who had served as press attaché in the South Vietnamese embassy in Washington until January. Closely allied with Thao in the abortive uprising were Brig. Gen. Lam Van Phat, ex-interior minister, who had been dropped from the army after being acquitted in Oct. 1964 of participating in an unsuccessful coup in September, and Col. Huynh Van Ton, who had lost his command of the 7th Division because of his participation in the September coup. The rebels demanded Khanh's ouster as armed forces commander, denounced him as a demagogue and said he was "power hungry." The insurgents charged that Khanh was remiss in pursuing the war against the Viet Cong. But they said their actions were not directed against the government of Premier Quat.

As the rebels seized Saigon, Khanh flew to Cap Saint-Jacques to command the military counter-action. Also eluding the rebels were Adm. Chung Tan Cang, navy commander, who dispatched his fleet to the river port of Nhabe, south of Saigon, to keep his ships out of rebel hands, and Marshal Ky, who remained at the Bienhoa Air Base, near Saigon. Ky warned Gen. Phat by phone that his planes would bomb Tansonnhut Airport and staff headquarters if rebel troops did not withdraw from those 2 points. Ky withdrew the threat after Gen. William C. Westmoreland, U.S. forces commander, had warned that bombing Tansonnhut would endanger the 6,500 U.S. troops stationed there.

Khanh Feb. 20 dispatched troops from Bienhoa and Cap Saint-Jacques to Saigon. The pro-Khanh forces reoccupied the capital without bloodshed as the insurgents offered no resistance and retreated. Suu appealed to both sides Feb. 20 to negotiate, and Phat then announced the capitulation of his forces. Later Phat, Thao and Ton disappeared, as did a 4th leader of the coup, a civilian identified as Vann Buu. (A military tribunal in Saigon May 7 sentenced Phat, Thao and Buu to death *in absentia*. 36 other officers and civilians who had been seized received prison sentences ranging from life to 3 months.)

Council Ousts and Exiles Khanh

The Armed Forces Council met in Bienhoa and dismissed Gen. Khanh Feb. 21 as council chairman and armed forces commander. Some of the generals who had sided with Khanh during the coup were among the council members who took this action after adopting a resolution expressing "no confidence" in Khanh's handling of his duties. Khanh was temporarily replaced as armed forces commander by Gen. Minh, who retained his post as chairman of the Joint Chiefs of Staff.

Immediately after the council vote to oust him, Khanh phoned military commanders throughout the country from Cap Saint-Jacques in an effort to rally support. Failing to win adequate backing, Khanh phoned council headquarters in Saigon Feb. 22 and announced his acceptance of the council's decision. Khanh was then appointed "roving ambassador" in an apparent move to get him out of the country. Gen. Thieu announced Feb. 23 that Khanh's first assignment would be to go to New York to present to the UN evidence that North Vietnam was directing the war in South Vietnam. (Khanh arrived in New York Mar. 2.)

Thieu was elected head of the council Mar. 3 and was given the new title of secretary general. The council appointed these 3 generals to serve under Thieu as a governing committee: Air Vice Marshal Ky (serving as commissioner for foreign affairs), Gen. Vinh (as commissioner for political affairs) and Brig. Gen. Pham Van Dong, capital military district commander of Saigon (as commissioner for security).

Armed Forces Council Dissolved

The Armed Forces Council dissolved itself May 6. The council's secretary and armed forces minister, Gen. Thieu, explained May 7 that the civilian régime of Premier Quat was capable of governing the country without the aid of the 20-man military body. Thieu said the council members also wanted to prove that they had no political ambitions.

The council Apr. 11 had purged 2 of its members and several other military officers who were accused of corruption and profiteering. Among those ousted were Rear Adm. Chung Tan Cang, navy commander, and Brig. Gen. Pham Van Dong, Saigon's military governor.

The officers' ouster prompted Roman Catholic leaders to tell Quat Apr. 12 that they feared a possible purge of Catholic military leaders. The Catholics believed that Gens. Minh and Thieu were among top officers slated to be replaced because of alleged Buddhist pressure to end the war against the Communists. The Catholics were reported to be planning a military defense in South Vietnam if the country were to come under complete Communist domination.

Catholic opposition to the government was further heightened by the disclosure May 9 of the formation of a new Catholic political organization, the Greater Unity Force. A force communiqué urged the election of a national congress "in the shortest period of time." It called for "invading and holding" North Vietnam "to deliver our compatriots from the yoke of Communist dictatorship." The force assailed the government for "bowing under the pressure of lackeys of the Communists . . . and eliminating a number of first-class nationalist elements who had anti-Communist records."

(A Buddhist 16-year-old novice and a Buddhist monk burned themselves to death in Saigon Apr. 21 and Apr. 24 in protest against the war.)

Opposition to Quat Intensifies

The stability of Quat's government was seriously shaken with the discovery May 20-21 of an alleged plot to assassinate the premier and with the development May 25-31 of a cabinet crisis due to a dispute over ministerial appointments.

South Vietnamese authorities arrested 40-50 of the alleged plotters May 20-21. Quat charged in a radio address that the plotters had cooperated with "Viet Cong elements." Most of those arrested were Roman Catholics, and about ⅔ were military personnel, including 5 junior officers. The seized dissidents had complained that Quat was not firm enough in dealing with pro-Communist and neutralist factions in government.

A Catholic delegation met with Chief of State Suu June 1 and demanded a halt in what they called politically motivated arrests. The delegation demanded Quat's resignation and charged him with "repressing the Catholics by kidnaping, arresting and torturing" them and by unfair trials. The Catholics had claimed in other statements that Quat's government had been partial to the Buddhists.

The government crisis developed May 25 when Suu refused to sign a decree of Quat's effecting a series of cabinet changes. The issue was further complicated by the refusal of Interior Min. Nguyen Hoa Hiep and Economy Min. Nguyen Van Vinh to resign. Quat wanted to replace them with Tran Van Thoan, a Saigon tribunal prosecutor, and Shell Oil Co. executive Nguyen Trung Trinh. Suu called the cabinet changes "unconstitutional."

Suu modified his position May 31 when he confirmed the appointment of 4 ministers. But he continued to oppose the replacement of Hiep and Vinh. The 4 approved cabinet appointees: Gen. Thieu, ex-head of the former Armed Forces Council, defense; Trinh Dinh Chinh, information and psychological warfare (to replace Brig. Gen. Linh Quang Vien); Tran Thanh Hiep, labor (vacant post); Lam Van Tri, agriculture (to replace Nguyen Ngo To).

The National Legislative Council June 4 upheld Quat's right to demand the dismissal of Hiep and Vinh.

Quat Resigns, Ky Replaces Him

Unremitting Roman Catholic opposition finally forced Quat and his civilian government to resign June 12. The Quat régime was replaced June 19 by a military-dominated government headed by Air Vice Marshal Ky as premier.

The military June 13 had formed a ruling triumvirate, the National Leadership Committee, headed by Gen. Thieu as chairman. Its other 2 members were Ky and Brig. Gen. Nguyen Huu Co, II Corps commander. The committee was expanded to 10 members June 14 as it began the task of forming a new government. The new members included all 4 corps commanders. The committee was to exercise supreme executive and legislative powers. But power was to be at least partly delegated to a 14-member Central Executive Council, designated as a "war cabinet." The council was subordinate to the Leadership Committee, which in turn was to be outranked by a Congress of the Armed Forces made up of generals from all service branches. Ky was appointed chairman of the council, a post equivalent to premier.

U.S. officials in Saigon supported the new military government but expressed regret at Quat's resignation. On returning to Saigon June 14 from consultations in Washington, however, U.S. Amb. Taylor was reported to have objected to Ky's appointment as council chairman on the ground that Ky's additional post would make it difficult for him to perform his duties as air commander. Ky was said to have assured Taylor that he would relinquish his military command if he became premier.

The Catholic leadership June 12 expressed satisfaction over Quat's resignation. A Catholic leadership statement June 14 opposed any "religious monopoly" and warned the government against displaying favoritism toward the politically militant United Buddhist Church. The Catholic declaration was supported by the rival Vietnamese General Buddhist Church (representing southern Buddhists) and the Cao Dai and Hoa Hao sects. United Buddhist Church officials June 15 called on Thieu to appoint civilians rather than military men as members of the Executive Council.

In a move to enforce strict discipline, the National Leadership Committee June 16 decreed the death penalty for Viet Cong terrorists, corrupt officials, speculators and blackmarketeers. Executions were to be carried out without trial if there was tangible proof of guilt.

Ky accepted the premiership and was sworn in June 19 with a 14-member Executive Council and a 10-member Leadership Committee. Thieu was given the title of chief of state. In an acceptance speech, Ky declared that the war against the Viet Cong was going badly and that South Vietnam was beset by political turmoil, economic collapse, war profiteering and injustice. Ky said his government would soon undertake a series of measures to cope with the country's problems. Ky expressed "hope in a few months to be able to return power to a civilian government at which time I will go back to the air force."

Ky announced the promised austerity measures June 24. Under the decrees: (1) The current martial law was expanded to a state of war. (2) Effective June 25 Saigon's

2 a.m.-to-4 a.m. curfew was to be expanded to 10 p.m.-2 a.m. (3) Price controls were to be imposed. (4) Government employes would no longer get free housing and transportation. (5) Leading government officials would have their pay cut 50%. A series of demonstrations were held in Hué Aug. 22-29. The demonstrators denounced the South Vietnamese government and demanded the removal of Chief of State Thieu, whom they characterized as an "ambitious and incompetent dictator."

An All Servicemen Convention, called by the ruling generals, met in Saigon Sept. 11 and adopted a resolution stating that the military would continue to rule for a while because of the unsettled political situation.

Montagnard Revolt Fails

Montagnard tribesmen staged a series of unsuccessful coordinated uprisings against South Vietnamese government authority in the Central Highlands Dec. 18-19. 35 Vietnamese soldiers and civilians were killed. The abortive revolt was carried out by the Unified Front for the Struggle of the Oppressed, an organization that sought autonomy for the Central Highlands' 700,000 tribesmen.

The most serious incident occurred Dec. 18 at Phuthien, district headquarters of Phubon Province, when 97 Rhade and Jarai tribesmen, soldiers in a government Regional Forces company, mutinied and killed 30 government troops. After holding the district headquarters for several hours, the rebels fled into a forest. They surrendered Dec. 19 to Vietnamese authorities.

A South Vietnamese court-martial in Pleiku Dec. 27 sentenced 4 montagnard tribesmen to death for their rôles in the uprising. 15 others received prison terms ranging from 5 years to life. One tribesman was acquitted.

Saigon Ends French Ties

South Vietnam severed diplomatic relations with France June 24 but retained consular ties. In announcing the diplomatic break, Foreign Min. Tran Van Do charged that France "has always directly or indirectly helped our enemies." Do said the break would not affect the 17,000 French citizens living in South Vietnam or Vietnamese residing in France.

Relations between France and South Vietnam had been cool since 1963, largely because of French Pres. Charles de Gaulle's advocacy of neutralization of Vietnam and his opposition to the U.S.' military rôle in Vietnam. Neither country had had an ambassador in the other's capital for months.

U.S. DOMESTIC DEVELOPMENTS

Johnson Administration Reaffirms Stand

The U.S. commitment to defend South Vietnam against Communist aggression had been reaffirmed by Pres. Johnson Jan. 4 in his State-of-the-Union message. Addressing a joint session of Congress and an audience that included senior Administration officials and foreign diplomats, Mr. Johnson declared: "In Asia, communism wears a[n] . . . aggressive face. We see that in Vietnam. Why are we there? We are there, first, because a friendly nation has asked us for help against the Communist aggression. 10 years ago our President pledged our help. 3 Presidents have supported that pledge. We will not break it now. 2d, our own security is tied to the peace of Asia. Twice in one generation we have had to fight against aggression in the Far East. To ignore aggression now would only increase the danger of a much larger war. Our goal is peace in Southeast Asia. That will come only when the aggressors leave their neighbors in peace. What is at stake is the cause of freedom, and in that cause America will never be found wanting. . . ."

Defense Secy. Robert S. McNamara declared Feb. 18 that the U.S. had no choice but to remain in South Vietnam to help defeat the Viet Cong. In his annual defense review, submitted to the House Armed Services Committee, McNamara said: "The choice is not simply whether to continue our efforts to keep South Vietnam free and independent, but rather whether to continue our struggle to halt Communist expansion in Asia. If the choice is the latter, as I believe it should be, we will be far better off facing the issue in South Vietnam," where the situation was "grave but not hopeless." The loss of South Vietnam to communism would "greatly increase the prestige of Communist China among the non-aligned nations and strengthen the position of their following everywhere." McNamara predicted that eventually China would "produce long-range ballistic missile systems and arm them with thermonuclear warheads." "Given the hostility the régime [Peiping] has shown, this is a most disturbing long-term prospect," he said.

Pres. Johnson asked Congress May 4 to appropriate an additional $700 million for fiscal 1965 "to meet mounting military requirements in Vietnam." The President could have obtained the money by transferring Defense Department funds, but, as he said in his special message to the Congress, "this is not a routine appropriation." Those supporting his request, he said, were "also voting to persist in our effort to halt Communist aggression in South Vietnam. Each is saying that the Congress and the President stand united before the world. . . ." The message expressed regret for "the necessity of bombing North Vietnam" but said that its purpose was to force Hanoi to negotiate peace.

Congressional action on the President's request began immediately May 4: the House Armed Services Committee voted unanimously to give full jurisdiction over it to the Appropriations Committee, where it was approved by a subcommittee the same day. The House passed it May 5 by 408-7 vote, and the Senate approved the measure the next day by 88-3. Mr. Johnson signed it May 7.

Mr. Johnson asked Congress Aug. 4 for an additional $1.7 billion in defense appropriations to help the U.S. meet its Vietnamese war commitments. Defense Secy. McNamara testified before the Senate Defense Appropriations subcommittee the same day in support of the request. McNamara disclosed that the Army would be increased by one division; this would bring the total to 17 divisions and increase total Army manpower to 1,188,000 men (up 235,000 men). The Navy was to be increased by 35,000 to a total of 720,000 men, the Marine Corps by 30,000 men to a total of 223,000 and the Air Force by 40,000 men to a total of 849,000 men. The increases would raise combined armed forces strength by 340,000 to 2,980,000.

In a TV panel program Aug. 23, Rusk said that in future negotiations with the Communists the U.S. was willing to accept restoration of the military balance envisaged for Vietnam in the 1954 Geneva agreements. The U.S. insisted, he said, on withdrawal of North Vietnamese forces from South Vietnam and on Hanoi's halting of infiltration of the south. Although these were the basic U.S. conditions for peace, "there are many details which can't be elaborated because we are not at a negotiating table," he said. As for reunification of Vietnam, Rusk suggested postponement of the matter because North Vietnam appeared to want it only on the basis of Communist rule over the entire country. "The people of the South don't want reunification on that basis," Rusk emphasized.

U.S. policy in Vietnam was reaffirmed Aug. 23 in a White House pamphlet restating Washington's commitment and objectives and in a summary of U.S. conditions for a truce to end the fighting, delivered by State Secy. Rusk, U.S. Amb.-to-UN Arthur J. Goldberg and Special Presidential Asst. (for National Security Affairs) McGeorge Bundy in a joint TV appearance.

The White House pamphlet, a 27-page booklet called *Why Vietnam?*, contained statements made previously on the Vietnam situation by Pres. Johnson and members of his Administration and by ex-Pres. Dwight D. Eisenhower and the late John F. Kennedy. The pamphlet contained the text of the original message sent to the late Premier Ngo Dinh Diem by Eisenhower Oct. 1, 1954 offering U.S. aid "in developing and maintaining a strong, viable state, capable of resisting attempted subversion or aggression through military means." (The 1954 message had become a source of controversy after Eisenhower had explained Aug. 17 that it actually had been meant as an offer of economic, not military aid. Pres. Johnson often had cited the letter as the basis for his Administration's military commitment to South Vietnam. In an effort to dispel reports that he disagreed with Mr. Johnson's Vietnam policies, Eisenhower further explained at a news conference in Gettysburg Aug. 19 that "I support the President" on Vietnam.)

(In an apparent rebuttal, the House Republican Committee on Planning & Research issued a "white paper" Aug. 24 assailing the Administration's actions in Vietnam. The white paper charged that the Administration "glosses over a messy situation with optimistic pronouncements and predictions." Accusing the Administration of a lack of candor, the document asserted that "neither the Congress nor the public is being accurately and fully informed about the nation's involvement in Vietnam." But the GOP statement said "all Americans must support whatever action is needed to put a stop to Communist aggression and to make safe the freedom and independence of South Vietnam.")

Political Leaders Debate War

The Johnson Administration's Vietnam policy was the subject of sharp domestic debate during 1965. Opposition to the Administration's handling of the Vietnam problem stemmed largely from liberal Democrats who favored limiting or ending the U.S. military intervention and from some Republicans who demanded intensification of the air war against North Vietnam and steps to assure a military defeat of Communist forces in South Vietnam. Despite the vociferous objections from both groups, which included respected members of the Senate, an overwhelming majority of Democrats and Republicans continued to support Mr. Johnson in his resolve to press the war until Communist forces withdrew from South Vietnam or accepted unconditional peace negotiations.

Among views voiced by American political leaders during the year:

• Senate minority leader Everett M. Dirksen (R., Ill.) proposed Jan. 2 that Pres. Johnson call an immediate conference to decide whether the U.S. should continue the war in Vietnam or withdraw. Asserting that "a hard decision now has to be made," Dirksen suggested that a meeting of "the best military, intelligence and other authorities" be held to "come to a united decision on what ought to be done." He said advice should be sought from Congressional leaders of both parties. Dirksen warned that "to give up in Vietnam means a loss of face throughout the Orient" and the loss of this Asian rice bowl to China.

● Senate majority leader Mike Mansfield (D., Mont.) said Jan. 3 that neutralization of Southeast Asia "perhaps would offer some hope for the future." Interviewed on NBC-TV's "Meet the Press," Mansfield conceded that Washington faced the dilemma of not being able to withdraw from South Vietnam or to expand the war to North Vietnam lest it become involved in a major war with Communist China.

● Sen. Wayne Morse (D., Ore.), a leading opponent of the war, said Jan. 5 that State Secy. Rusk's statements had convinced him "more than ever that the State Department's program in South Vietnam is bankrupt." Terming the U.S. presence in Vietnam an "open violation" of the UN Charter and of international law, Morse called on the U.S. to work through the UN towards a "fair, negotiated settlement."

● An AP survey of 83 U.S. Senators Jan. 6 showed the lawmakers divided on the Vietnam question. Among comments reported: Sen. Mansfield—"Expansion [of the war] will not resolve the problem. It is more likely to enlarge it, and in the end we may find ourselves engaged all over Asia in full-scale war." . . . Sen. Allen J. Ellender (D., La.)—The U.S. should withdraw from South Vietnam "without any ifs or ands." . . . Sen. Strom Thurmond (R., S.C.)—The U.S. should increase its military efforts in South Vietnam and stop "providing sanctuaries for the Communists." "Give the South Vietnamese all the supplies they need and whatever aid they need to bomb the North Vietnamese, but, if necessary, bomb them with United States troops, planes and ammunition." . . . Sen. Olin D. Johnston (D., S.C.)—"I suggest the UN handle it, set up a buffer zone between North and South Vietnam and police it." . . . Sen. John Sparkman (D., Ala.)—"I am not in favor of expanding the war to the Communist North, except to the extent . . . necessary to destroy the supply lines from North Vietnam to the Communists." . . . Sen. Wallace F. Bennett (R., Utah)—U.S. policy should be aimed at winning the war, even though "this may involve sending in combat units, or . . . crossing into the North using Vietnamese units."

● Ex-Vice Pres. Richard M. Nixon asserted Jan. 26 that the U.S. was "losing the war in Vietnam." Nixon, speaking in New York, warned that unless there was a change in strategy "we will be thrown out in a matter of months—certainly within the year." He proposed that the U.S. Navy and Air Force be used to interdict Communist supply routes to the guerrillas in South Vietnam and to destroy Communist staging areas in North Vietnam and Laos. He conceded that direct action might bring the U.S. into conflict with Communist China. But proposals to "negotiate" with the Viet Cong or "neutralize" South Vietnam would be tantamount to "surrendering on the installment plan," he said.

● Democratic and Republican Congressional leaders Feb. 8 voiced strong support of Pres. Johnson's decision to order retaliatory air strikes against North Vietnam. Senate majority leader Mansfield said : It was Mr. Johnson's aim "to achieve stability if possible so that the Vietnamese government can manage its own affairs within South Vietnam. I think he is proceeding cautiously and carefully, and he has a very full appreciation of all the elements involved in any move he directs." Senate GOP leader Dirksen said that "if we hadn't given an adequate response, we might have given the impression we might pull out" of South Vietnam. The U.S. air strikes were assailed, however, by Sens. Morse and Ernest Gruening (D., Alaska). Calling the attacks "a black page in American history," Morse suggested that "this threat to world peace" be negotiated at an international conference through the UN or the 1954 Geneva accords on Indochina. Gruening also proposed that the South Vietnamese war "be brought to the conference table, the sooner the better."

● Ex-Pres. Harry S. Truman, in a prepared statement issued Feb. 16 in Independence, Mo., expressed support for Mr. Johnson's Vietnamese policies. Truman said : U.S. troops were in South Vietnam "to help keep the peace, and to keep ambitious aggressors from helping themselves to the easy prey of certain newly-formed independent nations. If we abandon these to the new marauders and the 'little Caesars,' we are again headed for deep trouble." Truman derided "irresponsible critics" and "sidelines hecklers" of Pres. Johnson's policies "who neither have all the facts—nor the answers."

● A statement issued Feb. 17 by the joint Senate-House Republican leadership rejected negotiations while infiltration of South Vietnam continued from the north. The statement expressed full support for the U.S. air strikes on North Vietnam. It said any differences of opinion within the GOP stemmed from, "the belief that these measures might have been applied more frequently." Senate minority leader Dirksen charged Feb. 18 that Senate speeches made the previous day advocating negotiation of the Vietnamese war were tantamount to "run[ning] up the white flag" of defeat. Dirksen's position was supported by Sens. Leverett Saltonstall (R., Mass.) and George A. Smathers (D., Fla.). In an address to a national Young Republican leadership group, House minority leader Gerald Ford (R., Mich.) declared Feb. 18 that negotiations would be a "retreat to Pearl Harbor."

● Ex-Sen. Barry M. Goldwater (R., Ariz.) said in Washington Feb. 21 that Pres. Johnson should order air strikes against Hanoi itself "if that were necessary." He said the raids should be extended to such targets as "strategic depots, matériel-gathering points, much as I think we should have done in Korea." Goldwater conceded that such action might bring Chinese and North Vietnamese troops into South Vietnam. But he said they could be defeated with South Vietnamese ground troops and U.S. air and naval attacks.

● Sen. Gale McGee (D., Wyo.) said in a radio interview Feb. 22 that it was "imperative to force a showdown" with the Communists over Vietnam. He suggested that the U.S. bomb North Vietnamese military installations if Hanoi ignored a Washington ultimatum to stop sending troops into South Vietnam. He added: If such infiltration continued despite U.S. raids, the U.S. should bomb North Vietnam's bridges, highways and railroads; if these attacks did not stop the infiltration, "then we should announce that we will bomb [North Vietnam's] industrial centers."

• Sen. Thomas J. Dodd (D., Conn.) Feb. 23 described proposals that the U.S. withdraw from Vietnam and negotiate
as a form of a "new isolationism" that arose from a "national
weariness with cold-war burdens." In a 2½-hour speech on
the Senate floor, Dodd proposed the formation of "a North
Vietnamese Liberation Front" that would send anti-Communist guerrillas into North Vietnam. The demand for negotiations, Dodd said, "is akin to asking Churchill to negotiate
with the Germans at the time of Dunkirk or asking Truman
to negotiate with the Communists when we 'stood with our
backs to the sea in [Korea's] Pusan perimeter."

• Sen. George Aiken (R., Vt.) Apr. 23 urged a halt in U.S.
air attacks on North Vietnam. He said the raids "will not
put the North Vietnamese in a mood to negotiate" and might
stiffen their resistance. Aiken and Sen. Joseph S. Clark (D.,
Pa.) said most mail from their constituents expressed opposition to the Administration's policies in Vietnam.

• Chrmn. J. William Fulbright (D., Ark.) of the Senate
Foreign Relations Committee declared in a Senate speech
June 15 that U.S. policy in Vietnam "should remain one of
determination to end the war at the earliest possible time by
a negotiated settlement involving major concessions by both
sides." Fulbright said such negotiations were vital because
"it is clear to all reasonable Americans that a complete military victory in Vietnam, though theoretically attainable, can
in fact be attained only at a cost far exceeding the require-
ments of our interest and our honor." Fulbright expressed
opposition to "unconditional withdrawal of American support
from South Vietnam." He said "such action would betray
our obligation to people we have promised to defend" and
"would have disastrous consequences, including but by no
means confined to the victory of the Viet Cong in South Vietnam." Fulbright voiced equal objection to escalation of the
war. Contending that the air strikes against North Vietnam
had thus far "failed to weaken the military capacity of the
Viet Cong," Fulbright said escalating the conflict would provoke a large-scale North Vietnamese invasion of South Vietnam, which in turn "would probably draw the United States
into a bloody and protracted jungle war" and eventually

would precipitate "either massive Chinese military intervention in many vulnerable areas in Southeast Asia or general
nuclear war."

• Senate minority leader Dirksen June 24 opposed negotiating with the Viet Cong movement, even if it were part of a
North Vietnamese delegation, at any Vietnamese peace conference. Dirksen also questioned the advisability of a new
Congressional resolution (suggested by Sen. Jacob K. Javits,
R., N.Y.) to endorse the Administration's extended involvement in the conflict. Such a resolution, Dirksen warned, could
"knock the socks off the morale of our troops in Vietnam."
But Sen. Frank Church (D., Ida.) June 24 urged the Administration to express its desire for peace by appealing for UN
involvement in the dispute, by approving the presence of the
Viet Cong at any conference and by supporting "genuine
self-determination" for the South Vietnamese people.

• Criticizing recent actions of South Vietnam's Ky government, Senate majority leader Mansfield said June 26 that "it
is a good time to note that the commitment we made years
ago in Vietnam was to the people of Vietnam, and it was
made through the government of Pres. Ngo Dinh Diem, who
was the only one of this parade of governments in Saigon
which received any formal endorsement from the people of
Vietnam in elections." The U.S.' commitment to Saigon.
Mansfield pointed out, "is still intended for the people of
Vietnam and solely to bring about their peace and freedom."

• Ex-Vice Pres. Nixon visited South Vietnam Sept. 3-5 and,
in a statement made in Saigon Sept. 5, declared: "There is
only one basis for negotiations on South Vietnam, and that
is for a Communist withdrawal of their forces and for the
Communists to agree to quit infringing on the independence
and territorial integrity of South Vietnam." "Anything less
than that," Nixon warned, "would be defeat or retreat for
the United States and for the forces of freedom in Asia."

• Sen. Fulbright, interviewed Oct. 24 by NBC's "Meet the
Press" panel, suggested repeating the May 13-18 suspension
of air attacks on North Vietnam and for a longer period in
order to stimulate negotiations. Fulbright said the May 13-18

raid suspension "was not a very long time to allow any kind of negotiations to get under way." He recalled the arguments of the Soviet Union and other countries that the raids blocked peace talks. He added: "I have felt that we should take them up on this and at least stop it for a reasonable time"; if Hanoi did not respond by agreeing to negotiations "then you could always resume it and there would be no commitment never to resume it." Fulbright implied that the Defense Department was exerting more influence in foreign affairs than the State Department, particularly on Vietnam. He attributed this to Defense Secy. McNamara's "great persuasive powers" and the fact that the Defense Department controlled more than 50% of the nation's budget and negotiated "enormous contracts" with industry throughout the U.S. Fulbright also questioned the CIA's rôle in foreign affairs. The CIA, he said, was "supposed to be an intelligence agency only, and not an operating agency in the execution of foreign policy."

● Sen. Robert F. Kennedy (D., N.Y.) Nov. 5 defended "the right to criticize and the right to dissent" from Administration policy on Vietnam. Speaking at a news conference in Los Angeles, Kennedy said he favored donating blood to North Vietnam because it would be "in the oldest tradition of this country." "I'm willing to give blood to anybody who needs it," he asserted. But he said such blood donations to Hanoi should be given only "with concurrence of the government and the supervision of the Red Cross." (Ex-Sen. Goldwater charged at the Western States Republican Conference in Albuquerque, N.M. Nov. 6 that Kennedy's statement on blood for North Vietnam and pro-Viet Cong remarks that had been made by Rutgers University Prof. Eugene Genovese "come closer to treason than to academic freedom." Goldwater asked: "Why should . . . [Genovese] be defended by liberal leaders when he states publicly that he would welcome a victory for America's Communist enemies in Vietnam? Or why the silence today when a United States Senator said last night there was nothing wrong in sending American blood to our enemies?")

● Chrmn. L. Mendel Rivers (D., S.C.) of the House Armed Services Committee called Nov. 22 for the bombing of Haiphong and Hanoi. He said it was "folly to continue to let the port of Haiphong and military targets at Hanoi remain untouched and unscathed while war supplies being used against our troops are pouring into that port." Rivers said that although U.S. troops in South Vietnam were "inflicting heavy losses on the enemy, we were doing so at a heavy cost to ourselves." Therefore, he said, it was necessary to reverse the policy of trying "to match the Chinese and North Vietnamese man for man" and to increase air and sea attacks' so "we can drive the Viet Cong to their knees."

● Sen. Gruening (D., Alaska) declared Dec. 10 in New York that the U.S. had not made "a solemn pledge" to support South Vietnam, that the fighting in Vietnam was a civil war and that U.S. security was not threatened by events in Vietnam. Challenging Pres. Johnson's repeated contentions that previous Administrations had promised to help Saigon against Communist aggression, Gruening quoted the 1954 correspondence between Pres. Eisenhower and Ngo Dinh Diem to support his argument that Washington had promised Saigon limited economic assistance, not military aid. Gruening said that "one of the special myths on which we base our action is that the whole trouble stems from aggression from Hanoi." He quoted a statement in which the late Pres. Kennedy in 1963 had referred to "the civil war which has gone on for 10 years."

● Pres. Johnson's refusal to order the bombing of Hanoi and Haiphong was supported in a letter sent to the President Dec. 12 by 17 Democratic members of the House of Representatives. The letter contended that the bombing of the Hanoi-Haiphong industrial area could increase the war, not end it, and result in high U.S. casualties. The letter was signed by Reps. Jonathan B. Bingham (N.Y.), Benjamin S. Rosenthal (N.Y.), Donald M. Fraser (Minn.), Paul H. Todd (Mich.), George E. Brown Jr. (Calif.), Patsy T. Mink (Hawaii), Leonard Farbstein (N.Y.), Richard W. McCarthy (N.Y.), Phillip Burton (Calif.), John G. Dow (N.Y.), Don Edwards (Calif.), Robert W. Kastenmeir (Wis.), James H. Scheuer (N.Y.), Edith Green (Ore.), William F. Ryan (N.Y.), Henry S. Reuss (Wis.), John Conyers Jr. (Mich.).

War Protest Movement

The U.S.' growing involvement in Vietnam—and its extension of the war to North Vietnam—gave focus to several small but vociferous groups of Americans opposed to such intervention. Heartened by the division on Vietnam among U.S. political leaders, the opponents of the war sought to carry their views to the public through "teach-ins" and protest rallies and marches. Although generally leftist, the movement was diverse politically. It included religious and doctrinaire pacifist elements. Its aims ranged from simply halting the bombings of North Vietnam and facilitating peace negotiations to the outright withdrawal of U.S. forces and the probable abandonment of South Vietnam to Communist rule. The majority of Americans did not seem moved by the protests, despite the presence of many prominent professionals and intellectuals in their ranks.

Among major events in the protest movement during 1965:

'Teach-ins'—The "teach-in" movement originated in March at the University of Michigan, where Profs. Eric J. Wolf, William A. Gamson and Arnold S. Kaufman organized the first of the series of all-night meetings devoted to readings and lectures on the problems of Vietnam and Asia. From its inception, the teach-in movement became the voice of academic opposition to the war; and within a month teach-ins had been organized on college campuses from New York to Berkeley, Calif.

The teach-in movement reached its widest audience with a 15½-hour meeting held in a Washington, D.C. lecture hall May 15-16 and broadcast over a radio-and-telephone hook-up to more than 100 college campuses throughout the nation. Many Administration officials and prominent educators participated in the debate. The major defender of U.S. policy was University of California Prof. Robert Scalapino; major critics were Prof. Hans J. Morgenthau of the University of Chicago and Dr. George McT. Kahin of Cornell University. Other participants included Arthur Schlesinger Jr., historian and former White House aide, Isaac Deutscher, writer on Marxism, Leo Cherne of the International Rescue Committee and Walt W. Rostow, chairman of the State Department's

Policy Planning Committee. Eric Wolf of the University of Michigan was moderator of the event and chairman of the group sponsoring the teach-in, the Inter-University Committee for a Public Hearing on Vietnam.

Kahin attacked the "domino theory" that the loss of Vietnam to communism would precipitate the fall of other Asian nations to the Communists. "So long as Southeast Asian governments are in harmony with their countries' nationalism, and so long as they are wise enough to meet the most pressing economic and social demands of their peoples, they are not likely to succumb to communism," he said. Scalapino retorted that if the U.S. was to negotiate realistically with the Viet Cong and North Vietnam, the U.S. must recognize them as Communists and not harbor delusions that it was dealing with Asian nationalism.

Presidential Asst. McGeorge Bundy had been scheduled to take part in the teach-in but was forced to leave the U.S. on a mission to the Dominican Republic. Bundy participated, however, in a radio-TV debate on Vietnam held June 21 at Georgetown University in Washington. Appearing with him were Morgenthau, Prof. O. Edmund Clubb of Columbia University, Prof. Zbigniew Brzezinski of Columbia and Guy Pauker of the Rand Corp. Defending the Administration against attacks by Morgenthau and Clubb, Bundy declared that the only real alternative to the current U.S. policy was an extension of the war to North Vietnam and, possibly, Communist China.

State Secy. Dean Rusk Apr. 23 had derided the academic community's criticism of U.S. policy in Vietnam as "nonsense." In a speech before the American Society of International Law in Washington, Rusk said: "I sometimes wonder at the gullibility of educated men and the stubborn disregard of plain facts by men who are supposed to be helping our young to learn—especially to learn how to think." "We are asked to stop hitting bridges and radar sites and ammunition depots—without requiring that the other side stop its slaughter of thousands of civilians and its bombing of schools and hospitals and railways and buses." (Sen. Wayne L. Morse [D., Ore.] Apr. 26 attacked Rusk's remarks as "shocking." He said it was an insult to the academic community, 80% of whose members, according to Morse, opposed Administration policy on Vietnam.)

Peace marches—Nationwide demonstrations against U.S. policy in Vietnam were held Oct. 15-16 in about 40 U.S. cities. The demonstrations were organized by the National Coordinating Committee to End the War in Vietnam, a student-run organization set up in August with headquarters in Madison, Wis, near the University of Wisconsin campus. Major demonstrations occurred in New York and Berkeley, Calif. In New York, a parade was held Oct. 16, and more than 10,000 demonstrators marched in it despite heckling and threats from counter-demonstrators. In Berkeley, several thousand students attempted to march Oct. 15 and again Oct. 16 to the Oakland Army Base for a mass "sleep-out"; on both occasions they were turned back at the Oakland city limits by Oakland police. The Berkeley marches were directed by the Vietnam Day Committee, a university-centered group that had organized similar demonstrations near the Oakland base earlier in the year. Frank Emspak, 22, a zoology graduate of the University of Wisconsin and chairman of the National Coordinating Committee to End the War in Vietnam, said in Madison Oct. 17 that 70,000-100,000 persons had taken part in the demonstrations.

Marchers estimated to number from 15,000 to 35,000 converged on the White House Nov. 27 in a "March on Washington for Peace in Vietnam." The demonstration had been initiated by the National Committee for a Sane Nuclear Policy (SANE), under the sponsorship of an *ad hoc* committee that included prominent American authors, artists, churchmen and civil rights leaders.* After circling the White House for

---

* Members of the *ad hoc* committee included writers Saul Bellow, Michael Harrington, John Hersey and Arthur Miller, civil rights leaders Bayard Rustin and James Farmer, psychiatrist Erich Fromm, Socialist leader Norman Thomas, Unitarian-Universalist Association Pres. Dana McLeen Greeley, ex-Pres. Edwin Dahlberg of the National Council of Churches, educator Harold Taylor, medical specialists Albert B. Sabin and Benjamin Spock (the latter SANE co-chairman), cartoonist Jules Feiffer, sculptor Alexander Calder, actors Tony Randall and Ossie Davis and the latter's wife, actress Ruby Dee.

2 hours, carrying placards with such slogans as "Respect the 1954 Geneva Accords" and "Stop the Bombing," the demonstrators marched to the Washington Monument to hear speakers, among them Dr. Benjamin Spock, Norman Thomas, Mrs. Martin Luther King Jr. and Rep. George E. Brown Jr. (D., Calif.). 17 authorized march slogans had been issued, but members of the leftist Youth Against War & Fascism joined the march with placards bearing such unauthorized slogans as "Bring the GIs Home Now." A few Viet Cong flags, also unauthorized, were carried by members of the Committee to Aid the National Liberation Front. Attempts by counter-demonstrators (numbering about 100 and including members of the American Nazi Party) to tear down Viet Cong flags accounted for most of the isolated scuffles between demonstrators and counter-demonstrators. 13 arrests were made on disorderly conduct charges. Other organizations whose members participated in the march included: Women Strike for Peace (WSP), Students for a Democratic Society (SDS), the Student Nonviolent Coordinating Committee (SNCC) and the National Coordinating Committee to End the War in Vietnam.

White House Press Secy. Bill D. Moyers told newsmen in Austin, Tex. Nov. 26 that Pres. Johnson believed that the anti-Vietnam war demonstrations in the U.S. were "a part of the freedom guaranteed all Americans." But Moyers pointed out that Mr. Johnson was "obviously impressed also by the other kind of demonstration taking place in South Vietnam, where tens of thousands of Americans are serving their country and offering themselves in support of freedom." The President was convinced, Moyers said, "that the great majority of Americans do support our course of action in Vietnam."

A student peace march had been staged in Washington earlier in the year by Students for a Democratic Society, a leftwing non-Communist group with chapters at 63 universities. The rally, held Apr. 17, was supported by such groups as Women Strike for Peace and the Student Nonviolent Coordinating Committee. An estimated 15,000 demonstrators first picketed the White House and later marched to the Washington Monument for a series of addresses. One of the speakers, Sen. Ernest Gruening (D., Alaska), called for "the immediate cessation of our bombing in North Vietnam."

SANE had sponsored a rally June 8 in Madison Square Garden in New York to protest U.S. policy in Vietnam. Addressing a gathering of 17,000, Sen. Wayne Morse (D., Ore.) charged that the Administration's policies were leading the U.S. to the "abyss of war." Referring to Pres. Johnson's concept of government by "consensus," Morse asserted that the consensus on Vietnam "is not the consensus of our people, nor even the community of nations; it is a consensus among the State Department, Defense Department, Central Intelligence Agency and the White House staff."

Suicides—At least 2 American pacifists committed suicide by fire during 1965 to protest the U.S. military intervention in Vietnam.

Norman R. Morrison, 32, a Quaker of Baltimore, Md., burned himself to death in front of the Pentagon in Arlington, Va. Nov. 2. Some witnesses said that Morrison, who had driven up to the building with his one-year old daughter, first placed the child 15 feet away and then doused himself with kerosene or gasoline and set himself afire. Other witnesses said he had held the baby as his clothes caught fire and dropped her only after witnesses shouted to him. According to a statement issued by Morrison's wife, Ann: "Norman Morrison has given his life today to express his concern over the great loss of life and human suffering caused by the war in Vietnam."

Roger Allen LaPorte, 22, of the leftist Catholic Worker movement, burned himself in front of UN headquarters in New York Nov. 9 as a protest against war. LaPorte died of his injuries Nov. 10. The youth had sat down cross-legged in front of the UN building at about 5 a.m., doused himself with gasoline and then set himself ablaze. A policeman quoted LaPorte as saying in an ambulance as he was being rushed to a hospital that he had set himself afire because "I'm a Catholic Worker. I'm against wars, all wars. I did this as a religious action."

Draft-card burnings—Several extreme opponents of the Vietnam war—most of them youthful pacifists—burned their Selective Service cards publicly to dramatize their defiance of the Administration's policies and of a new law making it a crime to "knowingly" destroy or mutilate a draft card. The law, signed by the President Aug. 31, carried penalties of up to 5 years in prison and a $10,000 fine for violators. It had been submitted specifically to deal with an expected outbreak of draft-card burnings.

The first pacifist known to have broken the new law was David J. Miller, 22, a volunteer worker in a relief program run by the Catholic Worker movement. Miller burned his draft card publicly Oct. 15 at a pacifist rally staged outside the N.Y. City Armed Forces Induction Center. He was arrested by FBI agents Feb. 18 in Hookset, N.H.

Steve Smith, 20, a University of Iowa student, burned his draft card in public Oct. 20 in Iowa City; he was arrested Oct. 22.

5 pacifists burned their draft cards in New York's Union Square Nov. 6 at a rally to protest the Vietnam war. A heckler in the crowd sought to disrupt the action by dousing the 5 with a fire extinguisher. The draft cards were drenched, but the pacifists managed to dry them with a cigarette lighter and then burned them. The 5 card-burners were Thomas C. Cornell, 31, Marc P. Edelman, 20, Roy Lisker, 27, James E. Wilson, 21, and David McReynolds, 37. All but McReynolds were indicted Dec. 21 by a federal grand jury in New York.

Paul Booth, national secretary of the Students for a Democratic Society, announced in Chicago Nov. 18 that SDS leaders had dropped plans to promote a program of conscientious objection to the military draft. The group's local chapters had rejected the idea in a referendum by 56% vote. Citing opposition from the chapter at Harvard, Booth said the group there reasoned: "A major national push on the draft issue would obscure the central issue, . . . the war."

The outbreak of draft-card burnings and the SDS draft-objection plan had led Atty. Gen. Nicholas deB. Katzenbach Oct. 17 to announce a Justice Department investigation of

Communist influence in the war protest and anti-draft movements. Katzenbach had confirmed that SDS was one of the groups under study although he conceded that its leadership was largely non-Communist. The Justice Department probe was attacked Oct. 23 by Americans for Democratic Action as an attempt to "stifle criticism" of the Administration's Vietnam policy.

Rep. Emanuel Celler (D., N.Y.) Dec. 21 accused Lt. Gen. Lewis B. Hershey, 72, director of Selective Service, of "demeaning the draft act" by approving the draft reclassification of students who demonstrated against Administration policies. Celler had requested a clarification of Selective Service policy after 10 University of Michigan students convicted of trespassing in an Oct. 15 sit-in demonstration at the Ann Arbor draft board had been declared delinquent and reclassified as 1-A. In a reply made public by Celler Dec. 21, Hershey said that protesting U.S. policy in Vietnam was not cause for reclassification. 103 law school professors sent to Pres. Johnson Dec. 22 a letter voicing "deep concern about recent statements by officials of the Selective Service System which warned those demonstrating against Administration policies that student draft deferments can be revoked for actions 'against the national interest.'"

Rights leadership's stand—At its annual convention in Birmingham, Ala. Aug. 13, the Southern Christian Leadership Conference authorized its leader, the Rev. Dr. Martin Luther King Jr., to "turn the full resources" of the civil rights organization "to the cessation of bloodshed and war" in Vietnam "in the event of perilous escalation of the . . . conflict." King had said at an SCLC rally Aug. 12 that he planned to appeal to Pres. Johnson and the leaders of the Soviet Union, Communist China, and North and South Vietnam to end the war. Although conceding that Pres. Johnson had "demonstrated a greater desire to negotiate than the Hanoi and Peiping governments," King urged the President to issue "unconditional and unambiguous" pleas for peace talks.

King discussed the Vietnamese situation and other world problems with U.S. Amb.-to-UN Arthur J. Goldberg at UN headquarters in New York Sept. 10. King said the U.S. should state "unequivocably and unambiguously its willingness to negotiate with the Viet Cong" and consider a halt in the bombing of North Vietnam. But he expressed regret that North Vietnam and Communist China had not "responded with a positive attitude" to peace overtures.

Churches shun protests—Despite the participation of many clergymen—Protestant, Roman Catholic and Jewish—in war protest activities, the principal U.S. religious bodies generally declined during 1965 to take a public position on the protests and their aims. There were, however, 2 notable exceptions: the governing bodies of the Reform Judaism movement and of the National Council of Churches, embracing Protestant and Orthodox churches with a membership of 40 million.

The 48th general assembly of Reform Judaism's Union of American Hebrew Congregations in San Francisco Nov. 17 adopted a resolution calling on Pres. Johnson to order U.S. forces in Vietnam to cease fighting to permit the immediate start of peace talks. Rabbi Jacob Weinstein, president of the Central Conference of American Rabbis (Reform), had charged at the assembly's session Nov. 16 that American critics of U.S. Vietnam policy were being suppressed "not so much by government decree as by public hysteria carefully aided by the mass media."

The National Council of Churches Dec. 3 announced its support of certain aspects of Administration policy on Vietnam but urged new U.S. initiatives in seeking peace. The council's views were set forth in a message to churches and in a policy statement adopted by the council's general board in Madison, Wis. by 93-10 vote (6 abstentions). The policy statement noted "with approval" the Administration's commitment to unconditional discussions on the Vietnam war, the U.S. policy of not bombing North Vietnamese population centers and UN Secy. Gen. U Thant's "readiness to use his good offices to bring about a cessation of hostilities."

Speaking at a news conference Oct. 21 following the 6th World Order Study Conference of the National Council of Churches in St. Louis, ex-Minnesota Gov. Harold E. Stassen, Union Theological Seminary Pres. (the Rev. Dr.) John

C. Bennett and the Rev. Dr. Harold Row of Elgin, Ill. called for an end to bombing in Vietnam and for negotiations to include the Viet Cong. They criticized charges that anti-war demonstrators were Communist-inspired but warned that extreme forms of protest "may completely wipe out the real gains we have made in America in dealing with sincere conscientious objectors to military service."

About 500 persons led by Protestant, Roman Catholic and Jewish clergymen held a silent vigil before the Pentagon in Washington May 12 to protest U.S. policy in Vietnam. Defense Secy. Robert S. McNamara met for about 75 minutes with the leaders, who included Dr. Edwin T. Dahlberg, ex-president of the National Council of Churches; Dr. A. Dudley Ward, general secretary of the Methodist Board of Christian Social Concerns; the Right Rev. Daniel Corrigan, director of the Home Department of the Episcopal Church, New York; and Rabbi Leon I. Feuer, president of the Central Conference of American Rabbis.

50 Roman Catholic college students, most of whom attended Fordham University, picketed for 3 hours Dec. 4 in front of the N.Y. City chancery of Francis Cardinal Spellman, Roman Catholic archbishop of New York. (Spellman was at the Ecumenical Council in Rome.) The group, carrying signs with slogans such as "End Power Politics in the Church," said it was protesting the "suppression" of 3 Catholic clergymen actively opposed to U.S. policy on Vietnam.

The 3 priests were identified as Daniel Berrigan, Daniel Kilfoyle and Frank Keating, all of whom were Jesuits. Frank Carling, 20, chairman of the Fordham Student Committee for Religious Liberty, said that the Rev. Berrigan had been transferred to Cuernavaca, Mexico as a means of ending his participation in the Clergy Concerned About Vietnam Committee, a interreligious group opposed to U.S. Vietnam policy. Carling said the other 2 priests had withdrawn from the committee.

INDEX

Note: This index follows the Western usage in regard to most Vietnamese names. A Vietnamese individual, therefore, would be listed not under his family name but under the last section of his full name. *E.g.,* Ngo Dinh Can would be indexed thus: CAN, Ngo Dinh (not NGO Dinh Can). Exceptions are usually the cases of monks or others (*e.g.,* Ho Chi Minh) who use adopted names; such persons are generally listed under the first sections of their names (HO Chi Minh, not MINH, Ho Chi).